THE CATHOLIC UNIVERSITY OF AMERICA
CANON LAW STUDIES
No. 136

THE PRIVATION OF CHRISTIAN BURIAL

AN HISTORICAL SYNOPSIS AND COMMENTARY

A DISSERTATION

Submitted to the Faculty of Canon Law of the Catholic University of America in Partial Fulfillment of the Requirements for the Degree of

DOCTOR OF CANON LAW

BY

CHARLES A. KERIN, M.A., S.T.B., J.C.L.
Priest of the Society of Saint Sulpice

THE CATHOLIC UNIVERSITY OF AMERICA PRESS
WASHINGTON, D. C.
1941

NIHIL OBSTAT:

HIERONYMUS D. HANNAN, S.T.D., J.C.D.,
Censor Deputatus.
Washingtonii, D. C., die XXVIII Maii, 1941.

IMPRIMATUR:

✠ MATTHAEUS F. BRADY, D.D.,
Episcopus Burlingtonensis.
Burlingtonii, die XXX Maii, 1941.

AUSPICE MARIA

TABLE OF CONTENTS

PART ONE — HISTORICAL SYNOPSIS

PART TWO — THE CANONICAL COMMENTARY

FOREWORD

The privation of Christian burial is a loss that is most keenly felt by the faithful. Not only does it include the loss of the prayers and the blessings of the Church, but it also constitutes a brand of public unworthiness upon the deceased and a source of humilation for his family.

That no one appreciates the severity of this privation more than the Legislator is abundantly demonstrated by the rigid conditions prescribed by the law for inflicting it. Christian burial is denied by the positive law only when the case is indubitably clear; by the divine law only when the higher right of the good of souls must prevail over any individual right.

Because of this obvious preoccupation of the Legislator with the restricting of the privation and because of the necessity of fully understanding the conditions under which it must be applied, the subject of this dissertation has seemed worth while.

The work is divided into an historical synopsis and a canonical commentary. In the historical synopsis an effort is made to trace the law to its sources. The canonical commentary endeavors to define what is to be understood by *Christian burial* as this term appears in the Code of Canon Law; to give the principles that govern its privation; and to determine the classes of people to whom it applies.

The author wishes to express his sincere thanks to the Society of St. Sulpice for the opportunity to pursue higher studies, to the members of the Faculty of the School of Canon Law for their generous assistance and helpful direction in the preparation of this work and to all others, especially the Reverend Louis A. Rausch, M.A., S.T.B., who have in any way contributed to its production.

PART ONE
THE HISTORICAL SYNOPSIS

PRELIMINARY NOTIONS

From antiquity and amongst all peoples the innate respect for the mortal remains of men after death has dictated a ceremonial care relative to the provision of a final and suitable resting place for them. It has always been repugnant to think of men being left unburied as animals are. The ceremonial of burial was usually religious, but even when it was not religious, it was at least an act of humanity.[1]

Far from being any exception to this rule, the early Christians exercised the fondest care at all times in the burial of the faithful departed. Ancient sources record that the faithful, singing psalms, escorted the body of the deceased Christian to the cemetery, and there the Scriptures were read and the Sacrifice was offered for his soul.[2]

The reverence and devotion bestowed upon the body of the departed Christian were founded upon the doctrine of the resurrection, according to which the body is destined to enjoy, with the soul, the joys of eternal happiness in heaven. Moreover, as the temple of the Holy Spirit and the tabernacle of the Eucharist it was most fitting that it be honorably and reverently placed in a safe and becoming place.[3]

The Christian manner of burial was therefore a religious act, an ecclesiastical rite, and as such it has come down sub-

[1] André-Condis, *Dictionnaire de Droit Canonique* (3 vols., Paris, 1901), III, 503; Moulart, *De Sepulturis* (Louvain, 1862), pp. 1-4; Wernz, *Ius Decretalium* (6 vols., Romae et Prati, 1906-1913), III, 773.

[2] *Didascalia*, lib. VI, c. 22, n. 2—Funk, *Didascalia et Constitutiones Apostolorum* (2 vols., Paderbornae, 1905), I, 381. Van Hove states that this is a work of the early third century, and that it depends in many parts upon the even older *Didache*, which most probably dates from the close of the first century, and certainly not later than from the early second century,—*Prolegomena ad Codicem Iuris Canonici* (Romae: Dessain, 1928), pp. 92, 94; Duranti, *De Ritibus Ecclesiae Catholicae Libri Tres* (Romae, 1591), lib. 1, c. 23, nn. 9, 12.

[3] Origen, *Contra Celsum* VIII—*MPG* XI, 1562; Augustine, *De Civitate Dei*, lib. I, cc. 12-13—*MPL*, XLI, 26-28; *De Cura Pro Mortuis Gerenda*, c. III—*MPL*, XL, 595.

stantially unchanged through the centuries.[4] Christian burial has traditionally consisted of three parts: the escorting of the body to the church or cemetery, the religious rites at the house, the church or the cemetery, and the burial in ground set aside by the authority of the bishop for the burial of the faithful.[5]

However, the term has been used to refer to many aspects of the subject of Christian burial. Thus under this one name may be understood the right of Catholics to have ecclesiastical burial; the place of burial itself; the religious ceremonies connected with the burial; or the right of a pastor to perform the ceremony of Christian burial for the members of his parish.[6]

Therefore it should be made clear that the sense in which the term is to be understood in this history is that of burial in blessed ground. The term as here used will refer, in the main, to that right which belongs to the faithful who are worthy to have their bodies interred in blessed ground, or at least in that place that has been set aside by the authority of the bishop for the burial of the faithful, whether it is as yet blessed or not. The interment is to be accompanied then by the liturgical honors and rites that are presrribed for the ceremony. And the denial of Christian burial will mean privation of burial in blessed ground, or in ground set aside for Christian burial, and will include the denial of the ceremonies and rites that accompany that right.[7]

The term is not strictly defined in the old law, but is used either in the broad sense, including the three parts of Chris-

[4] Coronata, *De Locis et Temporibus Sacris* (Taurini: Marietti, 1922), 127; Many, *De Locis Sacris* (Paris, 1904), 140.

[5] Wernz, *Ius Decretalium*, III, 780; Barbosa, *Libri Tres Iuris Universi Ecclesiastici* (Lugduni, 1660), II, c. X, n. 2.

[6] Wernz, *Ius Decretalium*, III, 773; Ferraris, *Prompta Bibliotheca canonica iuridica moralis theologica necnon ascetica polemica rubricistica historica* (8 vols., Romae, 1885-1892), VII, 57, v. "Sepultura."

[7] Wernz-Vidal, *Ius Canonicum*, IV, 577 ff.; Many, *De Locis Sacris*, 222.

tian funerals, or in the stricter sense, denoting the actual burial in blessed ground. Santi states that the principal text of the decretal law, that of Gregory IX, *liber* III, *titulus* 28, is to be understood as referring to the narrower and stricter sense of the term, that is, either to the actual place of burial or to the right of worthy Christians to burial in blessed ground.[8] Also Reiffenstuel[9] and Wernz[10] declare that in general the term Christian burial refers to burial in blessed ground. Moreover, both Many[11] and Piat[12] hold with the majority of commentators on the Constitution "Apostolicae Sedis", that the term is therein used in the sense of interment, regardless of whether the religious rites are observed or not.

The extent of the meaning of the term will therefore depend frequently upon the context, but it is always to be understood as including burial in blessed ground, unless the text states otherwise.

The privation of burial has always been considered one of the worst indignities that can befall one. This is as true of non-Christians as it is of Christians. The Egyptians, Greeks and Persians all held this privation to be a dread calamity,[13] while the Romans, as appears from the testimony found on their monuments, felt that to be unburied was a disgrace and a dishonor.[14]

Roman law contains no specific reference to denial of burial

8 *Praelectiones Iuris Canonici* (4. ed., 5 vols. in 3, Ratisbonae, 1904), lib. III, tit. 28, n. 1.

9 *Ius Canonicum Universum*, lib. III, tit. 28, n. 2.

10 *Ius Decretalium*, III, 773.

11 *De Locis Sacris*, n. 224.

12 *Commentarius in Constitutionem 'Apostolicae Sedis'* (Parisiis, 1881), n. 240.

13 Moulart, *De Sepultura et Coemeteriis* (Lovanii, 1862), p. 58.

14 "C'était la un sort réservé aux derniers des hommes et dont nous trouvons le mention dans les inscriptions, mais toujours avec la forme de malédiction attachée à la non-sépulture."—Bosio, *Roma Sotteranea* (Romae, 1862)—Cabrol-Leclercq, *Dictionnaire d'Archéologie Chrétienne et de Liturgie* (14 vols., Paris: Letouzey et Ané, 1924-), I, 784.

as a penalty, but does imply it as a consequence of other penalties. Thus it provided that those guilty of patricide were either to be thrown into the sea or to the beasts, and were not to be buried.[15] Heretics must have been denied Christian burial from the severe laws that were enacted against their gatherings. They were forbidden to have either public or private worship,[16] were ordered to live outside the cities and compelled to keep away from all association with the other citizens.[17] Violation of these laws was punished with deportation and exile.[18] Obviously, then, they could not be buried among orthodox Christians. These laws were substantially repeated later in the Code of Justinian.[19]

Furthermore, those who were put to death for their crimes were often left unburied. This is implied in a law that permitted their heirs or relatives to ask for their bodies. However this request was not infrequently refused, especially with regard to those guilty of treason.[20]

The Jews also had the deepest horror of not receiving burial among their own people. Abundant evidence of this is to be found in the Old Testament.[21]

15 C. Th. (9. 15) 1.

16 C. Th. (16. 15) 11.

17 C. Th. (16. 5) 13 ss.

18 C. Th. (16. 5) 48, 53.

19 C. (1. 5) 3 ss.

20 D. (48. 24) 13; C. (3. 44) 11. The existence of such a law readily explains the action of Joseph of Arimathaea, who asked Pilate for the body of Christ that he might bury it.

21 Jeremias, XVI: 4, 6; Numbers, XIV: 29, 32; III Kings, XIV: 11, 13; XV: 4; XXI: 19, 23, 24; II Machabees, V: 10; XIII: 7, 8.

Chapter I

THE EVIDENCE OF THE PRIVATION OF CHRISTIAN BURIAL IN THE FIRST THREE CENTURIES

Art. 1—Evidence From the Christian Burial Places.

What may be called an indirect evidence of the privation of Christian burial at a very early date is the existence from the infancy of the Church of burial places exclusively Christian. For it is obvious that, given such places, those not of the Church must have been denied burial therein.

The cemeteries of Rome afford a good testing ground because of the eminence of that city and the preservation of the relics of ancient days that are to be found there. In Rome, the Christians seem to have had their own burial places from the dawn of Christianity.[1] However, in the earliest years, before the hostility that later separated them from the Jews had broken out, they were most probably buried among the latter; for they were, for some time after the death of Christ, still closely associated with them in many ways.[2]

The Jews had always buried their dead apart from the pagans, preserving after death that strict separation which in life divided the worshippers of the true God from the heathen.[3] It was the Jews also who in other lands than Palestine had nevertheless adapted the Palestinian form of burial to local conditions, in opposition to the Roman custom of cremation.[4]

The desire to avoid contact with the idolatrous rites of the pagans, and to escape the abuse and insults of the Jews would

1 Cabrol-Leclercq, *Dictionnaire d'Archéologie Chrétienne et de Liturgie*, III, 1630, v. "*cimetière*."

2 Acts V: 6; VIII: 2; IX: 37; XVIII: 12-17.

3 Smith-Cheetham, *Dictionary of Christian Antiquities* (2 vols., Hartford, 1880), I, 330, v. "cemetery"; Hastings, *Encyclopedia of Religion and Ethics* (10 vols., New York, 1912), IV, 456, v. "death."

4 *Encyclopedia of Religion and Ethics, loc. cit.*

naturally have led the Christians to follow the example set them by the latter and to provide their own burial places.[5] Moreover, it seems highly improbable that the Jews would long tolerate the burial in their midst of Christians with pagan antecedents. The rising hostility between Jews and Christians must, therefore, have forced a separation between them as regards burial arrangements, and though this development is not clearly traceable, such a separation must have taken place by the close of the first century, if not before.[6]

The first distinctly Christian burial places were private and individual. They were usually the private tombs or gardens of wealthy converts who had opened them to those of the faithful who had none of their own.[7] Beginning with these family tombs, the Church gradually made provision for the burial of all its members. Accordingly in the suburbs of every considerable city there arose Christian burial places, and catacombs.[8]

More evidence of the existence and number of these cemeteries is found in Tertullian's account of an attack upon the Christians at Carthage in 203, while they were gathered in a cemetery there.[9] And Eusebius refers to a decree of Emperor Valerian (253-260) closing the cemeteries and catacombs of the Christians around the year 257 because of the charge that they were being used as assembly places for forbidden worship.[10] Finally, in a letter from the Emperor Gallienus (260-

[5] *Dictionary of Christian Antiquities*, I, 252, v. "burial."

[6] *Encyclopedia of Religion and Ethics*, IV, 456, v. "death."

[7] Fliche-Martin, *Histoire de l'Eglise* (6 vols., Paris, Bloud & Gay, 1935-1938), I, 413; *Dictionary of Christian Antiquities*, I, 331, v. "cemetery." Cf. also Spence-Jones, *The Early Christians in Rome* (2. ed., London, 1911), p. 245.

[8] *Encyclopedia of Religion and Ethics*, IV, 456, 457, v. "death."

[9] *Epist. ad Scapulam*, c. 3—*MPL*, I, 701.

[10] *Historiae Ecclesiasticae Libri Decem* (ed. Henrici Valezii, Paris, 1659), lib. VII, c. 11—*MPG*, XX, 666; Thomassinus (1619-1695) also speaks of the assembling of the Christians in the catacombs and cemeteries for Mass.—*Vetus et Nova Ecclesiae Disciplina circa Beneficiaria et Beneficiarios* (10 vols., Parisiis, 1786-1787), pars III, lib. I, c. 65, n. 4.

268) to certain bishops, at the time that he revoked Valerian's decree, there is found mention of these burial places in the clause in which he writes that he permits the Christians to recover "what they call their cemeteries."[11]

The reservation of the Christian burial places to Christians alone is convincingly recorded in two very ancient monuments which are believed to have been erected even before the persecution period. Both are Roman, and neither of them, from their frankly Christian inscription, reflects any fear of anti-Christian legislation. But what is most significant is that both clearly state that the burial places that they mark are for Christians only.[12]

It seems, clear, therefore, from all this testimony that the Christians had their own burial places, first private, then communal, from the earliest times, and that they had their own cemeteries by the third century.[13]

In general, the works that speak of the early Christian cemeteries conclude that they were reserved exclusively for Christians.[14] Not only were non-Christians excluded from these burial places, but also the unworthy Christians could not be buried there. An interesting passage from the ancient *Constitutiones Apostolorum* (c. 400), in describing the traditional funeral service, states that the Christians accompanied the body to the cemetery, singing psalms as they went, and that when they had arrived they read the Scriptures and

11 Eusebius refers to this also in his *Historica Ecclesiastica*, lib. VII, c. 13—*MPG*, XX, 666.

12 Northcote-Brownlow, *Roma Sotterranea* (London, 1869), p. 62.

13 *Dictionnaire d'Archéologie et de Liturgie*, III, 1630, v. "*cimetière*"; Hornstein, *Les Sépultures* (Paris, 1868), p. 229; Batiffol, *Primitive Christianity* (translated by H. Brianceau from the fifth edition of *l'Eglise Naissante*, revised by the author, New York: Longmans, 1911), p. 34.

14 *Dictionnaire d'Archéologie et de Liturgie*, III, 1630, v. "*cimetière*"; Hornstein, *Les Sépultures*, p. 201; *Catholic Encyclopedia* (15 vols., New York, 1907-1912), III, 505, v. "cemetery."

offered the Sacrifice, *if the deceased had been faithful in Christ.*[15]

The exclusion of heretics and schismatics is further implied in the fact that the Novatians were allowed to keep their own cemeteries.[16] The Donatists, probably copying the example of the Catholics, even went so far as to exclude the latter from the cemeteries which they seized from them.[17] The Donatists also had eventually to decide against the practices of a sect whose members were called the Circumcellions and to exclude them from burial in Donatist cemeteries.[18] Moreover, Catholics had been forbidden by the Council of Laodicaea (343-381) to frequent the cemeteries and the "martyries" of heretics.[19]

St. Cyprian (200-258) shows how important it was that the Catholics should make use of their own cemeteries exclusively when he makes his accusations against the lapsed Spanish bishop, Martial. The latter was charged with the practice of associating with members of a heathen funeral confraternity and especially with having buried his sons in the cemetery over which the heathen had charge. For this he was deposed.[20]

And St. Hilary of Poitiers (315-366) in his commentary on the words of Our Lord, "Let the dead bury their dead," refers to the aversion of the Christians to burial among infidels.[21]

15 Lib. VI, c. 30, n. 2—Funk, *Didascalia et Constitutiones Apostolorum*, I, 381. Although this work was, at the earliest, a compilation of the late fourth century, Van Hove states that the first six books were taken from the *Didascalia*, of the third century—*Prolegomena*, 107.

16 C. Th. (16.5), 2.

17 *Libri VII Optati Milevitani*, liber VI, c. 7—*Corpus Scriptorum Ecclesiasticorum Latinorum* (68 vols., Vindobonae, apud Geroldi filium, 1865), vol. XXVI (a. 1883), 155. Hereafter this collection will be referred to with the abbreviation *CSEL*.

18 *Libri VII Optati Milevitani*, lib. III, c. 4—*CSEL*, XXVI, 82, 83.

19 Can. 9—Mansi, II, 565.

20 *Epist. LXVIII, Ad Clerum et Plebes in Hispania*—*MPL*, III, 1030.

21 Matt., VIII: 22.

He reminds the faithful that the Master *"admonuit non admisceri memoriis sanctorum mortuos infideles."* [22]

Were these ancient burial places blessed? No direct testimony in regard to this has been obtained beyond the well known allusion found in a letter of St. Gregory of Tours (538?-539?), in which he cautions against the burying of anyone in a place that had not yet been blessed by the bishop.[23] Authors conclude from this letter that the custom of blessing cemeteries was already well established by that time, but the practice has not been definitely traced further back in these early ages because of the lack of testimony.[24]

One opinion is that the solemn blessing of cemeteries came into being along with that of churches, of which there are signs even in the fourth century.[25]

After the close of the persecutions the faithful were zealous in seeking out and honoring the tombs of the martyrs. This was done by building a church over the grave, or in the cemetery, where Mass was offered, or by transporting the remains, or even a relic of them, to a new church.[26] It then became a much sought after privilege to be buried as near these martyrs as possible, if not in the church, then around it. There are many records of the burial of noted people in the churches at that time.[27] Thus the cemeteries and the churches became

22 *Commentarius in Evangelium Matthaei*, c. VIII, n. 2—*MPL*, IX, 958.

23 *De Gloria Confessorum*, c. 106—*MPL*, LXXI, 906.

24 Many, *De Locis Sacris*, n. 139; Duranti, *De Ritibus Ecclesiae Catholicae Libri Tres* (Romae, 1591), lib. I, cap. XXIII, n. 9.

25 *Dictionnaire d'Archéologie et de Liturgie*, III, 1641, 1644, v. "*cimetière*."

26 C. 29, D. I, *de cons.*

27 St. Gregory of Nyssa (*De Vita St. Macrinae*—*MPG*, XLVI, 994) speaks of his sister's being buried with the holy martyrs; St. Ambrose prepared his own tomb under the altar of his church—*Epist. XXII*, n. 13—*MPL*, XVI, 1023; Constantine was buried in the Church that he built—Eusebius, *De Vita Constantini*, lib. 4, n. 60—*MPG*, XX, 1210, 1211; St. Chrysostom records the burial of emperors in the churches—*Homil. XXVI in Epist. II ad Cor.*—*MPG*, LXI, 582.

associated through this desire of the people to be buried near their Christian heroes, and to benefit from the prayers there offered; and the blessing of the church must have included the blessing of the cemetery around it.[28]

Moreover, burial has always been considered even in pagan lands a religious function, a sacred rite. Christian burial seems similarly always to have been regarded not only a duty of humanity, but a strictly religious duty.[29] Thus Christian cemeteries appear to have derived their sacred character both from the religious end they served and from the blessing they received.[30]

Moulart proposes an interesting opinion, namely, that the simple blessing of cemeteries—the ordinary invocation of the blessing of God upon something set aside for His service—dates from the beginning of the Christian era. The basis for this opinion he finds in the respect and veneration that the burial places have always received; from St. Cyprian's mention of the crime of the Spanish bishop, Martial, who had allowed his sons to be buried in a "profane" cemetery;[31] and from a text of St. Augustine in which this Doctor of the Church asserts that those customs which are universally observed, but for which there is no written record, are to be considered either as of Apostolic tradition or derived from the general councils.[32] The question need not be further considered here. It suffices to know that places were set aside for the exclusive burial of the faithful members of the Church almost from the beginning, that the custom of blessing them is immemorial, and that the exercise of the public authority of the bishop in segregating them is very ancient.

28 Moulart, *De Sepultura*, pp. 75-77; Duchesne, *Christian Life and Worship*, translated by M. J. McClure (5. ed., London; Society for the Promotion of Christian Knowledge), p. 406 ff.

29 Wernz-Vidal, *Ius Canonicum*, tom. IV, vol. I, n. 561, footnote 16; Duranti, *De Ritibus*, lib. I, cap. XXIII, n. 14.

30 Wernz-Vidal, *loc. cit.*

31 *Epist. LXVIII, Ad Clerum—MPL*, III, 1030.

32 *Epist. LXIV, Ad Januarium*, c. 1.—*MPL*, XXXIII, 200.

If the matter of cemeteries has been considered at some length, it is because of the importance of understanding adequately what it means to be buried in a Catholic cemetery, and accordingly what a great loss it is to be denied that privilege. From the most ancient times Catholics have associated reverence for cemeteries with their most intimate and religious convictions. They have always considered them as places sacred and inviolable. The right to find final rest therein has always been esteemed the privilege of those alone who died in communion with the Church, a right that has never been conceded to those outside the fold, or to those unworthy members who have been expelled from it.

Art. 2—Evidence from the Early Penitential Discipline

Although direct evidence of the denial of Christian burial is extremely scarce in the earliest centuries of Christianity, there is a considerable amount of evidence which insinuates that this penalty must have been inflicted from the beginning. In the first three centuries there was no written ecclesiastical law to which appeal could be made. There existed rather the collective mind of the Church, a common rule which was formulated and applied as the occasion arose. One reliable source of information as to what this was is the severe discipline of the Church in regard to grave sin.[33]

In the early days of great faith and intense fervor, public discipline was prescribed for public sins, and for the various classes of offenders there were various types of penance, some severe, others not. For the most grevious sins penance could be granted but once. For sins of lesser malice penance and pardon could be had more often.[34] A practice of the Church

[33] Swete, *Essays on the Early History of the Church and the Ministry* (2 ed., London: MacMillan, 1921), p. 358.

[34] Morinus, *Commentarius Historicus de Disciplina in Administratione Sacramenti Poenitentiae Tredecim Primis Seculis in Ecclesia Occidentali et huc usque in Orientali Observata* (Parisiis, 1651), lib. VI, cc. 2-18 (Hereafter this work will be referred to as *De Admin. Sacr. Poenit.*); Origen, *Homilia XV*, n. 2—*MPG*, XII, 560; Tertullian, *De Pudicitia*, c. 19—*MPL*, II, 1020.

of the first three centuries, unique in the history of ecclesiastical discipline, was the denial of absolution to the dying apostates and excommunicates who had waited until death to ask for it. The particular malice of their offence was that they had bargained on the pardon of the Church; that is, they sinned grievously, and then remained in that state willingly, in order to escape the rigors and privations of public penance. When danger of death threatened, they sent for the priest and expected to be absolved, planning by this strategy to enjoy life and yet to win heaven. In refusing them absolution, the Church in no way implied that their sins were unpardonable, but simply that their disposition was not felt to be truly contrite.[35]

St. Cyprian (252) testifies to this general feeling against such presumption especially at a time when so much pressure was brought upon all the faithful to desert their faith. Strong action had to be taken lest this practice be encouraged and lest those who were trying to live up to their religion take scandal and be persuaded to follow such a course.[36] Further notice of this very severe discipline is found in a letter of Pope Innocent I in the year 405, which contrasts the discipline of earlier times with the more benign attitude of his own period.[37]

The use of the words *"comunio"*, *"veniam"*, and *"pacem"* in the centuries before Novatian signified full reconciliation with the Church, including, therefore, both absolution and the reception of Communion (Eucharist).[38] The general conviction of the insincerity of these last-minute seekers after absolution, and the popular belief that they were outside the fold is

[35] Morinus, *De Admin. Sacr. Poenit.*, lib. X, c. 1, n. 3.

[36] *Ep. LII, Ad Antonianum*, c. 23—*MPL*, III, 789.

[37] *Epist. VI, Ad Exsuperium*, 5.—*MPL*, XX, 498.

[38] Morinus, *De Admin. Sacr. Poenit.*, lib. IV, c. 21, n. 1; lib. X, c. 1, n. 6; Galtier, *De Poenitentia* (Paris: Beauchesne, 1923), n. 301; Moriarty, *The Extraordinary Absolution from Censures*, The Catholic University of America Canon Law Studies, n. 113 (Washington, D. C.: The Catholic University of America), pp. 15, 18, 21.

demonstrated by their being denied both the public prayers and the Sacrifice of the Mass after their death.[39] From the severity of both the words and tone of Morinus it is clear that in the eyes of the faithful they were considered as deserters and contemners of the Church.[40] Moreover, as excommunicated persons, their names were removed from the diptych, the roster containing the names of the "saints," [41] as the congregation of the faithful was called, a custom carried over from the Jewish practice with regard to those expelled from the fold.[42] The significance of this ceremony of the erasing of the names of the excommunicates included the privation of burial among the faithful so long as they remained out of the Church.[43]

The impenitent apostates and excommunicates here considered are not to be confused with the so called capital offenders, namely, those who had committed the grievous sins of adultery, murder or apostasy,[44] but who had repented and asked for penance. Though the commission of such grave offenses incurred excommunication from the fold, hope was not lost, for the offenders could ask for penance and pardon. The historical controversy over whether or not they could be pardoned on earth cannot be considered here beyond

39 Morinus, *De Admin. Sacr. Poenit.*, lib. X, c. 3, n. 5.

40 Morinus, *De Admin. Sacr. Poenit.*, *loc. cit.*, Tertullian, *De Poenitentia*, cc. 10, 11—*MPL*, I, 1245, 1246; *Didascalia*, II, 41, 9 (ed. Funk, I, 132); Watkins, *A History of Penance* (2 vols., New York; Longmans, 1920), I, 61, 65.

41 Acts, IX: 13; Rauschen, *Eucharist and Penance* (authorized translation from the second German edition, St. Louis: Herder, 1931), p. 153. Funk, *A Manual of Church History* (second impression from the authorized translation of the fifth edition, 2 vols., St. Louis: Herder, 1910), I, 68.

42 Luke, VI: 22.

43 Bingham, *Antiquities of the Christian Church* (2 vols., London, 1878), I, 892.

44 Acts, XV: 20, 29; XXI: 25; Tertullian, *De Pudicitia*, c. 19—*MPL*, II, 1020.

mention of the prevailing opinions which held that they were pardoned.[45]

All agree that they could be allowed to do penance, and it is this that separated them from the impenitent; for this penance in some way, at least, included them in the fold, and though it might not bring pardon on earth, it gave them hope of pardon in the next world. Tertullian urges them to ask for this penance and to embrace it.[46]

From the consideration of all this, it appears that the severe opinion which the faithful had of these calculating sinners hardly allowed for their burial among those who had sacrificed life and fortune to practice the faith. In fact, the whole tenor of ecclesiastical discipline at all times has excluded one class of people especially from the honor of Christian burial, namely, all those who died in contempt for the laws of the Church.[47]

This severity continued into the fourth century, according to Rauschen.[48] Certain it is that clear evidence of it can be found in the decree of the I Council of Arles (314), which stated that those who had committed capital sins and had postponed asking for penance until they were in danger of death, were to be refused reconciliation with the Church.[49]

Whether the Council of Elvira (305) can be considered a criterion of the discipline of the time is doubtful. In general

[45] Rauschen, *Eucharist and Penance,* pp. 153, 154; St. Cyprian reflects this diversity of practice in an epistle on the subject: *Epist. LII, Ad Antonianum,* c. 21.—*MPL,* III, 787; Cappello (*De Sacramentis* [3. ed., 3 vol., Romae: Marietti, 1932-1939], Vol. II [1938], nn. 68-72) opposes the opinion that absolution was denied by the early Church; Galtier (*De Poenitentia, Parisiis;* Beauchesne, 1923, nn. 300-304) takes the view that it was, carefully remarking that it was not because the Church felt incapable of giving it, but because discipline at that time dictated the denial; Cf. Morinus, *De Admin. Sacr. Poenit.* lib. X, c. 3, n. 5.

[46] Tertullian, *De Pudicitia,* c. 3—*MPL,* II, 986. Cyprian also speaks of this—*Epist. XII*—*MPL,* LV, 259.

[47] Bingham, *Antiquities of the Christian Church,* I, 892.

[48] *Eucharist and Penance,* p. 207.

[49] Can. 22—Mansi, II, 473.

it appears that the rigorous legislation of this council was due to the pressing evils of the time in its vicinity, and its influence does not seem to have extended beyond Spain and northern Africa.[50] This Council listed over one dozen sins for which absolution was to be denied even at the hour of death.[51] Its whole tenor and wording convey the most solemn warning to those committing the sins so condemned, and it stands out as especially severe legislation. Its sternness seems to imply the denial of Christian burial along with the denial of absolution at death. A logical consequence of its decrees, aimed at correcting the current, pernicious and persistent abuses and evils of the time of Diocletian's persecution, would indeed have been to deny to the offenders a final resting place among the faithful.

But by the time of the Council of Nice (325) the more merciful view had prevailed. This Council forbade the denial of absolution to any one who asked for it at the hour of death, or when in danger of death.[52] Hefele-Leclercq believe that this is the first instance in which it is so plainly stated that any sinner whosoever, if contrite, must be allowed to receive reconciliation when in danger of death.[53] This decree of the Council of Nice was recorded by Gratian in his *Decretum.*[54]. Innocent (402-417) states that absolution at death was finally granted to all who asked it in order to refute the contention of the Novatians that the Church could not absolve capital offenders.[55]

50 Morinus, *De Admin. Sacr. Poenit.*, lib. X, c. 2, n. 4; Rauschen, *Eucharist and Penance*, p. 177; Swete, *Essays on the Early History of the Church and the Ministry*, p. 376. Swete says of this Council: "The severity of this Council may be either a survival of the rigorist tradition, or it may be due to the deplorable situation in Spain at that time."

51 Cc. 1, 2, 6, 7, 8, 10, 12, 17, 19, 63, 66, 67, 70, 75—Mansi, I, 5-18.

52 Can. 13—Mansi, II, 681.

53 *Histoire des Conciles* (10 vols., Paris, 1907-1938), I, 595. Hereafter this collection will be cited simply as Hefele-Leclercq.

54 C. 9, C. 26, q. 6.

55 *Epist. VI, Ad Exsuperium*, n. 6—*MPL*, XX, 498.

But absolution at death, and later Christian burial, had always been denied, and continued to be refused, to those who died impenitent, as is illustrated in the fifth century in the letter of Pope St. Leo the great (440-461) to Rusticus, Bishop of Narbonne. Pope Leo informs him of the constant and unvarying tradition of the Church: *"Nos autem quibus viventibus non communicavimus, mortuis communicare non possumus."* [56]

This traditional rule was incorporated by Gratian in his *Decretum* and may be said to be one of the fundamental sources of the denial of Christian burial, for it states the principle that underlies the majority of reasons for excluding from burial among the faithful departed those who were either never in the Church, or those who had voluntarily deserted or had been expelled from it.[57]

In the conclusion of this chapter it is important to record what appears as the only explicit incident of the denial of Christian burial that has been found before the fourth century. It is recorded by St. Cyprian in one of his letters.[58] He speaks of the meeting of the bishops called at Carthage to consider a case of discipline.[59] A certain Victor Geminus had appointed, just before his death, a priest named Victor to be the guardian of his children. Since this was a task that demanded much time and care, an earlier Council had forbidden the appointment of priests to undertake it.[60] The decision of the Council was that no one should offer prayers for Victor Geminus, nor have Masses offered for his soul, for it was fitting that he who had tried to rob the altar of

56 *Epist. CLXVII—MPL*, LIV, 1206.

57 C. 1, C. 24, q. 2; c. 12, X, *de sepulturis*, III, 28; cc. 28, 29, X, *de sententia excommunicationis*, V, 39.

58 *Epist. LXVI—MPL*, IV, 410.

59 Hefele-Leclercq (*Histoire des Conciles*, I, 164-165) consider this to have been the Council of 249, and note that Mansi makes no mention of it.

60 Hefele-Leclercq (*loc. cit.*) suggest that this may have been a council held by Agrippinus between the years 218-222.

a priest should not benefit by priestly prayers. This severe punishment, says St. Cyprian, was decreed as being in accord with the prohibition of the earlier Council. It would appear from this that the sanction that bore such drastic effects must have been excommunication, and that it was thus considered that Victor Geminus had died outside the fold. The opinion is strengthened by the fact that St. Cyprian repeated this prohibition in the very same year in a letter which was later incorporated by Gratian in his *Decretum.*[61]

[61] C. 4, C. 21, q. 3. The *tutela* by testament is also prohibited with the same sanction in c. 40, C. 16, q. 1. However, the guardianship that a priest was bound to accept as unavoidable, i.e., of those who were left dependent upon him, was later permitted by the Council of Chalcedon (451) in canon 3—Harduin, *Acta Conciliorum et Epistolae Decretales ac Constitutiones Summorum Pontificum* (12 vols., Parisiis, 1715), II, 601. This work hereafter will be referred to as Harduin.

Chapter II

FROM 300 TO 1139

Art. 1—The Exclusion of Suicides, Public Sinners and Catechumens

The commission of suicide has always been universally condemned. One of the earliest recorded instances of the refusal of burial centers in this crime. The Circumcellions, a Donatist faction of the fourth century, were so eager to end this life and enjoy the bliss of heaven that they sought an early death. One of the favorite methods was deliberately to provoke public disorders in which numbers of them were killed. St. Optatus (c. 370) writes of them and tells of their being refused Christian burial by the Donatists, who considered their deaths indirect suicide.[1]

Palladius (c. 365-c. 432) recounts in his history an incident that further shows the antiquity of this ban on suicide. He writes of a nun who killed herself because she believed she had been calumniated. Her caluminator, upon hearing of her action, in turn killed himself, and Palladius states that both were denied the Sacrifice by the priest, which clearly showed that they were considered to have died out of the Church.[2]

Further, the *oblationes* were refused in the case of suicides. Originally the *oblationes* were gift-offerings brought to the altar by the faithful and offered to the priest. They consisted of bread and wine for the Sacrifice. The surplus that was left after the Mass was distributed to the poor.[3] This practice developed into the custom of making offerings to the Church on various occasions, especially that of a death, in order that the satisfaction of the offering might be enjoyed

1 *Sancti Optati Milevitani Libri VII*, lib. III, n. 4—*CSEL*, XXVI, 82, 83.

2 Lowther-Clarke, *The Lausiac History of Palladius* (New York: Macmillan, 1918), p. 116.

3 André-Condis, *Dictionnaire de Droit Canonique* (4 vols., Paris, 1901), III, 8.

by the soul of the deceased. In time, also, this offering took the form of money and was used for the support of the Church as well as of the poor.[4] For the Church to refuse to accept the offerings made for a particular deceased person, or for her to forbid the offerings to be made, clearly implied that such a one was not of the fold or that he had been excommunicated. Hence their refusal meant the refusal of Christian burial.[5] Moreover, on the occasion of the offering of the gifts the name of the person to be benefitted was inscribed in the diptych, the register of the faithful, and thus he shared in the prayers offered by the faithful for those whose names were there inscribed. Obviously, one not of the fold could not be so inscribed, and one to whom this inscription was refused by the rejection of the *oblationes* was not of the fold.[6]

Pope Gregory III (c. 732) clearly declared that the *oblationes* were not to be accepted for the intention of the unworthy, even if they were Catholics; his statement was incorporated by Gratian in the *Decretum*.[7] With this preliminary explanation, it will now be seen that several councils of very early times refused Christian burial, by refusing the *oblationes*. Thus the II Council of Orleans, in 533, ordered that the offerings be refused for "those laying violent hands upon themselves," suicides, and for those who were killed in the act of committing a crime, for they were indirect suicides in as much as they had wilfully caused their own death.[8] By

[4] *Dictionnaire de Droit Canonique, loc. cit.*

[5] Cf. Gonzalez-Tellez, in reference to can. 28 of the Council of Elvira (305): "Privatione sepulturae consequens est ne pro his defunctis oblationes recipiantur, . . . unde pro illis quibus denegatur sepultura ecclesiastica oblationes non admittebantur."—lib. III, tit. 28, c. 11, n. 6.

[6] *Dictionnaire de Droit Canonique*, III, 8.

[7] "Sancta sic tenet Ecclesia ut quisque pro mortuis vere Christianis offerat oblationes, atque presbiter eorum faciat memoriam, et quamvis peccatis omnes subiacemus, congruit ut sacerdos pro mortuis Catholicis memoriam faciat et intercedat; non tamen pro impiis (quamvis Christiani fuerint) tale quid agere licebit"—c. 21, C. 13, q. 2.

[8] Can. 15—Harduin, II, 1175. The same was later decreed in the Council of Auxerre (578), can. 17—Harduin, III, 446.

the same method the Council of Vaison (442) not only manifested a relaxation in the administration of penitential discipline, but also implied that burial had been theretofore denied, when it permitted the offering and acceptance of *oblationes* for the public penitent who had died suddenly or while on a journey.[9]

Whether Catechumens were refused burial in the early centuries of the Church does not seem clear, for there appears to be some diversity in the opinions of the Fathers. Thus, St. John Chrysostom (+ 407) was quite definitely opposed to it, for he recommended that private prayers and private offerings were to be made for them since they could have no part in the public offices of the Church.[10] But St. Ambrose, (+ 397) in his famous discourse on the death of Valentinian II, (375-392) may be considered to have implied that the latter had received Baptism of desire and therefore died in the Church. For, he says, as the martyrs who die before receiving Baptism receive it in the shedding of their blood, so Valentinian received it by the fervor of his desire, which was known to all.[11] One phrase in this sermon, however, gives rise to much speculation: *"solemniter non sunt celebrata mysteria,"* for it may be construed to mean either the ceremonies of Baptism or of the funeral Mass. If the latter, it would be a strong indication that Valentinian was denied Christian burial. But the context seems to favor the former meaning.[12]

St. Augustine's opinion is not entirely free of doubts, for he praises very highly the worth of a good catechumen: *"—nec ego dubito cathechumenum Catholicum caritate divina flagrantem haeretico baptizato anteponere, sed etiam in ipsa intus Catholica bonum catechumenum malo baptizato ante-*

[9] Can. 2—Harduin, I, 1787; the II Council of Arles (443) enacted an identical decree in can. 12—Harduin, II, 774.

[10] *Hom. III in Epist. ad Phillip.*, n. 4—*MPG*, LXII, 204.

[11] *De Obitu Valentiniani*, n. 51—*MPL*, XVI, 1375.

[12] Moulart thinks the contrary, namely, that this is a clear indication that the funeral services were not celebrated for him—*De Sepultura*, p. 62.

ponimus."[13] He insists also on the great value of faith when Baptism cannot be had: "*Etiam atque etiam considerans, invenio non tantum passionem pro nomine Christi id quod ex Baptismo deerat posse supplere, sed etiam fidem conversionemque cordis, si forte ad celebrandum mysterium Baptismi in angustiis temporum succuri non potest.*"[14] However, he is quite plainly opposed to the opinion that a catechumen's holiness will avail him anything if he is not baptized: ". . . *ita sanctificatio catechumeni, si non fuerit baptizatus, non ei valet ad intrandum in regno coelorum, aut ad peccatorum remissionem.*"[15] Gratian quotes Augustine as clearly opposed to any idea that catechumens are saved without Baptism: "*Catheclumenum, quamvis in operibus bonis defunctum, vitam habere non credimus, excepto dumtaxat nisi martyrio sacramentum compleat.*"[16]

From the sum of the evidence it would seem to be fairly certain that catechumens were not considered members of the Church as far as Christian burial was concerned.[17] Similarly, when infants of Catholic parents died without Baptism they also were refused Christian burial.[18]

With the I Council of Braga (561) legislation somewhat more specific is discovered, although there is still considerable opportunity in some instances for the process of deduction to discover the denial of Christian burial. There still is evidence of this privation under ambiguous terms, as in the foregoing times, but, on the whole, this period deserves to be considered as manifesting an advance in the development of legislation on the subject.

13 *De Baptismo*, lib. IV. c. 21, n. 28—*MPL*, XLIII, 172.

14 *Op. cit.*, lib. IV, c. 22—*MPL*, XLIII, 173.

15 *De Peccatorum Meritis et Remissione Libri IV*, lib. II, c. 26, n. 42—*MPL*, XLIV, 180.

16 C. 37, D. 4, *de cons.*

17 Many, *De Locis Sacris*, n. 217; Schmalzgrueber, *Ius Ecclesiasticum Universum*, (5 vols., Romae, 1843-45), lib. III, tit. 28, n. 6; cf. Moulart, *De Sepultura*, pp. 60-63, 268-269.

18 C. 112, D. 4, *de cons.*

The Council of Braga took decisive action on several prevailing evils. It forbade Christian burial to suicides and to those who were put to death for their crimes.[19] In canon 15 the Council renewed the prohibitions against communicating with heretics in any way, *"sicut antiqua canonum continent statuta."*[20] Catechumens also were denied Christian burial by canon 17 in so far as the Council denied it to all who had not been baptized.

With regard to those who were condemned to death, a mitigation of the severity of the Council of Braga is found in the decree of the Council of Mayence (847), which ordered that anyone condemned to death was not to be denied Christian burial, since God does not punish the same crime twice.[21] This law was incorporated in Gratian's *Decretum,* in the gloss to which it is noted that the permission of the civil authority was to be obtained that the act be licit.[22]

Those who died in tournaments, jousts or like forbidden contests wherein the danger of death was always probable, were to be deprived of Christian burial. The III Council of Valence (855) considered them to be suicides, and on that ground refused them Christian burial, even though death did

[19] Can. 16—Harduin, III, 351. This canon is not as clear as could be desired, for it states that suicides are not to be *solemnly buried with psalms:* "neque cum psalmis ad sepulturam eorum cadavera deducantur." That it did include privation of the entire ceremony of Christian burial is stated in the gloss to c. 12, C. 23, q. 5, of Gratian's *Decretum,* in which the decree of Braga was incorporated, v. *ad sepulturam:* "videtur quod tales sepeliuntur . . . sed hoc non est verum et intelligas illud de canina sepultura." It was presupposed, however, that the act of suicide was voluntary, for those who killed themselves while they were irresponsible were not excluded from Christian burial; cf. gloss of c. 12, C. 23, q. 5, v. *voluntarie:* "secus si per furorem; tunc non imputetur."

[20] Harduin, *loc. cit.*

[21] Can. 27—Harduin, V, 13.

[22] C. 30, C. 13, q. 2; gloss, v. *in patibulis:* "licite sepeliuntur suspensi et concremati dummodo hoc fiat auctoritate principis."

not occur until after the battle. In the latter event, they could be given the last sacraments, but no Christian burial.[23]

This legislation was in the spirit of that issued earlier by Pope Eugene II in 824 when he forbade the granting of Christian burial, *"Sepultura Christianorum"*, to those who lost their lives in contests forbidden by the Church as dangerous to life, even were they to receive the last sacraments before death.[24] Other councils took similar action.[25]

To be killed in the act of committing a crime was considered cause for the denial of Christian burial; for, to all appearances, it meant dying in sin. The Council of Chelsea in England (787) forbade the granting of Christian burial to such persons who had died without repentance or confession.[26] And the Council of Tribur (895) decreed that no public prayers were to be said nor any oblations to be received for those who died in this manner.[27]

Similar laws against those who died in crime were passed by the Council of Rouen (1074) [28] and the Council of Nîmes (1096).[29]

What may appear unusually severe was a decree of Pope Eugene II (824) in regard to advocates. It warned them that if they betrayed the trust reposed in them by misappropriating to themselves or to others what did not belong to them, and if they died unabsolved from this sin, they would be deprived of Christian burial.[30] Presumably the decree was necessitated by a certain amount of abuse and unscrupulous practice.

[23] Can. 12—Mansi, XV, 9.

[24] *Decretum* VII—*Decreta Eugenii Papae II*—Mansi, XIV, 416.

[25] Council of Rheims (1148), c. 12—Mansi, XXI, 716; III General Council of the Lateran (1179), c. 14—Mansi, XXI, 529.

[26] C. 20—Mansi, III, 2080.

[27] C. 31—Mansi, XVIIIA, 174.

[28] C. 9—Hefele-Leclercq, V, 113.

[29] C. 11—Hefele-Leclercq, V, 449.

[30] *Decretum* V—*Decreta Eugenii Papae II*—Mansi, XIV, 415.

Art. 2—The Exclusion of Pagans and Infidels

The attitude of the Church against the granting of Christian burial to pagans and infidels is very definitely stated in this period, as is evidenced in Gratian's *Decretum* in two important passages that he incorporated from the *Liber Decretorum* (c. 1012) of Burchard of Worms. Both express the strongest prohibition against the burial of these people in consecrated ground. The first declares that the ground in which a *pagan* has been buried cannot be consecrated, and that Mass cannot be celebrated there until the remains are exhumed, cast out, and the place has been purified.[31] The second states substantially the same with regard to *infidels*.[32] These two de-

[31] C. 27, D. 1, *de cons.;* Burchard, *Libri XX Decretorum*, lib. III, c. 13—*MPL*, CXV, 676.

[32] C. 28, D. 1, *de cons;* Burchard, lib. III, c. 38—*MPL*, CXV, 679. These two canons of Burchard were taken from two councils, according to his incomplete references to them; canon 27 from a Council of Orleans, and canon 28 from a Council of Agrippa. But Berardi (*Gratiani Canones Genuini ab Apochryphis Discreti* [4 vol., Venetiis, 1777], pars. I, cc. 29, 57) declares that they will be sought in vain there, for they were taken by Burchard from the *Capitula Regum Francorum*, which in turn received them from the Penitential of Theodore of Canterbury (Archbishop from 688-690). Acording to Berardi, Burchard deliberately invented the sources he gave because he did not wish to attribute them to the *Capitula Regum Francorum*, which, at the time, were not fully accepted by the Germans, among whom he was writing. Obviously, he did not know of their origin beyond that. Berardi allays any doubts as to their value by describing Theodore as a leading intellectual of the times, expert in both Eastern and Western customs and traditions, whose Penitential was the first and the model for later ones in the West. MacNeil & Gamer (*Medieval Handbooks of Penance* [New York: Columbia University Press, 1939], p. 199, nn. 4, 5) confirm this importance of Theodore's Penitential by their high estimation of his learning and influence. They also give the two sources of the canons that appeared in Gratian, and they are substantially the same as Gratian recorded them—Book II, c. 1, of the Penitential. As for Theodore's source, no mention is made of it and the value of the texts rests therefore upon the value of his reputation which seems to have been of the highest. It may very safely be assumed that he was interpreting the discipline of his time throughout the Church.

crees form one of the principal bases for later legislation on the denial of Christian burial to the unbaptized, according to Samuellius († 1660).[33] They are also a main source of the denial of Christian burial to the unbaptized children of Catholic parents.[34]

Art. 3—The Exclusion of Those Who Died Suddenly or in Childbirth

In the sixth and seventh centuries Christian burial was sometimes refused to those who died suddenly, without the sacraments, according to testimony concerning the practice in Ireland.[35] The same was refused to those dying in childbirth.[36] The refusal seems to have been based on a supposed manifestation of God's displeasure. But the practice does not appear to have been universal, for the XI Council of Toledo (675) provided that those who had manifested regret for their faults, even if death had overtaken them before their full reconciliation to the Church, were to be admitted to Christian burial.[37]

In later legislation this merciful tendency seems to have prevailed, for in the laws of King St. Stephen of Hungary (1000-1038), in the early eleventh century, it was provided that they who died suddenly were not to be denied Christian

33 *Praxis Nova Observanda in Ecclesiasticis sepulturis Christi Fidelibus Catholicis Tradendis* (Lucae, 1650), tract. 2, controv. 4. concl. 12. Hereafter this work is referred to as *De Sepulturis*.

34 Gloss, c. 28, D. 1, *de cons.*, v. "*celebrare*": "sed quid dices de muliere pregnante mortua? . . . consuevit tamen aperiri et foetus extrahi et extra coemeterium sepeliri."

35 In re Irish cemeteries of the period, cf. *Dictionnaire d'archéologie et de liturgie*, III, 1658, v. "*cimetière.*"

36 *Dictionnaire d'archéologie et de liturgie, loc. cit.*

37 C. 12; this canon reflects the diversity of opinion on the subject: "De his qui accepta poenitentia antequam reconcilientur ab hac vita recesserint, *quamquam diversitas praeceptorum de hoc capite habeatur*, illorum tamen nos sententias placuit sequi qui multiplices numero de hujusmodi decreverunt, ut et memoria talium in ecclesiis commendetur et oblatio pro eorum dedicata spiritibus accipiatur"—Mansi, XI, 144.

burial: *"nam occulta et divina judicia nobis sunt incognita."* [38] And the Council of Rouen late in the same century (1074) specified that both those who died suddenly and those who died in childbirth were not to be refused Christian burial, unless they were known to have committed suicide.[39]

Art. 4—The Exclusion of Heretics and Excommunicates

The principle for the denial of Christian burial to heretics and excommunicates was ably worded by Pope St. Leo, in the middle of the fifth century, in a letter that he wrote to Rusticus, the Bishop of Narbonne. In this letter he replied to several questions of the bishop in regard to discipline. Among them, the bishop had asked what was to be done with those who died unreconciled with the Church? Pope St. Leo replied that their lot is in the hands of God, for Whom it is to judge them, for since they were not in communion with the Church when they lived, they also were not when they died: *"Nos autem quibus viventibus non communicavimus, mortuis communicare non possumus."* [40] This text aptly described the attitude of the Church with regard to those who died outside the fold, and became the classical text for many later decisions and decrees, as will be noted in later history. It reflected a condition of fact and clearly showed that the denial of Christian burial was not an act of vegeance or of spite on the part of the Church, but merely the recognition of a real situation; namely, one was or one was not in communion with the Church, and upon that hinged the granting of Christian burial.

Another letter of the same saintly pontiff shows that excommunication places one outside the Church, for he wrote that if one is found to have been excommunicated by mistake, his name is to be *re-inscribed* in the diptych.[41] To have had one's name removed from this register of the members of the

[38] *MPL*, CLI, 1247.

[39] C. 9—Hefele-Leclercq, V, 113.

[40] *Epist. CLXVII*—*MPL*, LIV, 1205-1206.

[41] C. 6, C. 24, q. 2.

Church signified expulsion by a custom that dated back to the days before the infant Church had become completely independent of the Jewish congregations.[42]

St. Augustine leaves no doubt that excommunication meant the cutting off of the individual from the Church, giving him over to Satan, when he wrote that not only do they not belong to the Church who are separated from it by their manifest exclusion, but also they who, though corporally united, are cut off from it by their wicked life.[43]

The separation from the faithful of all heretics and excommunicates was therefore total in the early period of the Church. Excommunication in those days extended not only to separation in religious matters, but also in civil or profane affairs.[44] It seems obvious that in early legislation heretics were included in the ban on all excommunicates and that no formal edict by the Church was necessary to establish the fact of excommunication in their case. Their excommunication was implied in the fact, already mentioned in the Scriptures, that the faithful were to regard them as dangerous traitors and consequently to keep aloof from them.[45] This may be gathered from the acts of the Council of Antioch held in 341, which forbade the faithful to pray with excommunicates. Such absolute separation necessarily impled the denial of Christian burial.[46] Gonzalez-Tellez († 1649) clearly states that Christian burial was forbidden to excommunicates from the times of the Apostles.[47]

The strong tradition among the common people of the time

42 Luke, VI: 22.

43 C. 8, C. 24, q. 3; c. 32, C. 11, q. 3.

44 Hyland, *Excommunication, Its Nature, Historical Development and Effects*, The Catholic University of America Canon Law Studies, n. 49 (Washington, D. C., The Catholic University of America, 1928), p. 35.

45 Romans, XVI: 17; Titus, III: 10; I Cor., V: 9.

46 Hefele-Leclercq, I, 715.

47 Lib. III, tit. 28, c. 12, n. 56: "Cum omnis communio prohibita sit cum excommunicatis jam a temporibus Apostolorum, recto statutum est ne excommunicatum sepulturae ecclesiasticae tradamus."

against the Christian burial of heretics, excommunicates and others unworthy of the privilege, is reflected in many pious fables concerning the strange happenings that were reported to have followed the burial of such persons. Thus St. Gregory the Great (540-604) recounts that two nuns who had been excommunicated were buried in a church near the tomb of a martyr. An old servant who had attended them in life related that each time that the Deacon at Mass summoned the faithful to Communion, she saw the two spirits emerge from their tomb and leave the church.[48] The same author speaks of a sacristan who was reported to have seen the spirit of an excommunicated person, who had been buried in the church dragged before the altar and there consumed in flames. Other similar stories are told by St. Gregory of Tours (528-593) in his *De Gloria Martyrum*. This is not the place to discuss the genuineness of these stories. They are cited only as an indication of the popular opinion and reaction concerning the Christian burial of excommunicates.[49]

Renewing the ancient penalty against having anything to do with heretics and excommunicates, the Council of Ravenna (877), under the presidency of Pope John VIII, added a provision that was frequently repeated in later legislation, namely, that to remain excommunicated for one year, was to incur the loss of both communion with the Church *after* death and inclusion in the suffrages and prayers of the Church for the faithful departed.[50]

In general, the absolute avoidance of heretics and excommunicates that had been constantly enjoined since the days of the Apostles[51] was being relaxed—not however, in regard to Christian burial—and indications of this are clear in the decree of the Council of Rome (1079), in which it was per-

[48] *Diolog.* II, 23—*MPL*, LXVI, 178.

[49] *Dictionnaire d'Archéologie et de Liturgie*, I, 501, v. "*Ad Sanctos.*"

[50] Can. 9—Mansi, XVII-A, 338. In reference to this penalty, Gonzalez-Tellez (lib. V, tit. 13, c. 2, n. 8) adds that it deprived one of Christian burial, even after the reception of the last sacraments.

[51] I Cor., V: 11.

mitted that the family of an excommunicate might associate with him.[52]

The Council of Ravenna (877) implicitly denied Christian burial to those who were violators of churches or who struck clerics, when it decreed that, if after three warnings they still persisted in their excommunication without any effort to remove it, they were to be shunned by all Christians: *"ab omni consortio Christianorum repellantur."* [53]

Incendiaries, murderers and their helpers and abettors were warned by the Council of Ravenna (877) that they were excommunicated, and that if they failed to seek absolution from the penalty after a third warning they were to be shunned: *"ab omni collegio Christianorum separentur."* [54]

Appreciation of the severity of these decrees and of the evils that they were combating leaves little room for doubt that Christian burial was denied to those who died in a state of revolt against the law.

In the II General Lateran Council of 1139 Pope Innocent II (1130-1143) renewed a decree that had been promulgated by the Council of Rheims, 1131, over which he had also presided, enunciating once more the severest penalties against those who dared lay violent hands upon the clergy or religious. Their absolution was reserved to the Pope, except when they were in danger of death, and they were to present themselves before him and to accept the penance that he would impose.[55] Obviously, one dying under such an excommunication was considered out of the Church and therefore was denied Christian burial.[56]

The same Council issued Pope Innocent's scathing denunciation of incendiaries, in which he ordered that all those guilty of this horrible and most evil offence, which he condemned in

52 C. 103, C. 11, q. 3; c. 110, C. 11, q. 3.

53 Can. 5—Mansi, XVII-A, 338.

54 Cc. 7, 8—Mansi, XVII-A, 338.

55 Can. 15—Mansi, XXI, 530.

56 Gratian, in reference to Cause 17, q. 4, says that this offense was considered sacrilege.

the name of God and the Apostles Peter and Paul, should be excommunicated. He added that if one died with such a crime on his soul he was to be refused Christian burial. Nor was he to be absolved in this life before he had made full satisfaction, within his power, and had sworn never to commit such a heinous crime again. As a worthy penance for incendiarism the Pope suggested a year either in Spain or in the Holy Land in the service of God against the infidels.[57]

Art. 5—The Exclusion of the Interdicted

The evidence of the period points to an increasing difficulty in regard to excommunications. They were being too frequently endured passively without any effort to obtain absolution. The Church seems thus to have been frustrated in many of her attempts to remedy the evils of the times by the use of this penalty. It may possibly be that therein lies the origin of the interdict. The definition of this ecclesiastical penalty as known today is: "a censure by which the faithful, while remaining in communion with Christian society, are forbidden to use certain sacred things . . . these sacred things are the liturgical services, some of the sacraments and Christian burial."[58] The origin of this penalty, however, is not clear. Some place it as early as the late sixth century;[59] others later.[60]

The character of this penalty has been substantially the same from the time of its origin, so that no further treatment of it is needed here. The classic example of it is the interdict which was inflicted upon his diocese by Hincmar, Bishop of Laon, in middle of the ninth century. He had been summoned

57 Cc. 18, 19—Mansi, XXI, 531; c. 32, C. 23, q. 8.

58 Ayrinhac-Lydon, *Penal Legislation in the New Code of Canon Law* (New York, Benziger Bros., 1936), pp. 95, 96.

59 Crnica, *Modificationes in Tractatu de Censuris per Codicem Iuris Canonici Introductae* (St. Mauritii Agaunensis, 1919), p. 136.

60 For details of this, cf. Conran, *The Interdict*, The Catholic University of America Canon Law Studies, n. 56 (Washington, D. C.: The Catholic University of America, 1930), pp. 16-25.

to appear before a synod to answer for his misdeeds. Trying to forestall his condemnation, he ordered that no Mass be celebrated, that no sacraments be administered and that no one be given Christian burial in his diocese. Hincmar, Archbishop of Rheims, and uncle of the Bishop of Laon, records this affair in his letter to the latter, who was in prison.[61]

What may have been one of the origins of the "Truce of God" is contained in the threat of an interdict by the Council of Limoges in 1031. The Council was striving to diminish the number of private wars that were devastating the Viscounty of Limousin during that period. Having asked the nobles of the provinces to swear to keep the peace, and having received their refusal to cooperate, the bishops threatened them with an *excommunication upon the whole province,* during which there would be no church services of any kind, or Christian burial.[62] Thus the Council of Limoges laid down one of the first clearly distinguishable interdicts, and it marked the emergence of this penalty from the era of its obscurity and of its confusion with excommunication.[63]

Thomassinus refers to this same Council, but with regard to a different matter, namely, excommunication. He recounts that it was reported to the assembled bishops that a certain excommunicated man had been buried secretly in blessed ground by his friends. Soon after, the body was discovered mysteriously disinterred, and lying outside the limits of the cemetery, although the grave was completely undisturbed. The bishops concluded that this was proof to all that he who died outside the communion of the Church was to be denied Christian burial.[64]

Another example of interdict appears in a decree of the Council of Poitiers (1078). In its first decree it excom-

61 *Epist. III* Harduin, V, 1373.

62 Mansi, XIX, 541.

63 Hefele-Leclercq, IV, 956; Conran, *op. cit.*, p. 24.

64 *Vetus et Nova Ecclesiae Disciplina,* pars III, lib. I, c. 68, n. 2.

municated all those who seized Church property, and it placed under interdict any church so seized and held.[65]

The rising difficulties between the religious and the bishops over the question of jurisdiction, and the evasion sometimes practised by Catholics through intrigues with the regulars in escaping episcopal and synodal laws, are revealed by the decree of the Council of Nimes (1096), in which it was ordered that the regular clergy were not to grant Christian burial or any religious function to those who were excommunicated, interdicted, or guilty of robbery.[66] Furthermore, it insisted that the sanctions should be applied to those who withheld the tithes and the offerings of the Church. Among these it included those who seized a portion of a cemetery or sacred edifice, and it warned all such offenders that they were to be excluded from all contact with the faithful.[67]

Thus the period closes with a clear and strong enunciation of the penalty of the privation of Christian burial for those who died in grievous sin. The legislation developed from the less distinct forms of denial in the earlier part of the period to the unmistakable and specific forms of denial found in the later part. The period witnessed the growth of the interdict as a form of excommunication upon a community, a place, or a moral person, which differed from excommunication in that those upon whom it was laid were not expelled from the communion of the faithful. The privation of Christian burial during an interdict arose from the fact of closed churches and cemeteries.

The period about to be discussed witnessed the greatest development in the use of this penalty in the Church's struggle to save civilization from the chaotic elements which arose from the ruins of the empires of Rome and of Charlemagne. This period also saw the growth of new heresies and the strenuous efforts of the Church to stamp them out by extending her laws against them to all who in any way cooperated in their propagation.

65 Mansi, XX, 498.

66 Can. 16—Hefele-Leclercq, V, 449.

67 Can. 6—Hefele-Leclercq, *loc. cit.*

Chapter III

FROM 1179 TO 1614

Art. I—The Exclusion of Catechumens

By the time of Innocent III (1198-1216) catechumens were granted Christian burial, but only under certain conditions. They must have had the use of reason, have been instructed in the truths of faith necessary for salvation, have signified their intention and resolve to receive Baptism, and thereupon have died so suddenly that they could not previously receive Baptism.[1]

This benign legislation was occasioned by the sudden death of a priest, who, it was only then discovered, had never been baptized. The privilege seems to have been already generally conceded and it continued to be granted in the cases of those who, though properly prepared for Baptism, died suddenly before having received it, through no fault of their own.[2]

Art. 2—The Exclusion of Heretics

The legislation of the III General Lateran Council (1179) discloses the presence of new and growing heresies, after a period in which annoyance from that source had been comparatively slight. Alexander III (1159-1181) took firm steps to combat the new errors, which, he complained, were being openly flaunted, whereas formerly they had been kept secret. He inaugurated a period of legislation that was to be characterized by thoroughness and vigor.

In canon 27 of the Council it was decreed that all those who publicly professed heresy were to be anathema, together with all who were their *defensores*,[3] *receptatores*,[4] and all others who received heretics into their homes, allowed them

1 C. 2, X, *de presbytero non-baptizato*, III, 43, in VI°.

2 *Hostiensis Summa Aurea* (Lugduni, 1503), lib. III, *de presbytero non-baptizato*, n. 2; Many, *De Locis Sacris*, 217.

3 Those who in any way defended either the heresy or the heretic. Cf. Alterius, *Disputationes de Censuris Ecclesiasticis* (2 vols., Romae,

upon their lands, or in any way had anything to do with them.[5] This penalty provided that if any of those mentioned died unabsolved they were to be denied Christian burial. Since it was a General Council that made this law, it applied to the whole Church. Moreover, the legislation of the III General Lateran Council on the subject of heresy gave the tone to all legislation that was to follow.

The same penalty was enacted by Pope Lucius III (1181-1185) in the Council of Verona (1184), and was extended to include those who were openly suspected of heresy.[6]

In 1215 Innocent III, at the IV General Lateran Council, extended this law still further to include the *credentes*,[7] and *fautores*[8] of heretics[9] In 1229 Gregory IX (1227-1241) declared anathema[10] upon all heretics and their supporters.[11]

1616), Tom. I, lib. V, c. V, disp. 2. This work is referred to hereafter as *De Censuris*.

4 Those who sheltered or shielded heretics from the authorities. The offense had to be of a habitual nature rather than a single instance for the incurring of the penalty. Cf. Alterius, *op. cit.*, Tom. I, lib. V, c. IV, disp. 2.

5 Harduin, VI, 1683; c. 8, X, *de haereticis*, V, 7.

6 " . . . qui vero inventi fuerint sola Ecclesiae suspicione notabilis . . . simili sententiae subiacebunt"—c. 9, X, *de haereticis*, V, 7.

7 Those who assented to or believed heretics were considered to be as guilty as heretics; Cf. Suarez, *Opera Omnia* (36 vols., Parisiis, 1856-1861), vol. XII, *Tractatus de Fide*, disp. 24, sec. 1, n. 1.

8 Anyone who, broadly, acted favorably toward heretics; one who favored them in any way. Cf. Alterius, *De Censuris*, Tom. I, lib. V, cap. V, disp. 2.

9 Harduin, VII, 21; c. 13, X, *de haereticis*, V, 7.

10 "Anathema" before the time of Gregory IX meant the total cutting off of the offender from the Church of Christ and was deemed worse than excommunication, which meant separation from the faithful — c. 13, C. 24, q. 3; but from the time that Gregory declared that *excommunication* when used unmodified meant *major excommunication* (c. 59, X, *de sent. excom.*, V, 39), there was no difference between the two terms, *anathema* and *excommunication*, except in the solemnity used in declaring the former.

11 C. 15, X, *de haereticis*, V, 7.

And again, in 1254 Alexander IV (1254-1261) strengthened the foregoing legislation by declaring that anyone who knowingly gave Christian burial to heretics, their *credentes, receptatores, fautores,* or *defensores,* was *ipso facto* excommunicated. The offender was not to be absolved before he had, with his own hands, disinterred the deceased heretic and placed the body far from consecrated ground. Furthermore, the grave so desecrated was never to be used for burial again.[12]

This legislation was repeated by numerous councils, but by none more emphatically or comprehensively than it had been declared by these great pontiffs. The legislation enacted by Alexander IV was the model for all other legislation.

In 1280 Nicholas III (1277-1280) issued his Constitution *"Noverit universitas vestra,"* in which he renewed the legislation of his predecessors in the matter of heretics and their supporters. This Constitution was occasioned by the Pope's desire to warn the regular clergy, who had felt exempt from the law in this matter, that to grant Christian burial to those forbidden it by the laws on heresy was to incur excommunication *ipso facto,* from which they could be absolved only under the same conditions as those prescribed by Alexander IV.[13]

This strong body of legislation governed the matter until the appearance of the Constitution *"Ad evitanda"* [14] of Martin V in 1418, which divided excommunicates into two groups: those with whom the faithful could associate, the *tolerati,* and those who had to be avoided in all things, the *vitandi.*[15] The Constitution was issued to meet a situation that had developed from the large number of excommunicates. Up to the time of Martin V, all excommunicates were to be avoided in both

12 C. 2, *de haereticis,* V, 2, in VI°.

13 *Bullarium Romanum,* IV, 48.

14 *Fontes,* n. 45.

15 These terms are not used in the Constitution, but were first used by Dominicus Soto (1494-1560), according to Kober (*Der Kirchenbann nach den Grundsätzen des canonischen Rechts* [Tübingen], 1863, p. 267).

sacred and profane matters under the penalty of minor excommunication, which consisted in one's being deprived of the sacraments. The difficulties resulting from this prohibition of association with excommunicates were becoming increasingly complicated and relief was asked from the Holy See. By his decree the Pope declared that from that time forward only those excommunicates would be *vitandi* who had been excommunicated by name, whether by a judge or by public denunciation, and those who were notoriously guilty of having assaulted clerics.[16]

Considerable controversy developed over whether heretics who had not been denounced publicly were among the *excommunicati tolerati,* and, if they were, whether they could be given Christian burial. The difficulty arose from the very broad language of the Constitution in which the Pope mercifully stated that thenceforth no one was bound to forego association with any one *"praetextu cuiuscumque sententiae aut censurae ecclesiasticae, a iure vel ab homine generaliter promulgatae."* For, it was argued, if *tolerati* may associate with the faithful in life, they may also do so in death, and therefore be given Christian burial among the faithful. This adaptation in practice, it was stated, was but the application in positive form of the famous principle which Pope Leo I had proposed; *"Quibus viventibus non communicavimus, mortuis communicare non possumus"* [17]

The controversy is too long to be treated here; it will be sufficient to quote from the majority opinion which maintained that notorious heretics were not allowed Christian burial, even though they were not denounced or sentenced as heretics. Moulart[18] felt that the question was already settled by the same Pope in another constitution of the same year, concerning heresy itself. In that constitution, condemning the heresies of Wyclif and Huss, the Pope had expressly stated: *"Et*

16 Alterius, *De Censuris*, Tom. I, disp. VI, c. 1, D.

17 *Epist. CLXVII—MPL*, LIV, 1205-1206.

18 *De Sepultura*, p. 273.

si tales haeretici publici et manifesti, licet nondum per Ecclesiam declarati, in hoc gravi crimine decesserint, ecclesiastica careant sepultura." [19] Moulart believed that this shows that the Pope placed the reason for the penalty in the fact of heresy and not in the fact of the excommunication.[20] Many [21] reasoned that if heretics were to be considered only as excommunicates it was true that they could be granted Christian burial according to the Constitution *"Ad evitanda,"* if they had not been denounced. But he believed also that they were refused Christian burial because of their heresy itself, independently of their excommunication. He based his opinion on the decree of Alexander III in the III General Lateran Council (1179) which referred to the fact of heresy, and not to the presence of excommunication, as the ground for the penalty.[22] This opinion was supported by other authorities.[23]

Moreover, any relaxation of the old rule with regard to the heretics and all communication with them that might have arisen after the Constitution *"Ad evitanda,"* would seem to be nullified by the decree of the V General Lateran Council (1512-1517), in which it was enacted that the faithful were to shun all whose excommunication was public and notorious, even though they were not denounced.[24]

19 Const. *"Inter cunctas,"* in the Council of Constance, 22 Feb., 1418—*Fontes*, n. 43.

20 *De Sepultura*, p. 273.

21 *De Locis Sacris*, n. 219.

22 C. 8, X, *de haereticis*, V, 7.

23 Barbosa, *Libri Tres Iuris Ecclesiastici Universi*, lib. 2, c. 10, n. 43 (Hereafter this work will be referred to as *Ius Eccles. Univers.*); Raymond of Peñafort, *Summa Iuris* (Verona, 1744), lib. 1, tit. 15, *de sepulturis*, p. 133; Giraldi (*Expositio Iuris Pontificii*, 3 vols., Romae, 1769, pars. 1, lib. V, tit. 7, sec. 809) included those heretics who were not denounced, as long as the fact of their heresy was notorious; Samuellius (*De Sepulturis*, tract. II, disp. I. controv. 9, conclus. 3) wrote that all heretics are to be denied Christian burial if they are notorious, for the Church *"non intendit aliquem favorem praestare . . . quando indulsit ne vitaretur."*

24 Sess. XI—Mansi, XXXII, 968, *ad finem*.

The final authority, however, is found in the Ritual of Paul V (1614). Immediately after listing Jews, infidels and pagans among those to whom Christian burial was not to be granted, it extended the prohibition of Christian burial *"hereticis et eorum fautoribus."* [25]

ART. 3—THE EXCLUSION OF EXCOMMUNICATES

Before the Constitution *"Ad evitanda"* of Pope Martin V in 1418 all those who were under the *major* [26] excommunication were *vitandi,* that is, they were to be shunned by all the faithful both in secular and in sacred affairs.[27] This utter separation from the faithful, which was incurred by those whom the Church has declared expelled, was of apostolic origin,[28] and had been formulated for all time by Pope St. Leo the Great: *"Quibus vivis non communicavimus, nec mortuis communicare possumus."* [29]

The law of the early part of this period did not alter the ancient concept in any way. Thus it was simply the traditional

25 *Rituale Romanum Pauli V. Pont. Max. Editum* (Antverpiae, 1744), tit. *De Exequiis,—Quibus non licet dare Ecclesiasticam sepulturam.* (Hereafter this work will be referred to as: *Rit. Rom. Paul. V*).

26 *Major* excommunication was that excommunication which cut one off completely from the fold of Christ. It was called *major* in opposition to the *minor* excommunication, which was more of a penance, and which deprived one of the sacraments. Since minor excommunication did not expel a Christian from the Church, the term "excommunication," as used in the following pages, will not be employed in the latter sense if it is not specifically qualified by the word "minor." Cf. Hyland, *Excommunication*, pp. 31-34, for further details of the distinction between the two excommunications. Some authors held that even the minor excommunication, if it was public and notorious, prevented the granting of Christian burial: e.g., Panormitanus (lib. III, tit. 7, c. 1, n. 5) and Samuellius (*De Sepulturis*, tract. 2, disp. 1, controv. 9, concl. 2). But the more general opinion never accepted this theory. Cf. De Murga, *De Sepulturis*, trac. 2, disquis. 3, dubium 1, nn. 1-15.

27 Hyland, *Excommunication*, p. 35.

28 Hyland, *Excommunication*, pp. 35, 36.

29 *Epist. CLXVII—MPL*, LIV, 1205-1206.

doctrine which Pope Alexander III stated in his letter to the Archbishop of Canterbury (1175) on hearing that the Templars of that diocese had been granting burial to excommunicates who were so designated by name. He ordered the Archbishop to remind the Templars that not only was this severely forbidden, but it was forbidden to give *any* excommunicate Christian burial. Further, they were to exhume the excommunicates whom they had allowed to be buried.[30] Later the same Pontiff had to condemn the general violation of this law by both the Templars and the Hospitalers. This he did through a decree of the III General Lateran Council (1179).[31]

In the year 1200 Pope Innocent III quoted the words of Pope St. Leo I in decreeing that they who were cut off from the Church were not to have Christian burial unless they were absolved before death. If, contrary to this rule, they had been granted Christian burial, they were to be exhumed.[32] But if they had shown manifest signs of penance before death, and could not be absolved because of the lack of time, they were to be absolved from excommunication after death before being granted Christian burial. The Pope's reasons for this were that, though penance may absolve one before God, the excommunication of the Church still stands and must be removed. Further, absolution from the censure was to be imparted lest the faithful conceive the impression that all they needed at death was repentance, and that absolution was not necessary. For with this wrong impression some might lead sinful lives and neglect to call the priest when they were in danger of death, thus sparing themselves the burden of confession, and, perhaps, of restitution.[33] In 1213 the same Pope ordered that cemeteries in which excommunicates had been buried were to

30 C. 5, X, *de privilegiis et excessibus privilegium*, V, 33; Harduin, VI, 1816.

31 Can. 9—Harduin, VI, 1677; C. 3, *de privilegiis et excessibus privilegium*, V, 33.

32 C. 12, X, *de sepulturis*, III, 28.

33 C. 28, X, *de sententia excommunicationis*, V, 39.

be re-blessed *"sicut in dedicatione ecclesiae fieri consueverit."* [34]

When Pope Innocent III heard that some religious were granting Christian burial to those who were excommunicated, he reproved their action in the IV General Council of the Lateran (1215).[35]

Pope Boniface VIII (1294-1303) also showed the abhorrence in which such a breach of the law was to be held when he condemned those religious who were granting Christian burial to excommunicates under what they declared were their privileges.[36] Similarly, Pope Clement V (1305-1314) condemned those who were granting the favor of Christian burial to publicly excommunicated persons.[37] The Council of Ravenna (1311) denied Christian burial, even after the reception of the sacraments, to those who had deliberately remained excommunicated over one year without seeking absolution.[38]

The same difficulty that was discussed above in reference to *heretics*, i.e., the scope of the Constitution *"Ad evitanda,"* arose in this matter of excommunicates also. The question again was whether the *excommunicati tolerati* could be granted Christian burial. Many[39] held that though excommunicates had no *right* to Christian burial in view of their exclusion from the Church, they could be granted it if they were not *vitandi*. Arguing from the principle of St. Leo I, he concluded that whosoever did not have to be shunned in life, did not have to be shunned in death, provided his excommunication was not *"a iudice publicata vel denunciata specialiter et expresse,"*

[34] C. 7, X, *de consecratione ecclesiae*, III, 40.

[35] Can. 61—Harduin, VII, 63; c. 31, *de praebendis et dignitatibus*, III, 5.

[36] C. 8, *de privilegiis*, V, 7, in VI°. Cf. likewise the Council of Compiègne (1304), cc. 1, 3—Harduin, VIII, 1275, 1276.

[37] C. 1, *de sepulturis*, III, 7, in Clem. The gloss on this decretal states that "*publice*" meant that which was *publicly known*, and was therefore not restricted to that which was *publicly denounced*.

[38] Can. 28—Harduin, VIII, 376-377.

[39] *De Locis Sacris*, n. 218.

according to the words of the Constitution *"Ad evitanda."* [40] This opinion had been opposed by Reiffenstuel,[41] who held that the *excommunicati tolerati* were excluded from Christian burial by the common law and that this penalty was incurred by them if they died unabsolved. Moulart [42] followed the view of Reiffensteul and based his opinion upon the fact that the Consitution *"Ad evitanda"* itself clearly stated that *"per hoc tamen excommunicatis . . . non intendimus in aliquo relevare nec eis quomodolibet suffragari."* He believed also that notorious excommunicates, although they were not *vitandi,* incurred the penalty of the denial of Christian burial by the common law. Wernz [43] held the same opinion and cited in support of it Kober and Hollweck. This seems to have been the prevailing opinion and it also seems more consonant with the law as later found in the Ritual of Paul V, in which it was forbidden to give *"publicis excommunicatis majoris excommunicationis"* Christian burial.[44]

ART. 4—THE EXCLUSION OF APOSTATES, SCHISMATICS AND THE INTERDICTED

A. *Apostates*

Apostates were likened to heretics in the matter of Christian Burial.[45] They were, therefore, *ipso facto* excommunicated by the very fact of their apostasy.[46] Denial of Christian burial,

40 *Fontes,* n. 45; Many's opinion had been earlier maintained by Pirhing: lib. III, tit. 28, n. 68.

41 Lib. III, tit. 2, c. 3, nn. 85, 86.

42 *De Sepultura,* pp. 270-271.

43 *Ius Decretalium,* III, 499, footnote 45.

44 Rom. Rit. Paul V, tit. *De Exequiis,—Quibus non licet dare Ecclesiasticam sepulturam.*

45 "Les apostats ne se distinguent pas des hérétiques quant à la nature de leur faute,"—Vacant-Mangenot, *Dictionnaire de Théologie Catholique* (13 vols., Paris, 1903-), I, 1602 ff., v. "apostasie."

46 Cc. 8, 9, 13, X, *de sententia excommunicationis, suspensionis et interdicti,* V, 7.

then, was the legal consequence of their state if they died unrepentant.[47]

B. *Schismatics*

If schismatics were also heretics, they, of course, came under the strictures on heretics with regard to Christian burial. If they were not, they were still denied Christian burial in virtue of the major excommunication which they had incurred by their act of schism.[48]

C. *The Interdicted*

The legislation on the interdict in the period between 1179 and 1614 is so vast that no attempt will be made here to review it completely. Fortunately it lends itself to a summary treatment because of the consistency of its development.

It should here be recalled that an interdict is a censure by which the faithful, while remaining in communion with the Christian society, are forbidden the use of certain sacred things; these are: the liturgical services, some of the sacraments, and Christian burial.[49]

An interdict may be local—applying to a place—prohibiting the above mentioned acts from being celebrated there; or personal—applying to an individual—prohibiting them to a person no matter where he may be. Both the local and the personal interdict may be general or particular. A general local interdict would apply to a whole territory and all persons therein, while a particular local interdict would include, for example, a parish in a city in which there were other parishes. A general personal interdict would include all the people of a specific parish, city or state, but not those who were passing through, while a particular personal interdict would concern one or several determined persons.[50]

In 1179 Alexander III, in the III General Council of the

47 *Dictionnaire de Théologie Catholique*, I, 1608.

48 Hostiensis, *Summa Aurea, de schismaticis*, nn. 2, 3.

49 Ayrinhac-Lydon, *Penal Legislation in the New Code of Canon Law*, nn. 95, 96.

50 *Ibidem*, pp. 97, 98.

Lateran, issued a strong condemnation of the Knights Templars, who had been granting Christian burial even to those who were interdicted *nominatim,* and he threatened them with excommunication, for, he declared, those who are interdicted by name are *vitandi* whether they be religious or laymen.[51] Innocent III, writing to the bishops of Portugal in 1199, reminded them that an interdict is general whether it is laid upon a city, a town or a province.[52]

Since, however, the severity of the interdicts of the time was doing great harm to the faithful because of the prolonged privation of the sacraments, of religious burial and of the divine services, measures had to be taken to lessen their unfortunate effects.[53] Pope Innocent III stated some of the modifications that were gradually being introduced into the interdict to soften its harshness. He declared that although in general Christian burial was to be denied during an interdict, however, those clerics who had faithfully observed the interdict, if it was local, and not personal to them, and who had not been responsible for its infliction, could be buried in the cemetery of the Church but without any external pomp and in silence.[54] The Council of Cologne (1280) also provided that clerics could be given Christian burial during the interdict, but only in silence.[55]

Further mitigation of the severity of the interdict was introduced when Innocent III wrote to the Bishop of Ferrara in 1209 that preaching to the people was to be permitted during the interdict, but no divine services, and therefore no Christian burial.[56] He also permitted that one who had left his property to a monastery on condition that he be buried there after death could be granted that favor during an interdict, if he were not responsible for its infliction.[57]

51 Can. 9—Harduin, VI, 1677.

52 C. 17, *de verborum significatione,* V, 40.

53 Ayrinhac-Lydon, *Penal Legislation,* n. 100.

54 C. 11, *de poenitentiis et remissionibus,* V, 38.

55 Can. 18—Harduin, VIII, 834.

56 C. 43, X, *de sententia excommunicationis,* V, 39.

57 C. 24, *de privilegiis et excessibus,* V, 33.

Innocent had to repeat the warning of Pope Alexander III to religious who violated the interdicts by allowing Christian burial from their churches, reminding them that they thereby incurred excommunication *ipso facto.*[58]

Gregory IX (1227-1241) permitted Mass once a week during an interdict for the purpose of renewing the Blessed Sacrament, but insisted that there be no other religious service of any kind.[59]

It is from exceptions of this kind that an idea can be obtained, by way of contrast, of the great severity of the interdict in those days. Moreover, this legislation settles any doubt that the interdict prohibited not only Church funeral services but also burial in blessed ground. The specific privilege just mentioned relative to clerics without guilt did not apply, however, if the cemetery was itself interdicted with a local interdirt. In that case no one could be buried in the cemetery.[60] In some instances of the interdict exception was also made as to Christian burial for beggars, strangers, and children under two years of age.[61]

Boniface VIII (1294-1303) spoke of the interdict *ab ingressu ecclesiae.* He warned priests who were punished thus that they violated the interdict by offering Mass, and that if they died impentitent they would be refused Christian burial.[62] Under the same kind of interdict a layman was cut off from all divine services; if he died impenitent, he also was to be denied Christian burial with regard both to the ceremonies in the church and the burial in the cemetery.[63]

The same Pope further clarified the effects of the interdict of his time when he declared that a local interdict prohibited

58 C. 31, *de praebendis et dignitatibus,* III, 5; Harduin VII, 63.

59 C. 57, X, *de sententia excommunicationis,* V, 38.

60 De Murga, *De Sepulturis,* tract. 2, disq. IV, dubium 1.

61 Ducange, *Glossarium Mediae et Infimae Latinitatis* (10 vols., Parisiis, 1937-1938), "Interdictum," IV, 391; Conran, *The Interdict,* p. 39.

62 C. 20, *de sententia excommunicationis,* V, 11, in VI°.

63 *Loc. cit.;* cf. De Murga, *De Sepulturis,* tract. 2, disq. IV, dubium 5.

the granting of Christian burial in the place upon which the interdict was inflicted, while a personal interdict prohibited it everywhere for the person or persons so censured.[64] The gloss to this decretal mentioned that any interdict, whether local or personal, unless it was specifically modified, prevented the Christian burial of even children who had not yet attained the use of reason. This is not to be wondered at, continues the gloss, when it is recalled that the interdict by its very nature is a spiritual penalty that punishes the innocent for the faults of the guilty.[65]

De Murga, in the seventeenth century, concluded from this decretal that those who were responsible for the infliction of the interdict upon a place were, by that local interdict itself, made personally interdicted. According to this reasoning, those who were of the territory which was placed under interdict could, as long as they were not the guilty ones, receive Christian burial elsewhere, but the ones responsible for the penalty could not receive it anywhere.[66]

Again the necessity of correcting the abuses of certain religious in defiance of the Church's law of interdict called forth a new decree from Pope Boniface VIII. This decree stipulated that, regardless of any privileges, even if these had been obtained from the Holy See, any of the clergy, both secular and regular, who violated an interdict by granting Christian burial to anyone not entitled thereto would incur the interdict *ab ingressu ecclesiae*.[67] However, Boniface introduced some modifications in the rigor of the interdicts. He ordered that on the great feasts of Easter, Pentecost, Christmas and the Assumption, the churches under interdict were to be thrown open to all, and services were to be held in all solemnity.[68]

[64] C. 16, *de sententia excommunicationis*, V, 11, in VI°.

[65] Gloss to c. 16 *de sententia excommunicationis*, V, 11, in VI°, at the word: "*interdicti*."

[66] *De Sepulturis*, tract. 2, disq. IV, conclus. I, n. 21.

[67] C. 8, *de privilegiis*, V, 7, in VI°.

[68] C. 24, *de sententia excommunicationis*, V, 11, in VI°.

A controversy seems to have existed for some time as to whether this privilege allowed Christian burial to take place on these feasts.[69]

In the General Council of Vienne (1311-1312) Clement V renewed the prohibition against the granting of Christian burial to anyone during an interdict. Excommunication which was reserved to the one inflicting the interdict was the penalty.[70]

The thirteenth century seems to stand out as a time when interdicts were most numerous.[71] From the legislation of this period it appears that the denial of Christian burial was inflicted upon those who were interdicted personally and upon all who were in a place that was under local interdict, unless they were privileged, e.g., the clergy; and the penalty for the breach of this law was excommunication.[72]

No major change in the law occurred after this time. It is in a similar form that the legislation was incorporated into the Ritual of Pope Paul V: *"Negatur eclesiastica sepultura . . . interdictis nominatim et eis qui sunt in territorio interdicto, eo durante."* [73]

69 De Murga (*De Sepulturis,* tract. 2, disq. IV, dubium IV, n. 3) held that it did, for the interdict was suspended on those days. Alterius (*De Censuris,* Tom. II, disp. 6, c. 3) earlier in the seventeenth century had held the opposite view. He reasoned that the penalty of the denial of Christian burial was a penalty separate from that of the denial of divine services, and that therefore it was prohibited in itself, and not merely as a consequence of the denial of church services. He concluded that the lifting of the ban on the one did not necessarily affect the other.

70 C. 1, *de sepulturis,* III, 7, in Clem.

71 Council of Rouen (1212), can. 8—Mansi, XXII, 907; Council of Montpellier (1214), can. 29—Mansi XXII, 946; Council of Clermont (1268), can. 2—Harduin, VII, 606; Council of Nîmes (1284)—Harduin, VII, 922-923.

72 Barbosa, *Ius Eccles. Univers.,* part 2, lib. 2, c. 10, n. 41: Pax Jordanus, *Elucubrationes Diversae* (Lugduni, 1729), Tom. I, lib. 5, tit. 12, n. 131; Panormitanus, *Commentaria in Quinque Libros Decretalium* (8 vols., Venetiis, 1588), lib. III, tit. 28, c. 12, n. 7.

73 *Rit. Rom. Pauli V,* tit. *De Exequiis—Quibus non licet dare Ecclesiasticam Sepulturam.*

ART. 5—THE EXCLUSION OF THOSE WHO NEGLECTED TO MAKE THEIR "EASTER DUTY"

Before the year 1215 there was no uniform legislation with regard to the frequency of the reception of the sacraments of Penance and the Holy Eucharist.[74] However, the failure to receive the sacraments at least occasionally had always been a mark of weak faith. Thus it was ruled by the Council of Agde (506) that they who did not receive Communion at Easter, Pentecost, the feast of the Assumption and Christmas were not to be considered Catholics, nor to be numbered among the faithful.[75]

However, the first general law in this matter was issued by Innocent III in the IV General Lateran Council (1215). In this decree it was stipulated that, unless for some reasonable cause he was excused by his pastor, one who had attained the age of discretion and failed to receive the Sacrament of Penance at least once a year and Hoy Communion at Easter time should be barred *ab ingressu ecclessiae* while living, and, if he died in his sin, should be denied Christian burial.[76]

Some difficulty arose over the interpretation of this law. First, it was asked if one became liable to this penalty by neglecting Confession during a year when one felt that there was no mortal sin to be confessed. The answer was that one did not.[77]

A problem was presented also in the determination of the age at which the obligation became binding. In some Councils of the period it was determined to be at the age of fourteen.[78] However, the later common interpretation held that the *age*

[74] Schroeder, *Disciplinary Decrees of the General Councils* (St. Louis: Herder, 1937), p. 201, not. 24.

[75] Can. 18—Harduin, II, 1000; c. 19, D. 11, *de cons.*

[76] Can. 21—Harduin, VIII, 35; C. 12, X, *de poenitentiis et remissionibus*, V. 38.

[77] Gloss on the decretal asserts this at the words "omnia sua peccata"; Cf. also Panormitanus, lib. V, tit. 38, c. 12, n. 10.

[78] Council of Narbonne (1227), can. 7—Mansi, XXIII, 23; Council of Béziers (1351), can. 12—Mansi, XXVI, 250.

of discretion was the same as the *age at which one attained the use of reason.*[79]

Another question arose as to whether one was liable to the penalty by the very omission of the duty, i.e., was it *latae sententiae,* or only after a sentence, i.e., was it *ferendae sententiae.* This seems to have been decided by a decree of the Congregation of Bishops and Regulars in 1595. The Congregation declared that the penalty was *ferendae sententiae.* It could be made *latae sententiae,* however, by diocesan statute. However, if the omission was notoriously blameworthy, then the notoriety of fact in itself was equivalent to a sentence by an ecclesiastical judge, and Christian burial had to be denied unless there had been signs of repentance.[80] Moreover, the penalties were in reality distinct, so that the denial of Christian burial did not depend upon the previous infliction of the interdict *ab ingressu Ecclesiae.*[81]

The practice after the IV General Council of the Lateran (1215) does not appear to have been uniform. The Council of Toulouse (1229) decreed that the obligation of Confession and Communion was to be fulfilled three times a year, Christmas, Easter and Pentecost.[82] And the II Provincial Council of Milan (1569) ordered that neither penalty, that is, neither the interdict *ab ingressu ecclesiae* nor the denial of Christian burial, was to be inflicted until after two or three warnings. Then, if the offender remained obdurate, he was to be denounced and his name affixed to the Church door.[83]

The law of the IV General Council of the Lateran, however,

79 Conran, *The Interdict,* pp. 37-38.

80 *Collectanea S. C. Ep. et Reg.,* p. 635.

81 *Loc. cit.* For further information on this subject cf. Gasparri, *De SS. Eucharistia* (3. ed., 2 vols., Parisiis, 1897), n. 1167; Schaaf, "Catholic Burial"—*The American Ecclesiastical Review,* XCV (1936), 190; Clinton, *The Paschal Precept,* The Catholic University of America, Canon Law Studies, n. 73 (Washington, D. C.: The Catholic University of America, 1932), p. 38; Schroeder, *Disciplinary Decrees,* p. 263.

82 Can. 13—Hefele-Leclercq, V, 1498.

83 Can. 13—Harduin, XI, 738.

remained the principal legislation and the model for all other decrees. It was later decreed by the Council of Trent that to deny the binding force of the precept of the Lateran Council was to incur excommunication.[84] It is found substantially repeated in the Ritual of Pope Paul V: *"Negatur igitur Ecclesiastica sepultura . . . iis de quibus publice constat quod semel in anno non susceperunt sacramenta Confessionis et Communionis in Pascha et absque ullo signo contritionis obierunt."* [85]

In reference to the word *"publice"* of the Ritual of Pope Paul V, De Murga noted that unless the fault was *public* and *manifest,* i.e., not only so known that it could be proved, but also so known that it could not be concealed, Christian burial was not to be denied. For the presumption was always in favor of the deceased, who, unknown to his pastor, could have fulfilled the obligation elsewhere.[86]

Schaaf notes that at no time was there ever question of excommunication in reference to this fault.[87] This seems adequately substantiated by the action of the Council of Trent in imposing excommunication for *denying* the *precept,* not for breaking it.[88] Moreover, the increasing tendency towards leniency in the infliction of this penalty is already plainly discernible in the Ritual of Paul V, according to which the denial of Christian burial was to be enforced only when the one who had neglected Confession and Holy Communion departed this life without *any* sign of contrition. Perhaps the way was paved for the expression of this milder discipline by the very attitude of the Council of Trent, which emphasized the respect due to the law, rather than the penalty consequent upon the law's violation.

84 Sess. XIII, *de sacrosanctae Eucharistiae Sacramento,* can. 9.

85 Tit. *De Exequiis—Quibus non licet dare Ecclesiasticam Sepulturam.*

86 *De Sepulturis,* tract. 2, disq. XV, concl. 1.

87 "Catholic Burial"—*The Eccles. Review,* XCV (1936), 190 ff.

88 Sess. XIII, *De Sacrosanctae Eucharistiae Sacramento,* can. 9.

ART. 6—THE EXCLUSION OF OTHER PUBLIC SINNERS

A. Participants in Tournaments

The tournaments here under consideration designate those encounters and combats between individuals or groups of individuals at which the loss of life was a normal result for those engaged therein. They caused great harm to both the temporal and the spiritual welfare of society. They are not to be confused with those other tournaments in the same medieval period in which tests of skill and dexterity, or even of military prowess, were featured. For, although deaths sometimes resulted from the latter, these were not the normal result, but rather an unusual consequence. In the former death was probable, while in the latter it was both unexpected and unintended.

The former tournaments were condemned by the III General Council of the Lateran (1179); Alexander III decreed that those who died in them were to be denied Christian burial, even though they were to live long enough to receive the last sacraments.[89]

This unusually severe legislation was explained by Gonzalez-Tellez (+1649),[90] who stated that sometimes Christian burial was denied, even after the reception of the last sacraments, as a corrective and disciplinary measure. For, as he said, it did not harm the deceased whose soul had been taken care of by the sacraments, in as much as the denial of Christian burial could in no way effect the condition of the soul already before God.

Pope Alexander III later mitigated somewhat the severity of the law by declaring that it did not include those who had gone to such affairs as neutrals, and without any intention of participating. The specific case under consideration in the papal decretal was that of a merchant.[91]

It was disputed whether the penalty applied to those who

89 C. 1, *de torneamentis*, V, 13.

90 Lib. V, tit. 13, c. 1.

91 C. 2, *de torneamentis*, V, 13.

died later and elsewhere from wounds received in the contest.[92]

That the penalty was not applied to those contests of strength and skill in which the probability of death was remote is witnessed by Panormitanus in reference to this decretal.[93]

With the disappearance of such contests the law may have lapsed, for it is not mentioned in the Ritual of Pope Paul V.

B. *Participants in Duels*

A duel is a contest between two persons deliberately entered upon on private authority and agreed to by mutual consent. It is staged at a prearranged place and time. The special malice in it arises from the expectation that the effect will be death, mutilation or serious wounds.[94]

This evil had been early condemned by the Popes, who sought to eradicate it completely from society.[95] Alexander III condemned it as a pernicious evil,[96] and his condemnation was followed later by those of Julius II (1509),[97] Leo X (1519)[98] and Pius IV (1560).[99]

It was the Council of Trent, however, that enacted the most drastic legislation on this practice when it decreed that duels were absolutely forbidden; that those princes who allowed a

[92] De Murga held that it did not (*De Sepulturis*, tract. 2, disq. 9, conclus. 2, nn. 7-12); Hostiensis that it did (lib. V, *de torneamentis*, c. 1).

[93] Lib. V, *de torneamentis*, c. 1; Samuellius stated that bull-fights were included—*De Sepulturis*, tract. 2, disp. 1, controv. 8, concl. 1; and Gonzalez-Tellez (lib. V, tit. 8, c. 3, n. 7) declared that they were included in constitutions by Popes Pius V, Gregory XIII, Sixtus V and Clement VIII, but the prohibition seems to have been widely ignored.

[94] De Murga, *De Sepulturis*, tract. 2, disq. XI, n. 2.

[95] Nicholas I (858-867)—c. 22, C. II, q. 5; Celestine III (1191-1198)—c. 1, X, *de purgatione vulgari*, V, 35. The III Council of Valence (855) considered death by this means suicide, and that was indeed the general opinion.

[96] C. 1, X, *de clericis pugnantibus in duello*, V, 35.

[97] *Fontes*, n. 63.

[98] *Fontes*, n. 75.

[99] *Fontes*, n. 101.

place to be set aside for such affairs by that very fact lost their jurisdiction over those places; and that those who died in a duel were to be deprived of Christian burial. Moreover, cooperators with duelists, and spectators present at duels, if they went to see them deliberately, no matter what privileges or customs were alleged to justify the evil, were included in the excommunication.[100]

This legislation of the Council of Trent was renewed by Pope Gregory XIII (1572-1585) and was extended to cover private or secret duels.[101] Clement VIII (1592-1605) amplified the law to include among duels the arbitrary military procedures in the settling of an issue between two armies by a duel between two or more men from both sides. He also put upon the Index any and all literature favoring duels under whatsoever pretense, whether it was honor, glory, reputation or fame.[102]

This legislation was not mitigated in the Ritual of Pope Paul V. That Ritual declared that the penalty was nevertheless incurred by a man dying in the duel even if he repented before death.[103]

C. Usurers

The taking of interest for loans of money was condemned by the Church from early times.[104] But the period now under consideration stands out for the rigor of its legislation on this matter.

Alexander III in the III General Lateran Council (1179) took a strong stand on the question and decreed that anyone who was a manifest usurer was to be denied Christian burial, if he died in that sin.[105] And in one of his letters he wrote that one could not be absolved from this sin until he had

100 Sess. XV, *de ref.*, c. 19.

101 Const. "*Ad tollendum*," 5 dec. 1582—*Fontes*, n. 149.

102 Const. "*Illius vices*," 17 aug. 1592—*Fontes*, n. 176.

103 *Rit. Rom. Pauli V*, tit. *De Exequiis—Quibus non licet dare Ecclesiasticam Sepulturam.*

104 C. 1, C. IV, q. 3; c. 4, C. IV, q. 4.

105 Can. 25—Harduin, VI, 1683; c. 3, X, *de usuris*, V, 19.

made restitution according to his ability. He further specified that such restitution included *all* that had been received as interest, even if it had been used up or given away to relatives or others. Moreover, the law was retroactive and applied to any profit made by means of interest both before and after the decree. Even possessions acquired from the profits so gained were to be sold for the purpose of making due restitution. However, if the plea of poverty at the time of death prevented such restitution, and it was supported by the person's manifest condition, then the penalty was not to be applied.[106]

Gregory X in the II General Council of Lyons (1274) repeated the prohibitions and the penalty of Alexander III. He added the further sanction that Christian burial was to be denied until the offender had either made restitution before his absolution, or had solemnly promised it under bond furnished by those who would execute it if he defaulted.[107] Similar legislation was passed by other councils of the period.[108]

That the spirit of this legislation remained long unchanged is evidenced by the law of Clement V in the Council of Vienne (1311-1313), in which the Pope declared excommunicated anyone who dared to grant Christian burial to manifest usurers.[109]

In this delict, also, it was necessary that the crime was manifest. De Murga held that the term *manifest* in this connection was to be accepted in the broad sense, as not only capable of being proved, but also openly public and unconcealable.[110] The term was taken in a broader sense in this

106 Letter to the Archbishop of Salerno—Harduin, VI, 1780; c. 5, X, *de usuris*, V, 19.

107 Can. 2—Harduin, VII, 717; c. 2, *de usuris*, V, 5, in VI°.

108 Council of Clermont (1268), can. 2—Harduin, VII, 606; Synod of Paris (1212), can. 7—Harduin, VI, 2006; Council of Ravenna (1286), can. 6—Harduin, VII, 947.

109 Harduin, VII, 1321; c. 1, *de sepulturis*, III, 7, in Clem. In another Clementine decretal (c. 1, *de usuris*, V, 5, in Clem.) it is stated that one guilty of the crime of taking interest is to be punished in the same manner as heretics.

110 *De Sepulturis*, tract. 2, disq. 14, nn. 6, 7, 8; Cf. also the gloss to c. 1, *de sepulturis*, III, 7 in Clem., at the word "*manifestos*."

decree of Clement from the fact that manifest usurers were coupled in it with public excommunicates and such as were interdicted by name. Christian burial was to be denied to all three classes.

The law appears also substantially unchanged in the Ritual of Pope Paul V. That Ritual included usurers under the heading of public sinners who died without having given any signs of repentance.[111]

D. Divers Other Excluded Persons

1. *Robbers*

The crime of robbery was very common during the period under consideration. The highways on both land and sea were rendered dangerous by the number of robbers and pirates who lay in wait to loot travelers. The legislation against this crime shows an increasing tendency towards mercy for those who repented.

In the twelfth century Pope Eugene III (1145-1153) established the general norm that governed later law when he ordered that they who were manifestly guilty of the crime were to be denied Christian burial so long as they obstinately refused to make restitution and died in that state of mind.[112] If, however, they had refused restitution during life, but at death's approach repented, and if they then found themselves unable to make restitution, or to find heirs or relatives to do it for them, they were to be allowed burial in blessed ground, but without benefit of ceremony or clergy.[113] This mercy was shown because no one was to be held to the impossible, and one so situated could not make restitution. However, lest mercy be presumed and the crime thus encouraged among others, the prohibition of Church services and the denial of

111 *Rit. Rom. Pauli V*, tit. *De Exequiis—Quibus non licet dare Ecclesiasticam Sepulturam.* Wernz, *Ius Decretalium* III, p. 499, note 45.

112 C. 2, *de raptoribus*, V, 17. The word *manifest* in this decretal has the force of *notorious*, according to Panormitanus (lib. V, *de raptoribus*, c. 2, n. 4).

113 C. 2, X, *de raptoribus*, V, 17.

the assistance of the clergy were imposed that they might be deterred from postponing the duty of making restitution.[114]

Alexander III issued a similar decree in regard to a case in which absolution was to be granted but Christian burial denied. He urged that the strongest pressure be brought upon the heirs and relatives to make satisfaction in order thus to permit the deceased to have full Christian burial.[115]

Gregory IX went still further and ordered that the relatives be forced to make restitution under pain of censure, so that it would be rare that the full Christian burial should have to be denied to those who died truly repentant.[116] The tendency of the legislation, which at first glance appears to grow more exacting, is in reality all in favor of the deceased sinner. The increase of the rigor is upon those who survive. The concern of the Church that nothing stand in the way of final absolution, and that no one be afraid to ask for it, is increasingly evident. This is clearly apparent in the legislation as it was incorporated in the Ritual of Pope Paul V: *"Negatur Ecclesiastica sepultura . . . manifestis et publicis peccatoribus, qui sine poenitentia perierunt."* [117]

2. *Suicides*

The law in regard to those who had deliberately taken their own life showed no change at this time from the law decreed at the Council of Braga (561).[118] Voluntary suicide had always been regarded a crime. The tradition in this regard was immemorial. It may be said, however, that the presumption gained ground during this period that no one was ever to be considered guilty of the offense until it was proved. Many involved arguments were waged concerning the morality of

114 Samuellius, *De Sepulturis*, tract. 2, disp. I, controv. 4, concl. 11; cf. gloss at the word *"sepulturae"*; Panormitanus, in lib. V, *de raptoribus*, c. 2, n. 4.

115 C. 5, X, *de raptoribus*, V, 17.

116 C. 14, X, *de sepulturis*, III, 28.

117 *Rit. Rom. Pauli V*, tit. *De Exequiis—Quibus non licet dare Ecclesiasticam Sepulturam.*

118 Can. 16—Harduin, III, 351.

suicide committed in order to escape being seduced. They are too profuse to be retailed here. Suffice it to say that while in principle it was never held lawful to choose death to dishonor, yet those who did make such a choice usually did so out of invincible ignorance and were therefore considered excused.[119] Thus Innocent III, in a famous decree, ordered Christian burial to be granted to a woman who met death by drowning while fleeing from seducers; for, he declared, it was evident that she did not die of her own free choice and deliberate decision.[120]

Moreover, it was already then the opinion that for anyone found dead, even in circumstances that could indicate either suicide *or* accident, the presumption of death by accident was in favor of the deceased until death by suicide was established.[121] Further, if one attempted suicide but did not succeed, and upon revival confessed and was absolved, there was no longer any application of the penalty.[122]

The law appears in the Ritual of Pope Paul V in substantially the same form: *"Negatur igitur Ecclesiastica Sepultura . . . seipsos occidentibus ob desperationem vel iracundiam (non tamen si ex insania id accidat) nisi ante mortem signa dederint poenitentiae."* [123]

3. *Assaulters of Clerics*

In the days of feudalism, when civil wars and internecine strife were so general, it became necessary to protect the clergy from physical attack, especially since they were

119 Samuellius, *De Sepulturis*, tract. 2, disp. 1, controv. 5, concl. 1; De Murga, *De Sepulturis*, tract. 2, disq. 8, nn. 6, 7.

120 C. 11, X, *de sepulturis*, III, 28.

121 Barbosa, *Ius Univers. Eccles.*, Pars II, lib. 2, c. 10, n. 49; *De Officio et Potestate Parochi*, Pars. III, c. 26, n. 49; Samuellius, *De Sepulturis*, tract. 2, disp. 2, controv. 5, concl. 2; De Murga, *De Sepulturis*, tract. 2, disq. 8, n. 16; Pirhing, *Ius Canonicum*, lib. III, tit. 28, n. 89.

122 C. 28, *de sententia excommunicationis*, V, 39, in VI°.

123 *Rit. Rom. Pauli V*, tit. *De Exequiis—Quibus non licet dare Ecclesiasticam Sepulturam.*

usually not allowed to carry defensive arms. The deliberate laying of violent hands upon a cleric, and, by the favorable interpretation, upon any religious, had been branded as a most evil offence by Innocent II in the II General Lateran Council. (1139) [124]

Alexander III (1159-1171) repeated the law and its sanction. Those who committed this crime were excommunicated and their absolution was reserved to the Pope himself.[125]

The Council of Noyon (1344) ordered that captive clerics be released by their captors without ransom under pain of excommunication and the denial of Christian burial. It decreed the same penalty for those captors who made the clerics use some other garb than their proper clerical habit or forced them to stop wearing their tonsure.[126]

In the Constitution *"Ad evitanda"* (1418) Pope Martin V showed that there was to be no mitigation of the severity against this crime when he declared that, while only those excommunicates were to be regarded as *vitandi* whose excommunication had been inflicted by a decree or a sentence of a judge, the striking of a cleric, if it was notorious, automatically made its perpetrator an *excommunicatus vitandus.*[127]

Though there was no explicit mention of this offense in the Ritual of Pope Paul V, such offenders may be understood to be included under the heading of public sinners.[128]

4. *Confiscators of Tithes*

Christian burial was sometimes refused to those who in any way had interfered with the tithes or Church moneys, their collection and their transportation. This was not new law for

124 Can. 15—Mansi, XXI, 530; C. 29, C. XVII, q. 4.

125 Cc. 5, 8, X, *de sententia excommunicationis*, V, 39.

126 Cc. 6, 13—Harduin, VII, 1673.

127 *Fontes*, n. 45. It is to be noted that the act had to be deliberate; an act of anger, inadvertence, or ignorance lacked the requisite basis for the incurring of the penalty.

128 Wernz, *Ius Decretalium*, III, p. 499, footnote 45.

it was referred to in the earlier period.[129] The main legislation of this period was a decree of Alexander III in the III General Lateran Council (1179). It forbade the laity in any way to retain illegally, to misuse, or to divert the tithes and moneys due the Church, under penalty of excommunication and the denial of Christian burial.[130] The Council of Noyon (1344) issued a similar decree, warning the faithful to be just in regard to tithes, under threat of excommunication and denial of Christian burial.[131]

5. *Mutilated Persons*

It was forbidden under pain of excommunication to separate, by boiling, the flesh from the bones of a corpse. This may sound strange in these days, but it was not an unusual practice of the period here under consideration. It was often resorted to in order to make the transportation of corpses easier, or to allow burial in two or more different places. The law prohibiting this practice also banned the cutting up of the body for such purposes, and it denied Christian burial to bodies so mutilated.[132]

For the correct appraisal of this prohibition it should be added that the law did not prohibit the burial of mutilated bodies or mangled corpses if this condition resulted from acts of anger, hatred or war, or if it come about through disease, or if it followed from a legitimate surgical operation. It should also be understood that there was no injustice in depriving the body of Christian burial when the deceased was in no way responsible for the crime, for it must be remembered that the penalty here was a punishment of the crime perpetrated upon the body, and was not a punishment of the deceased.[133]

129 Council of Meaux (845), can. 11—Harduin, IV, 1496; Council of Nîmes (1086), can. 6—Hefele-Leclercq, IV, 449.

130 Can. 14—Harduin, VI, 1679-1680; c. 19, X, *de decimis*, III, 30. Religious were included in this law by a decree of the Council of Vienne (1311-1312)—c. 1, *de decimis*, III, 8, in Clem.

131 Can. 9—Harduin, VII, 1673.

132 C. 1, *de sepulturis*, III, 6, in Extravag. com.

133 Gloss on c. 1, *de sepulturis*, III, 6, in Extrav. com., at the word

6. *Blasphemers*

Abuse of the name of God, of the Virgin or of the saints, if public and manifest, was first punished by a penance. If the penance was rejected and the sinner remained obdurate, he was punished with an interdict *ab ingressu ecclesiae,* and, if he were to die in the sin, with the denial of Christian burial.[134]

7. *Incendiaries*

Alexander III ordered Christian burial to be granted to one to whom it had been refused because of his failure to make restitution for the crime of incendiarism. The Pope pointed out that the man had been absolved before death, and that he had accepted his penance. He was therefore not to be denied Christian burial, but his relatives were to be compelled to make restitution for his crime.[135] From the fact that the Pope accorded to this incendiary the right of Christian burial precisely in view of his penetential spirit and the consequent absolution bestowed upon him before his death, one may legitimately conclude that the crime of incendiarism, if unrepented, barred its perpetrator from receiving Christian burial.

8. *Debtors*

The deliberate neglect to pay one's debts while still living was a crime of serious magnitude in this period. Alexander III wrote to the Archbishop of Canterbury during the III General Lateran Council (1179) reminding him that those who left their debts unpaid before death, when they could have paid them, were to be denied Christian burial until their relatives made good the payment.[136] This Pope sent a similar letter to the Bishop of Lucca.[137] In 1227 the Council of Narbonne de-

"*sepultura*"; Panormitanus mentions the same penalty for this offense in his comments on another decretal—lib. V, *de torneamentis*, c. 1.

134 C. 2, X, *de maledicis*, V, 26.

135 C. 5, X, *de raptoribus*, V, 17.

136 Harduin, VI, 1834.

137 Harduin, VI, 1822.

creed that a priest should be called to witness the last will and testament, and that failure at least to call him would deprive the deceased of Christian burial.[138]

To die intestate in the twelfth and thirteenth centuries provided grounds for suspicion. Such an event was presumed to be an indication of one's dying in sin. Therefore it is not unusual to find that in those times a man was denied Christian burial on the ground that he was believed to have died with a view of defrauding his creditors.[139] The English civil law of the period was explicit in declaring this penalty for the offense.[140]

An outstanding instance of this penalty is that of the Bishop of Bayeux, who died in 1360 in debt to the Roman Curia. It is recorded that his body lay "unburied," i.e., buried privately in a château, until the debt was paid by a successor to the see, eighty years later. The bishop's body was then transferred to the cathedral and buried with pomp.[141]

Barbosa speaks of two other offenses for which Christian burial was also denied, namely, treason,[142] and the crime of clerics who refused to cease living in concubinage.[143]

Art. 7—Legislation Following the Council of Trent

The frequency of the application of the penalty of the denial of Christian burial during the period here considered is witnessed by the great number of private tombs of which relics still remain. They date back to the days of the frequent application of the penalties of excommunication and interdict. Generally they appear to have been built as temporary resting

138 Can. 5—Harduin, VII, 146.

139 Ducange, *Glossarium Mediae et Infimae Latinitatis*, v. "intestatio," IV, 399; Thomassinus, *Vetus et Nova Ecclesiae Disciplina*, Pars III, lib. 1, c. 14, n. 6.

140 Pollock and Maitland, *A History of English Law before the Time of Edward I* (2 vols., Cambridge, 1899), II, 358 ff.

141 *Gallia Christiana* (16 vols., Parisiis, 1874), IX, 374.

142 *Ius Univers. Eccles.*, Pars II, lib. II, c. 10, n. 39.

143 *Ibidem*, n. 53.

places for the bodies of the deceased, pending appeal against the sentence of denial. If the appeal was won, they were removed and deposited in blessed ground. It is recorded that one of the abuses that arose as an effect of the frequent application of the penalty was the following. The bodies of the dead who were denied Christian burial in the consecrated ground of the cemeteries would be placed in the trees that grew upon the cemeteries. By a statute which he issued to correct this atrocious abuse, an Archbishop of Rouen sheds an eery light upon a rather unhallowed by-product of the Church law forbidding Christian burial.[144]

The period from 1179-1614 is the most prolific one in regard to legislation on the denial of Christian burial. Yet, extensive though this legislation was, it did not obtain all the desired results for which it had been enacted. For, as late as 1583 the Council of Bordeaux complained that Christian burial was all too frequently being granted to those who died outside the communion of the Church. It specified the denial of Christian burial for the following: heretics, schismatics, manifest usurers and robbers, blasphemers, those who had neglected to make their "Easter Duty," suicides, duelists and those who had been executed for their crimes and had died impenitent.[145]

The Council of Rheims in the same year reminded the clergy that Christian burial was denied to the following: usurers, heretics, schismatics, suicides, those killed in duels, those who neglected to make their "Easter Duty," infidels, and excommunicates. It further reminded them that the denial of Christian burial consisted in the privation of *both* the services at the Church or house, *and* the interment in blessed ground.[146]

The issuing of the first Roman Ritual by Pope Paul V in 1614 did well, then, to list the sins for which one was to be denied Christian burial. That list sums up in a complete way the preceding legislation, and may be said to contain the law of

144 Bernard, *La Sépulture en Droit Canonique* (Paris: Loviton, 1933), p. 27.

145 Cc. 29, 30—Mansi, XXXIV-A, 783.

146 Can. 15—Harduin, X, 1289.

the period. It includes much that has been seen, although some of the classes penalized have been studied here under the general classification of public sinners who died without repentance.[147]

The Ritual of Pope Paul V thus stated the law on the denial of Christian burial:

> Negatur igitur Ecclesiastica Sepultura Paganis, Iudaeis, et omnibus infidelibus, haereticis, et eorum fautoribus; apostatis a Christiana fide; schismaticis, et publicis excommunicatis maiori excommunicatione; interdictis nominatim, et iis qui sunt in loco interdicto, eo durante.
>
> Seipsos occidentibus ob desperationem vel iracundiam (non tamen si ex insania id accidat), nisi ante mortem dederint signa poenitentiae.
>
> Morientibus in duello, etiamsi ante obitum dederint poenitentiae signa.
>
> Manifestis et publicis peccatoribus, qui sine poenitentia perierunt.
>
> Iis, de quibus publice constat quod semel in anno non susceperunt Sacramenta Confessionis et Communionis in Pascha, et absque ullo signo contritionis obierunt.
>
> Infantibus mortuis absque Baptismo.
>
> Ubi vero in praedictis casibus dubium occurrerit, Ordinarius consulatur.[148]

[147] Many (*De Locis Sacris*, n. 220) stated that the Ritual of Pope Paul V was the first authentic text that included in a general classification all public sinners subject to the penalty of the denial of Christian burial. Authors commonly held that the penalty aplpied only to those of whom it was known that they died impenitent. This opinion was based upon the gloss to c, 11, X, *de sepulturis*, III, 28 (v. "*communicabatur*"), in which it was declared that Christian burial should not be given to those who were known to have died in mortal sin ("*constat in peccato mortali decessisse*").

[148] *Rit. Rom. Pauli V*, tit. *De Exequiis—Quibus non licet dare Ecclesiasticam Sepulturam.*

Chapter IV

FROM 1614 TO THE CODE OF CANON LAW (1918)

Introduction

After 1614 the law of the Church with regard to the denial of Christian burial remained substantially unchanged. In fact, the law as incorporated in the Ritual of Pope Pius X, of 1915,[1] is dentical, word for word, with that of the Ritual of Paul V in 1614, although the ritual had been revised in the meantime by Benedict XIV and re-authorized by Leo XIII.

This does not mean, however, that there was no development. The interpretation of the law had to be continually clarified and adjusted according to the needs of the various times, places and people. Though the letter of the law remained unchanged, the Church had to make many allowances here and there in accordance with the changing conditions in the modern world, especially in so far as it was affected by the so-called Protestant Reformation. The great number of sects, and even the large body of non-Catholics with no sectarian tendencies, necessitated adjustments to fit the new circumstances, particularly in sections of the world in which Catholics were no longer in the majority. As a result of these adjustments, the law's interpretation took on a leniency and an adaptability necessitated by varied circumstances. Thus it is readily comprehensible that the decrease of active and vicious hostility to the Church could properly occasion a mitigation of the severity of older times. As a result, the modern period of the legislation on the denial of Christian burial is characterized chiefly by the mercy shown in its interpretation, a mercy that culminated in the adaptation which the letter of the law as now received into the Code of Canon Law most aptly reflects.

[1] *Rituale Romanum Pauli V, P. M., Iussu editum, a Benedicto XIV et a Pio X castigatum et auctum* (novissima editio, Taurini, 1915).

Art. 1—Difficulties in Excluding non-Catholics From Catholic Cemeteries After the Reformation

One of the results of the Reformation that offered particular difficulty in applying the laws on the denial of Christian burial was the necessity of the using of a common cemetery by Catholics and Protestants in many places where there was but one burial ground. This difficulty was early placed before the Holy See for solution and some of the replies will now be seen.

It was declared in 1637 that only in case of necessity was a common cemetery to be used by Catholics and non-Catholics, and then only if the Catholics could have their section apart. If this could not be had, the individual graves were to be blessed when the bodies were interred.[2]

Lest this sharing of a common cemetery appear too shocking to the modern reader, he should be reminded that there were many curious practices tolerated in countries largely Protestant after the Reformation. In Germany in the seventeenth and eighteenth centuries the Catholics and Protestants in many places used the same churches. In some of these the clergymen of the two congregations even participated in the services held by the other.[3]

In such a state of affairs the Church had to struggle to preserve even the essentials, overlooking out of necessity the sacrifices that had to be made to circumstances. There were even some canonists who excused communion with heretics in Protestant lands provided that no formal approval was given them. Thus they permitted what was not uncommon, that Catholics and Protestants of the same town should accompany each other's funerals to the church and to the cemetery, provided

[2] S. C. C., *Cathuren.*, 13 iul. 1635, referred to in a decree of the Sacred Congregation of the Propagation of the Faith, 29 aug. 1763—*Collectanea S. C. de Prop. Fide* (2 vols., Romae, 1907), n. 449. This work will hereafter be referred to as *Coll. S. C. P. F.*)

[3] For practices of this kind consult Nottarp, "Zur Communicatio cum haereticis, Deutsche Rechtszustände im 17 und 18 Jahrhundert,"—*Schriften der Königsberger Gelehrten Gesellschaft*, IX Jahr., Heft 4 (1933), pp. 100, 120, 121, 124, 133.

that the Catholic was buried in blessed ground.[4] This toleration of abuses never extended to Catholic countries, however, and Pope Clement VIII, on July 26, 1596, specifically forbade the participation of Catholics in heretical funerals.[5] Gregory XV, on July 2, 1622, renewed the ancient prohibition and censure against the favoring of heretics.[6]

As to the actual burial of heretics in Catholic cemeteries, that was to be tolerated only when it could not be resisted.[7]

In three councils of the same period, the early eighteenth century, the traditional refusal to allow the burial of non-Catholics in Catholic cemeteries was reiterated in widely different places.[8] Benedict XIV decreed that the burial of non-Catholics in Catholic cemeteries was to be suffered only to avoid a greater evil.[9] And the Holy Office granted only passive toleration of the burial of non-Catholics in Catholic cemeteries under the strictest necessity. No consent or approval was to be given and the indignity was to be endured only when greater evil threatened.[10]

In 1830, when asked about the common cemetery, the Sacred Congregation of the Propagation of the Faith replied that there should be two sections, one for Catholics and one for others, and two separate entrances.[11]

4 Pirhing, Tom. V, lib. V, tit. 7, sec. 2, nn. 24, 26; Layman, *Theologia Moralis in Quinque Libros Distributa* (Patavii, 1733), lib. 11, c. III, n. 6.

5 *Bullarium Romanum*, X, n. CXXXVI, pp. 279-280.

6 *Bullarium Romanum*, XII, n. LXVI, pp. 708-709.

7 S. C. C., 24 aug. 1579; 16 iun. 1668. Cf. Pallottini, *Collectio . . . S. C. C.*, XVI, "Sepultura," § III, nn. 43, 42, respectively; Reiffenstuel, lib. III, tit. 28, n. 78.

8 Synod of Albania (1703), pars. 2, c. 12—*Acta et Decreta Sacrorum Conciliorum Recentiorum* (8 vols., Friburgi Brisgoviae, 1870-1890), I, 323 (This work will hereafter be referred to as *Coll. Lac.*); Council of Mount Lebanon (Maronite) (1736), n. 12—*Coll. Lac.*, II, 158; Council of Avignon (1725), tit. 19, c. 3—*Coll. Lac.*, I, 512-513.

9 Const., "*Inter omnigenas,*" 2 febr. 1744—*Fontes*, n. 339.

10 S. C. S. Off., instr. (*ad ep. Scepusien*) 16 aug. 1781—*Fontes*, n. 843.

11 S. C. de Prop. Fide, 29 mart. 1830—*Coll. S. C. P. F.*, n. 812.

Notorious heretics are not to be honored with Catholic funeral rites, declared Gregory XVI to a bishop of Bavaria in rebuking him for having publicly announced prayers for the deceased Protestant Queen of Bavaria. The bishop had ordered recited in his churches the Ritual prayer: *"Pro omnibus in Christiana et Catholica societate defunctis"* for the queen.[12]

When asked, in 1853, whether Catholics and Protestants might share the same private burial place, the Holy Office replied that the answer given on Aug. 16, 1781,[13] was to be the norm and guide in this matter, and added that the bishop was to strive to have the law obeyed; if this could not be done without scandal, then he might tolerate the abuse.[14] Any apparent relaxation granted in that decree was not to be further extended, as appears in declaration of the Sacred Congregation of the Propagation of the Faith. This Congregation issued its own decree on February 12, 1862, to the effect that where no Catholic cemetery existed Catholics were to have their own section in the common one, or at least they were to have the individual graves blessed.[15]

Non-Catholics were never to have a Catholic funeral, no matter what other abuses might be tolerated out of necessity, according to the decree of the Holy Office in a warning to pastors that they were not to accept offerings for such services, since they could not perform them.[16]

Finally, Pius IX, in his Constitution *"Apostolicae Sedis"* (1869), renewed the excommunication of apostates, heretics, and schismatics, and those who ordered or forced by threats

[12] Epist. "*Officium,*" 16 febr. 1842—*Fontes,* n. 499. The same prohibition is found renewed in two later instances, as recorded in the *Analecta Iuris Pontificii,* IV (1860), 2390, 2391.

[13] Instr. (*ad Ep. Scepusien*)—*Fontes*, n. 843.

[14] "Curet episcopus ut cuncta fiant ad normam sacrorum canonum; quatenus vero absque scandalo id obtineri non possit, tolerari posse."—*Coll. S. C. P. F.*, n. 1089.

[15] (Ad. Ep. Rosen.) 16 apr. 1862—*Coll. S. C. P. F.*, n. 1227; Martigny, *Dictionnaire des antiquitées chrétiennes* (Paris, 1880), v. "sépulture," p. 731 ff.

[16] S. C. S. Off., 20 iun. 1866—*Fontes*, n. 994.

the granting of Christian burial to them, or to those excommunicated or interdicted by name.[17] Many held that the term "Christian burial" is here used in the *"strict"* sense, i.e., *interment* in ground set aside by the bishop for Catholic burial *and* blessed by him or by his authority.[18]

As late as the Vatican Council (1869-1870) however, abuses in regard to the granting of Christian burial to those not entitled to it were noted. The Neapolitan bishops protested that not only were the faithful neglecting to have the church services in connection with Christian burial, but also heretics and infidels were being buried indiscriminately in Catholic cemeteries.[19]

In America, the I Plenary Council of Baltimore (1852) took a rigid stand in the matter and ordered that any Catholic who was to be buried in a non-Catholic cemetery, in a place where a Catholic one was available, was to be refused ecclesiastical rites.[20] But the II Plenary Council, in 1866, sought to mitigate the severity of the older law, and declared that converts who wished to be buried among their Protestant relatives could be given Christian burial. Catholics who had had a lot in a non-Catholic cemetery from before 1852, or who had obtained one since then, *sine fraude legis,* could also be granted Christian burial.[21]

In the same article the Council added that it was tolerated by the Holy See that non-Catholic relatives of Catholics could

[17] Sec. I, nn. 1, 3; sec. IV, n. 1—*Fontes*, n. 552.

[18] *De Locis Sacris*, n. 223; Piat (*Commentarius in Constitutionem Apostolicae Sedis* [Parisiis, 1881], p. 240, 241), gave the opinions in the controversy as to whether the cemetery must be blessed or not for one to incur the censure for forcing the burial therein; those who held that it must are led by Schmalzgrueber (lib. III, tit. 28, n. 1); on the other side Reiffenstuel is the leading author (lib. III, tit. 28, n. 3).

[19] In the Appendix to the acts of the Council: "*Postulata Episcoporum Neapolitanorum*," pars. II, c. 4, n. 9—*Coll. Lac.*, VIII, 831.

[20] Art. 80—*Coll. Lac.*, III, 145.

[21] Art. 387—*Concilii Plenarii Baltimorensis II Decreta* (Baltimorae: Murphy, 1875), pp. 201, 202.

be buried in private Catholic family burial plots.[22] The Council had taken the exact wording of this statement from a decree of the Council of Prague (1860),[23] which, in turn, had thus formulated a decree of the Holy Office of the previous year.[24] That decree was in reply to a question whether non-Catholic relatives, by blood or by marriage, could be buried in Catholic private family lots. The Holy Office had replied: *"Curent Episcopi totis viribus ut cuncta fiant ad normam sacrorum canonum; quatenus vero absque scandalo et periculo id obtineri non possit, tolerari potest."* [25]

That the wording of both the Councils was too broad an interpretation of the decree of the Holy Office was evidenced by a later pronouncement of the Holy Office which objected to the liberal translation of its decree. It specified that the decree of Baltimore be interpreted *strictly* according to the response of 1859: *"adeo ut tolerantia de qua agitur sit tolerantia mere passiva ad praecavenda maiora mala."* [26] However, even with the strict interpretation, room was left for the toleration of the burial of non-Catholics in Catholic cemeteries whenever the danger of scandal or of greater harm following from the non-toleration dictated such a procedure.

Some controversy arose over the meaning of the term *"sepulcra gentilitia,"* as used in the decree, and for some time the toleration seemed restricted to the cases of burial in *mausoleums* and tombs. However, the misunderstanding was due largely to the term *"aedificantur,"* as used in the decree of the Holy Office, which inclined some to believe that only those burial places that were *built* were included.[27]

22 "Ex mente Sanctae Sedis toleratur ut in sepulcris gentilitiis, quae videlicet privata et peculiaria pro Catholicis laicorum familiis aedificantur, cognatorum et affinium etiam acatholicorum corpora tumulentur."

23 Tit. III, c. 13, n. 2—*Coll. Lac.*, V, 468.

24 S. C. S. Off., 30 mart., 1859—*Fontes*, 949.

25 *Loc. cit.*

26 S. C. S. Off., 4 iul. 1888—*Coll. S. C. P. F.*, n. 1173, note 1.

27 Sabetti-Barrett, *Theologia Moralis* (ed. 33, New York, 1931), n. 973, q. 3.

But this seems too strict a translation of the decree. By definition *"sepulcrum gentilitium"* is a burial place reserved to a family: "*—eligens sepulturam, designare potest* (*aliquis*) *eandem pro se et pro sua gente . . . ex qua facto habetur sepulcrum gentilitium.*"[28] Wernz speaks of this toleration as extending to family burial plots in cemeteries as well as to private tombs.[29] Further, Europeans speak in general of cemeteries and graves as being *built* or *constructed* or *erected,* so that the word *"aedificantur"* is not of necessity to be translated literally.[30] In his commentary Augustine includes family *plots* or *lots* in the term *sepulchra particularia,* which are similar to *sepulcra gentilitia*: " . . . permits *lots or vaults* (*sepulchra particularia*) . . . ",[31] and later in the same volume, " . . . ancestral *graves* or tombs: strictly family *plots* . . .".[32]

An article in the *Ecclesiastical Reveiw* apparently makes no differentiation between a *family tomb* and a *family lot* when it states: "If there is danger of scandal, then the bishop is free to exercise his discretion by admitting into consecrated ground one or another of those who, though belonging to Catholic families, have, nevertheless, neglected to prove their right to rest there by embracing the Catholic faith. This is a passive toleration to avoid greater evil, i.e., scandal." [33] The *Review* states in another passage: "If, as in the case of a mixed marriage, it happen that a non-Catholic dies in the bosom of a Catholic family, the Church, rather than see dissension and public scandal arise, would for the time yield a measure

[28] Rossi, *La "Sepultura Ecclesiastica" e l' "Ius Funerum" nel Diritto Canonico* (Borgamo: Arnaldi, 1920), p. 119.

[29] *Ius Decretalium,* III, p. 114, n. 470.

[30] Coronata, "*Institutiones Iuris Canonici* (Taurini, Marietti, 1931), II, n. 794; Wernz-Vidal, *Ius Canonicum,* IV, n. 595; Vermeersch-Creusen, *Epitome Iuris Canonici* (3 vols., Vol. I, 6. ed., Vols. II-III, 5. ed., Mechliniae-Romae: Dessain, 1934-1937), II, n. 519.

[31] *A Commentary on Canon Law* (8 vols., Vol. VI, St. Louis: Herder, 1921), VI, 110.

[32] *Ibidem,* p. 133.

[33] I (1889), 207, 208.

of her right and of her sacred discipline for the sake of peace and order." [34]

The French interpretation of this toleration is similar to the American. The toleration is to be merely passive. Only in cases in which it is too difficult because of the danger of scandal to carry out the fundamental law relative to burials in Catholic cemeteries may non-Catholics be permitted to be buried in Catholic family plots.[35]

Art. 2—Catholics Who Were Denied Christian Burial

A. *Duelists*

One paricularly persistent evil practice that continued to present great difficulty through the greater part of this period, as in the previous one, was the crime of dueling. The Church continued to legislate against this pernicious social crime, and already in 1619 a decree was issued restating the law in reference to the prohibition. Duelists were reminded that even after repentance, if they died as a result of such an affair, they would be refused Christian burial.[36]

The Sacred Congregation of the Council had again to refer to the matter in 1637, and it stated that the prohibition extended also to duels into which Christians might be tempted by the Turks.[37] However, this did not include duels that were not premeditated, that is, that were not arranged and planned. It excluded, therefore, the duels arising out of a chance encounter with an enemy, as also the blows struck in an act of rage.[38]

34 *Loc. cit.*

35 *Dictionnaire de Théologie Catholique* (13 vols., Vacant-Magenot, Paris, 1903-), "Hérésie, Hérétiques," VI, 2550; " . . . suo tamen jure cum summa prudentia uti debet pastor, ne inducantur scandala multo graviora quam foret inhumatio peccatoris"—Icard, *Praelectiones Iuris Canonici in Usu Seminarii S. Sulpitii* (6. ed., 3 vols., Paris, 1886), II, 479.

36 S. C. C., 24 aug. 1619—Pallottini, *Collectio . . .* S. C. C., VI, "sepultura," § III, n. 45.

37 S. C. C., *Catharen.*, 22 aug. 1637—*Fontes*, n. 2590.

38 S. C. C., 15 oct. 1644—Pallottini, *Collectio . . . S. C. C.*, XVI, "sepultura," § III, n. 46.

In 1647 a decree of the Sacred Congregation of the Council proclaimed that unless the buried bodies of duelists were indistinguishable from the others in a cemetery, they were to be exhumed and cast forth from blessed ground.[39]

In 1752 Benedict XIV issued a particularly severe prohibition against duels, in which he not only repeated the sanctions of the Council of Trent,[40] but also nullified the availability of almost all excuses which then were urged in justification of duels. The possible loss of position; the imminent loss of promotion or of well-deserved benefits; the knowledge that the proposed duel would never take place; the claim that a duel was the last feasible means of saving either one's honor or one's fortune—all these he rejected as excuses for the waging, or even simulated planning of duels.[41]

Benedict further added to the rigor of the law of the Council of Trent when, in the same Constitution, he declared that the penalty of the denial of Christian burial was incurred before any sentence was passed, whether the duel was public or private; whether one died on the field or elsewhere; and regardless of whether or not one repented of his act and was absolved; moreover, he took away from all bishops the faculty or power to dispense from or to interpret this law.[42] Wernz notes that this Constitution considerably added to the substance of the decree of the Council of Trent and removed from the bishops any power to change the law, directly or indirectly, expressly or tacitly.[43]

Pius IX renewed the legislation of Benedict XIV in his Constitution *"Apostolicae Sedis,"* [44] and Leo XIII confirmed the preceding legislation.[45]

Emphatic as was all this legislation, it did not entirely

[39] S. C. C., *Parisien.*, 14 dec. 1647—*Fontes*, n. 2678.

[40] Sess. XXV, *de ref.*, c. 19.

[41] Const. "*Detestabilem*," 10 nov. 1752—*Fontes*, n. 422.

[42] N. 9, *Fontes, loc. cit.*

[43] *Ius Decretalium*, III, 781, note 44.

[44] 12 oct. 1869, sec. II, n. 4—*Fontes*, n. 552.

[45] Ep. "*Pastoralis Officii*," 12 sept. 1891—*Fontes*, n. 612.

prevail, for in some places there soon arose a contrary custom by which those killed in duels were allowed burial in blessed ground, at least if they showed some signs of repentance.[46]

The positive legislation however remained unchanged until the present Code of Canon Law, in which it was mitigated so that Christian burial may be granted to duelists who showed some signs of repentance before death.[47]

B. *Excommunicates*

In regard to excommunicates the legislation during this period continues the trend to leniency already initiated in the previous period. The doubt concerning the *tolerati* seems to have been solved in thir favor, for in the mid-seventeenth century the opinion appeard to be that they could be granted burial in blessed ground.[48] This opinion held, however, that they could not have the favor, even if they had repented, unless they had been absolved before death.[49]

Moreover, it was held that one could grant Christian burial to even publicly known *tolerati,* without incurring excommunication, so long as they had not been denounced.[50] This concession did not extend, however, to those who were excommunicated by name or who were notorious assailants of clerics. To grant such as these Christian burial remained a sufficient cause for ecclesiastical censure.[51]

46 Santi-Leitner, *Praelectiones Iuris Canonici* (4. ed., 5 vol. in 3, Ratisbonae-Romae 1904), lib. III, p. 245, n. 23. Many, *De Locis Sacris*, n. 220; But Moulart (*De Sepultura*, p. 291) denies this was ever allowed.

47 Canon 1240, § 1, 4°.

48 *Salmanticensis Collegii Cursus Theologiae Moralis* (*editio novissima correctior*, Venetiis, 1714), I, 242 (this work is a later edition of the work begun in 1665) ; cf. Van Hove, *Prolegomena*, pars. IV, c. III, n. 325, p. 303.

49 *Loc. cit.*

50 *Salmanticensis Collegii Cursus Theologiae Moralis, loc. cit.* (This author based his conclusions upon the Constitution "*Ad evitanda*" of Martin V and the words of Pope St. Leo. "Quibus viventibus," etc.)

51 *Loc. cit.*

A special interpretation of the law by Benedict XIV was necessitated by conditions among the Christian peoples who were under Turkish domination. Among the offenses for which the denial of Christian burial along with excommunication was incurred were: request before death of the use of Turkish rites at the funeral; denial of the faith out of fear of the civil power; voluntary concealment of the faith by Christian women who married Turks, who entered their harem, and were thus removed from all possibility of practicing their religion; marriage with Turks before Turkish officials, unless, after repentance, the attempted marriage was rectified by the Church; marriage with several wives on the part of a Christian man; marriage by a Christian woman to a man with one or more wives; and finally, the persisting in concubinage with Turks on the part of a Christian woman.[52]

It was the same Pontiff who warned that public sinners were notorious not only by notoriety of law, i.e., upon the pronouncement of sentence by a judge, but also by notoriety of fact, i.e., if their state was so well known that it could not be concealed. Either notoriety was sufficient to effect the denial of Christian burial.[53]

Simulated apostasy begot the penalty of privation of Christian burial, as was evidenced by a reply to a question from the missions. Some Christians in China had been keeping idols in their homes to give the impression that they were still pagans, while they practiced Christianity secretly. The Sacred Congregation of the Propagation of the Faith declared that the practice could not be tolerated, for it was dissimulation, and if the ones guilty of the practice died after refusing to give it up, they could not be given Christian burial. Moreover, very definite signs of repentance had to be given—*"notabilia signa"*—to prove the sincerity of their conversion.[54]

An extraordinary stretching of the limits of tolerance in

52 Ep. encycl. *Inter omnigenas*, 2 febr. 1744, nn. 4-13—*Fontes*, n. 339.

53 *De Synodo Dioecesana* (3 vols., Romae, 1783), lib. 7, c. 2, n. 6.

54 S. C. de Prop. Fide, instr. (*ad Vic. Ap. Sutchuen*), 6 iun. 1817—*Fontes*, n. 4710.

the face of apparent impenitence is recorded in the reply to another difficulty from the missions. It was asked if Christian burial could be granted in a certain section of China to the natives who persistently refused the last sacraments, not through malice, but because of a peculiar local superstition. The Holy Office replied that since the fault was due to ignorance, they were to be allowed Christian burial, so long as there was any hope that they had died with signs of repentance.[55] Schaaf remarks that while this is a private reply for a particular case, as its wording implies, and therefore cannot be extended to others, it does reveal the clemency of the Church which is ever evailable, provided the careless Catholic has given some signs of a change of heart.[56]

The French used to include all actors among public sinners by virtue of their profession, since they were considered as ready to act evil rôles as virtuous ones.[57] Many declared, however, that the common law never sanctioned this broad inclusion of the members of the profession, but judged each actor according to his actions, not his profession.[58]

The forced burial of the unrepentant was in no way to be approved, declared the Sacred Penitentiary, when it ordered that the clergy was not allowed to assist at the compulsory burial in blessed ground of one notoriously unworthy.[59]

The increase of the number of civil marriages, due to the laws of the various nations in the later nineteenth century, contributed no little difficulty in the matter of Christian burial. Great pains were taken that Catholics be made to realize that civil marriage for them was not real marriage. In an instruction to the clergy, a gathering of the Bishops of the

55 S. C. S. Off., 14 febr. 1827—*Coll. S. C. P. F.*, n. 794.

56 "Catholic Burial of Public Sinners"—*Ecclesiastical Review*, XCV (1936), 191.

57 Icard, *Praelectiones Iuris Canonici in Usu Seminarii St. Sulpitii*, II, 479.

58 *De Locis Sacris*, n. 221.

59 S. Poen. Ap., 10 dec. 1860—*ASS*, I (1865), 563-564, ad 21.

Province of Prague (1868) ordered that they should remind their parishioners that unless the civil ceremony was followed by a Catholic one, the parties would be living in sin, and that if they died unrepentant, they could not have Christian burial.[60]

This gathering further urged the clergy, when called to attend dying persons guilty of this sin, that reparation of scandal was to be made before death, if possible. But Christian burial was not to be refused to one who had evidenced any desire before death to regularize his marriage. This merciful interpretation included those who, though unable at the time of their death to manifest any outward sign of their repentance, had previously given signs of it. If, however, scandal would arise from the granting of Christian burial, the pastor had to announce the repentance to the congregation on a Sunday or a Holy Day preceding the funeral, or, if this could not be done, at some time before the funeral, either at the house, or in the church, or, at least, at the grave. Finally, if Christian burial could not be accorded to those who had lived in a civil marriage, then it might at most be tolerated that they be interred in the cemetery, but the priest was not allowed to accompany the funeral, no ritual service of any kind could be held, Mass could not be offered for the deceased, the bells could not be rung to announce the death, and the *iura stolae* could not be received, for such acts would imply cooperation and participation of an altogether forbidden character.[61]

In a similar case the Holy Office gave the instruction that one who had died too suddenly for sacramental reconciliation was to be given Christian burial if there were any previous signs of repentance. However, there was to be no pomp or solemnity.[62]

The Constitution *"Apostolicae Sedis,"* at the same time that it forbade the granting of Christian burial to notorious

60 *Coll. Lac.*, V, 1406-1407.

61 *Loc. cit.*

62 S. C. S. Off., 6 iul. 1898—*Coll. S. C. P. F.*, n. 2007.

heretics, included in the same prohibition those who were excommunicated by name, *nominatim,* and those who were personally interdicted. It also declared those to be excommunicated who ordered or forced the granting of Christian burial to those who were denied it.[63]

The old excommunications levelled against manifest usurers [64] and against the abettors—*fautores*—of heretics[65] do not appear in the Constitution *"Apostolicae Sedis,"* and may therefore be said to have lapsed, for this Constitution listed all the excommunications that were to apply after 1869, and any former ones not included were abrogated.[66]

In general, therefore, the later tendency has been to grant Christian burial even to those who died before a sacramental reconciliation could be effected, provided there had been sufficient signs to indicate a change of heart before death. Testimony of relatives, of servants, or of anyone aware of these signs was deemed sufficient. Relative to their character, these signs could consist of various manifestations: the kissing of the crucifix or of a sacred image, the asking for a priest, the performance of any act of Christian devotion, or any other equivalent action or expression which in a normal way would be interpreted as betokening a desire for repentance. However, in the granting of Christian burial because of these manifestations it was deemed advisable to omit all pomp and solemnity.[67] By the denial of pomp and solmenity there was implied the silencing of bells and the privation of all chant and music. The funeral service was limited to the offering of a low Mass and the bestowal thereafter of the absolution in a hushed tone of voice.[68]

63 Sec. IV, n. 1—*Fontes*, n. 552.

64 C. 1, *de sepulturis*, III, 7, in Clem.

65 C. 2, *de haereticis*, V, 2, in VI°.

66 *Fontes*, n. 552; Many, *De Locis Sacris*, n. 224.

67 S. C. S. Off., 19 sept. 1877—*Fontes*, 1054.

68 Mothon, *Institutions Canoniques*, II, 574; Wernz, *Ius Decretalium*, III, 773.

C. Suicides

A clear tendency to give the benefit of the doubt to suicides is discernible especially in the nineteenth century. An outstanding example of this was the case of a suicide in Italy, in the town of Avezzano of the Diocese of Marsi. A man had killed himself after a quarrel with his wife. The pastor refused Christian burial, alleging that the man's sanity seemed established by his having had a public letter-writer write two letters for him before the deed. The bishop supported the pastor's refusal and the case was carried to Rome, where it was referred to the Congregation of Bishops and Regulars. The Congregation after examination, declared the appeal granted. It gave as its reason the general opinion of canonists that insanity is to be presumed whenever there is grave doubt as to its existence or non-existence:

> "Idem doctores tradunt quod si dubium sit an suicidium ex delicto vel insania ortum duxerit, pro secundo parte standum sit, iuxta regulam quod delictum tam grave de iure non praesumitur. Quae opinio maiorem ex eo confirmationem capit quod Suprema Inquisitio sepulturam suicidae largiendam esse definit, quando non sit 'probabilmente esclusa l'insania' ".[69]

The Sacred Congregation quoted as the sources of the law in the case the decree of the Council of Braga (561),[70] and the Ritual of Benedict XIV.[71] Further, it stated that no change of law had occurred since. Since the law of the Ritual of Pope Benedict XIV was identical with that of the Ritual of Pope Paul V in 1614, it is obvious that no change of legislation had occurred in this period on the matter of suicide. As canonists supporting the presumption in favor of insanity the Sacred Congregation quoted Reiffenstuel,[72] Pirhing,[73] Schmalzgrueber[74] and Zallinger.[75] The same Con-

69 S. C. Ep. et Reg., 7 aug. 1835—*Coll. S. C. Ep. et Reg.*, pp. 54-58.

70 Can. 16—Harduin, III, 351; C. 12, C. 23, q. 5.

71 *De Exequiis.*

72 Lib. III, tit. 28, n. 3.

73 Lib. I, n. 65.

74 Lib. III, tit. 26, n. 3.

75 Lib. III, tit. 28, n. 268.

gregation declared in addition that when a suicide has led a good life and a pious one, insanity is more easily presumed from even ambiguous signs.[76]

Another fact brought out in the case is that the opinion of the medical authorities is to be acceped by the pastor if there is no grave reason to doubt its impartiality. However, because of the long delays in the case, in view of the refusal of both the bishop and the pastor, and in order to avoid all scandal, the body was ordered to be buried in the cemetery quietly and at night.[77]

The Provincial Council of Prague (1860) ordered that when there is grave doubt as to the doctor's verdict of insanity, let the matter be referred to the Ordinary. If the doubt of the insanity remained, let the deceased be given Christian burial without any solemnity.[78] It should be added that the doubt here in question was one concerning the existence of *insanity;* for when a doubt arose as to whether death was by *accident* or by *intent,* no delay was necessary, for in such case the deceased received the benefit of the doubt and Christian burial was readily granted.[79]

The Sacred Congregation of the Holy Office gave a similar instruction to pastors and missionaries at Constantinople in 1866. It admonished them, in as far as it was possible for them to do so, to have recourse to the Ordinary when suicide cases were surrounded with doubt. The rule was: It was not allowed to grant Christian burial to those who killed themselves in a fit of desperation or in a fit of anger (excluding of course the case in which an insane person took his life), unless before death they had given signs of repentance. When there was certainty, therefore, of anger or despair, Christian burial was to be refused and the pomp and the solemnities of

[76] Ferraris, *Bibliotheca*, v. "*Sepultura*," n. 184.

[77] *Coll. S. C. Ep. et Reg.*, p. 58.

[78] Tit. III, c. 13, n. 2—*Mansi*, XLVIII, 264; *Coll. Lac.*, V, 486.

[79] *Loc. cit.*

the funeral service were to be foregone. But when there was certainty of insanity, Christian burial with its accompanying solemn exequies was to be granted. Finally, when a doubt remained whether a man took his life in insanity or in desperation, Christian burial could be granted, but without the pomp and the solemnities of the funeral service.[80]

This may be considered as having been the general mode of procedure up to the Code. *"Porro hanc insaniam benigna Mater Ecclesia facile praesumit. Insuper, animadvertendum est ipsum suicidium numquam praesumi sed esse probandum."* [81]

D. Those Who Ordered Their Own Cremation

The practice of cremation reappeared about the middle of the nineteenth century, strongly promoted by materialists, by members of the Masonic Order, and by other enemies of Christianity.[82]

The Holy Office in 1886 declared that many bishops had spoken of the new peril of the faith and had asked how it was to be met. The reply was that the faithful were forbidden to join cremation societies of any kind or to order their own cremation. Pope Leo XIII, in approving the decree, urged that the faithful be made acquainted with the malice underlying this new practice.[83]

The Holy Office again decreed, in 1886, that anyone who had willed his own cremation, and had not retracted the order, before his death, was to be refused Christian burial. The decree punished the intention and made no mention of the fact of cremation as being any cause of the denial.[84] According to this decree, then, although one had willed his own cremation, he would escape the penalty of the denial of Christian burial if he retracted his intention before death.

80 S. C. S. Off. (Constantinop.), 16 maii 1866—*Fontes*, n. 993.

81 Santi, *Praelectiones Iuris Canonici*, lib. III, tit. 28, n. 20.

82 Hornstein, *La Crémation* (Paris, 1886), pp. 319 ff.

83 S. C. S. Off., 19 maii 1886—*Fontes*, 1100.

84 S. C. S. Off., 15 dec. 1886—*Fontes*, 1103.

If however one was not responsible for his own cremation, but it was done at the orders of others, the rites and suffrages of the Church could be invoked both at the house and at the church, with all necessary safeguard against scandal. This safeguard could be assured by the announcement that the cremation was determined not by the will of the deceased, but by the desire of others. But when there was question of those who by their own decision determined their cremation and then certainly and notoriously adhered to this will up to the very time of their death, Christian burial had to be denied.[85]

If, finally, it was publicly known that a person had determined his own cremation, then his reception of the last sacraments, altogether apart from any proof that he had explicitly retracted his evil will, became the basis for a full presumption that he had retracted. Under these circumstances Christian burial could be granted.

That there is no intrinsic evil in cremation was demonstrated by a reply to a query from the missions. The question was asked whether pagan converts could be baptized and then granted Christian burial after death, when it was known for certain that they would be cremated according to the prevailing tribal customs. The reply was that since the practice was general, it was to be ignored by the priests and they were to remain passive toward it.[86]

In a later decree on the question of the attitude to be taken by the clergy when faced with the problem of compulsory cremation, the Holy Office warned that one who refused to withdraw the will to be cremated could not have public Mass offered for his soul—therefore no funeral Mass—nor could he be given the last sacraments. It would seem that such a one certainly could not have Christian rites after two such prohibitions. The Holy Office insisted that one may never cooperate formally in cremation, and only materially when it is sure there is no question of recognizing a practice of the

[85] *Loc. cit.*

[86] S. C. de Prop. Fide, 27 sept. 1884—*Coll. S. C. P. F.*, n. 1626.

enemies of the Church, or of aiding a sect or of showing contempt of Church law on this matter.[87]

The law remained unchanged up to the Code which incorporated the old law and forbade Christian burial to those who ordered their own cremation.

E. Those Who Neglected to Make their "Easter Duty"

The law of the IV General Lateran Council (1215) on the duty of annual confession and Easter Communion, as incorporated in the Ritual of Pope Paul V in 1614, remained the universal law throughout the modern period and up to the advent of the present Code of Canon Law.

The Synod of Baltimore of 1791 offers an exceptionally authoritative evidence of the interpretation of the law that was in use not only in America but also throughout a large part of the Church. There are several reasons why this Synod's action took on more importance than a diocesan synod's ordinarily would. It was, first of all, a national synod, legislating for the whole United States. Secondly, it was composed of men, in a large measure, recently arrived from various parts of Europe. The theologians of the synod had just arrived from France and could not but have brought with them the custom and practice of their homeland. It thus differs from a synod composed of clergy who are concerned with the affairs of a small region and who represent but a small group. Therefore the interpretation of the law as adopted by the Synod may be considered to reflect a wider practice than a synod's dercee normally would.

The Synod reminded the clergy and people of the United States of the law of the Church and also warned the clergy that the penalty of the denial of Christian burial was a *ferendae sententiae,* penalty and therefore not to be hastily applied. It ordered that no one should be denied Christian burial for a breach of this law without the pastor's having consulted the bishop or the vicar-general. Since, however, the great

87 S. C. S. Off., 27 iul. 1892, ad 3—*Fontes*, 1158.

areas of the new diocese would render this consultation impossible in a great many instances, the Synod outlined several conditions under which the pastor himself could impose the penalty. The pastor was to determine whether the deceased had missed his Easter Duty only once or numerous times; whether it was with contumacy or contempt of the law; whether the morals of the deceased were otherwise bad and his example pernicious. If *all* these conditions were present in the individual case, the Synod gave the pastors power to deny Christian burial, if they judged that it would be for the greater glory of God and the salvation of souls.[88]

The legislation of the First Baltimore Synod on the denial of Christian burial to those who neglected to make their "Easter Duty" remained the norm of procedure in the United States in later years. It is a clear testimonial of the mercy and toleration that was to be practiced in the administration of the law on the fulfillment of one's "Easter Duty."

The solution of a case by the Sacred Congregation of Bishops and Regulars in 1851 accurately sums up the more recent interpretation of the law. A young Neapolitan had been killed accidentally and suddenly, without time for any word or sign to anyone. His pastor, having consulted the Archbishop of Naples, refused Christian burial on the ground that he had neglected to perform his "Easter Duty" for several years. Having appealed the case to the Curia of the Archdiocese, and having lost the appeal, the mother of the young man took the case to Rome, where it was referred to the aforesaid Congregation.[89]

The attorneys for the mother urged that the man had not incurred the penalties of interdict and of the privation of Christian burial, since they were *ferendae sententiae* penalties according to the decretal law.[90] Further, they quoted a de-

88 *Statuta Synodi Baltimorensis anno 1791 Celebratae*, article 24—*Concilia Provincialia Baltimori* (Baltimori, 1842).

89 S. C. Ep. et Reg., "*Neapolitana*," 9 mart. 1855—*Fontes*, n. 1971.

90 C. 12, X, *de poenitentiis et remissionibus*, V, 38.

cree of the Congregation under date of July 24, 1595, to the same effect.[91]

The Sacred Congregation, however, pointed out that the man had died without manifesting any signs of contrition. Moreover, by Synodal law in the Archdiocese of Naples the interdict was established as a *latae sententiae* penalty. The Sacred Congregation then corrected the assertions of the attorneys by still further pointing out that the transgression had extended over several years and was notorious, thus coming under a provision of the same Congregation of the year 1696, which amended the decree of 1595 by adding that privation of Christian burial was *ipso facto* incurred not only when the neglect of one's "Easter Duty" was of a notorious character, but also when a synodal statute had established this penalty as one not requiring any intervening judicial sentence to contract it.[92]

The Sacred Congregation further pointed out that the two penalties of the law, namely, the interdict *ab ingressu ecclesiae* and the denial of Christian burial, were separte and independent; that therefore the latter could be inflicted, although the former had not been. It even quoted its authority for the distinction.[93]

The appeal of this case to the Sacred Congregation of Bishops and Regulars was lost not only in view of the existing diocesan statute which constituted the interdict *ab ingressu ecclesiae* and the privation of Christian burial as *latae sententiae* penalties, but also because of the transgression of

91 "Qui non confitentur et non communicant in Paschate non tamen sunt ipso interdicti, sed sunt interdicendi per sententiam; unde si ante declarationem moriuntur, non privantur ecclesiastica sepultura, modo obierint cum signis contritionis."

92 " . . . nisi intermissio esset notoria vel adesset statutum synodale in contrarium."—*Fontes*, n. 1971.

93 De Ameno, *De Delictis et Poenis*, Tom. III, tit. 5, 1, n. 12: "Una enim poena (interdicti) ut separata ab alia (privationis sepulturae) . . . et ex consequenti haec locum habet licet illa non fuerit inflicta."

the Paschal Precept which continued for some years as a notorious neglect of duty that had not been corrected before death by the manifestation of any sign of contrition or repentance. The case aptly shows that the sanction of the law was not to be sacrificed in the face of plain evidence of guilt. It restated the law of the period and its interpretation, and showed the vigor with which it had survived. Human weakness was one thing; but flagrant disregard of the law was quite another.

Wherever the enacted sanctions of interdict *ab ingressu ecclesiae* and of privation of Christian burial had remained *ferendae sententiae* penalties, consultation with the bishop was the normal procedure before the penalties were inflicted. This is evidenced by several nineteenth century councils which invariably stated that the penalties were not to be inflicted, or to be regarded as having been incurred, without previous consultation of the bishop for his authorized sentence or decision.[94]

Many asserted that the penalty of privation of Christian burial was not incurred unless the *habit* of neglecting the Paschal Precept had been fully established; moreover, both the failure to make one's "Easter Duty" and the subsequent lack of any manifestation of contrition or repentance had to be publicly known.[95] Moreover, according to Many, the almost universal custom was for bishops and pastors to interpret this law benignly.[96] It is therefore not surprising that this law does not appear in the present Code of Canon Law as an enactment prohibiting the granting of Christian burial.

94 Council of Avignon (1849), tit. V. c. 1—*Coll. Lac.*, IV, 342-343; Council of Ravenna (1855), pars III, c. 6, n. 6—*Coll. Lac.*, V, 189; Council of Vienna (1855), c. 14—*Coll. Lac.*, V, 189; Council of Venice (1859), pars. III, c. 26—*Coll. Lac.*, V, 343; Council of Smyrna (1869), sec. 2, c. 6—*Coll. Lac.*, VI, 572-573.

95 *De Locis Sacris*, n. 220. The same doctrine was declared in a decision of the Sacred Congregation of the Council, February 26, 1859—*Analecta Iuris Pontificii*, IV (1860), 1757.

96 *De Locis Sacris*, n. 220.

F. Members of Forbidden Societies

Modern Masonry may be said to have originated in the early eighteenth century, that is, the type of Masonry called *speculative* Masonry, which teaches morality by means of geometric symbols.[97]

The Church was not long in experiencing the evil effects of the new movement, nor was she slow to point out the menace that it cloaked for both State and Church. Pope Clement XII, in his Constitution *"In eminenti,"* [98] addressed to all the faithful a prohibiiton against joining or favoring the society under the penalty of excommunication. Nor could absolution be obtained before withdrawal from membership. One who died unabsolved was to be denied Christian burial, unless he had shown signs of repentance.

In 1751 Benedict XIV renewed verbatim the law of his predecessor [99] because of the doubt among many authors as to whether the earlier legislation was still in force. He stated emphatically that it was, and added urgent requests to the civil powers to root out the evil movement.

Similar renewals of the condemnation of Clement XII, called forth by recurring doubts as to the survival of the law, were issued by Pius VII [100] and Leo XII.[101] Pope Leo did not limit the condemnation to the Masons, but included all societies bound by a vow of secrecy, *"jusjurandum nefarium,"* and extended the penalties to all those who joined such societies in even the lowest "degrees."

The menace later called forth strong condemnation from Pius IX, who recalled the earlier laws and renewed their force.[102] This was not the first pronouncement on the question

97 Quigley, J., *Condemned Societies*, The Catholic University of America Canon Law Studies, n. 46, Washington, D. C.: The Catholic University of America, 1927, p. 11; *The Catholic Encyclopedia*, IX, 771-787, v. "Masonry."

98 April 25, 1738—*Fontes*, n. 299.

99 Const. *"Providas,"* 18 maii 1751—*Fontes*, n. 412.

100 Const. *"Ecclesiam,"* 13 sept. 1821—*Fontes*, n. 479.

101 Const. *"Quo graviora,"* 13 mart. 1825—*Fontes*, n. 481.

102 Allocut. *"Multiplices inter,"* 25 sept. 1865—*Fontes*, n. 544.

by this great Pope; he had condemned the secret societies earlier, but perhaps less vigorously and less specifically.[103]

His allocution was elecited by the same evasions that had caused his predecessors to repeat the condemnation of Clement XII: the constantly arising doubts as to the duration of the papal condemnations. Pius left no doubt as to their continuation and specified that no illusion should exist as to their applicability even in the states in which the civil power tolerated the movement.

In his Constitution *"Apostolicae Sedis"* Pius IX renewed the excommunication against all who enrolled their names in the Masonic Order or in secret societies of a like nature.[104]

Piat in his commentary on this Constitution declared that the phrase *"nomen dantes"* included all those who knew the nature of the society they joined. No contumacy or presumption on the part of those who enrolled was necessary to incur the penalty. It was sufficient that they were aware of the prohibition; ignorance, therefore, alone excused.[105] Far from mitigating the earlier laws, Pius IX extended the law to include all those who *favored* such societies.[106]

Finally, Leo XIII, in confirmation of the law of Pius IX, added that societies of a like nature are to Masonry as a *species* is to a *genus;* they are all of the same type and are all equally to be avoided, for they revolve around Masonry as a center.[107] Leo declared that though the animosity of some

[103] Ep. encycl. "*Quanta cura,*" 8 dec. 1864—*Fontes*, n. 542; *Syllabus Errorum* (a. 1864), IV—*Fontes*, n. 543.

[104] 12 oct. 1869, Sec. IV, n. 1—*Fontes*, n. 552.

[105] *Commentarius in Constitutionem Apostolicae Sedis*, p. 145, N. (1).

[106] Piat stated that among those favoring Masonry there were not to be included such persons as had attended one or two meetings of the society with no intention of joining, or simply out of curiosity. With regard to those who had once belonged and had later withdrawn, they were not allowed to pretend still to belong to the society. An exception to the latter prohibition was available only for those who were compelled to attend under threat of most grave harm, and of possible death—*Commentarius*, p. 147, note (5).

[107] Ep. encycl. "*Humanum genus,*" 20 apr. 1884—*Fontes*, n. 591.

of the members of such societies against the Church could be said to have diminished in some places, and though many members might even be well disposed, the essential evil of Naturalism was fostered and spread by the progress and growth of Masonic societies.[108]

The Councils of Baltimore constantly restated the Church's anti-Masonic legislation and insisted on its enforcement. As early as the IV Provincial Council (1840) a condemnation of secret societies in general was issued, without however naming the Masons in particular.[109] This Decree was repeated in 1866 in the II Plenary Council,[110] which devoted thirteen paragraphs to the question of Masonic and similar secret societies.[111] The Council contained also the reply that had been received from the Holy Office in answer to the question about the specific characteristics of condemned societies. The Holy Office stated that all societies that secretly worked against either the Church or the State were included in the papal condemnations, regardless of whether or not their members were bound by oaths of secrecy.[112]

The III Plenary Council of Baltimore (1884) likewise inveighed against any toleration of laxity in regard to the joining of secret societies. It defined as forbidden societies, over and above those condemned by Popes Pius IX and Leo XIII, all such societies whose aims and workings could not be revealed to the bishop of the diocese, or whose members were sworn to blind obedience. Absolution had to be refused to any and all members of the forbidden as well as the condemned societies as long as they retained their formal membership. Only upon withdrawal from the societies could such

108 *Loc. cit.*

109 Decree VII—*Concilia Provincilia Baltimori*, p. 172.

110 Art. 513—*Concilii Plenarii Baltimorensis II Decreta* (Baltimorae, 1875), p. 261.

111 Arts. 511-523—*op. cit.*, pp. 260-265.

112 S. C. S. Off., 5 aug. 1846—*Fontes*, n. 899; Quigley, *Condemned Societies*, p. 58.

persons hope for absolution.[113] Those who belonged to this particular type of forbidden societies were declared liable to the censure enacted with reference to heretics and schismatics.[114] Further, the Council forbade any compromising with the law or any dissimulation in its application and extent. It ordered the prohibition of the Church to be made public without any apologies.[115]

The Holy Office, in reply to specific inquiries, replied that Christian burial may not be granted to Masons unless they have shown clear (*clara*) signs of repentance.[116] Furthermore, no Christian burial could be granted to one who, though he had received the last sacraments, ordered that Masonic insignia be used on his bier. But if this was done upon the order of others, he was not to be penalized, provided that the insignia were removed.[117]

In a letter to the Ordinaries of Brazil, the Holy Office ordered Christian burial denied to all who did not withdraw from the society before death, and absolution could not be granted until they had severed their membership. If, however, they died too suddenly to effect this severance of membership and thereupon to obtain absolution, they could be granted Christian burial, if they had shown definite signs of repentance before death. No Masonic symbolism was to be connected with the funeral, especially with regard to the use of the Masonic ritual at the grave. If the interment of unreconciled Masons was forced by threats or by the civil authority, the clergy was not allowed to assist in any manner. Delegations of Masons could not be permitted to assist as a corporate body wearing its insignia at a Christian burial. If Masons were present at the Catholic funeral as individuals,

113 Art. 244-247—*Decreta Concilii Plenarii Baltimorensis Tertii* (Baltimorae, 1866), pp. 137-138.

114 Art. 249—*op. cit.*, pp. 140-141.

115 Art. 252—*op. cit.*, p. 142.

116 S. C. S. Off., "*Portus Aloisii*" 1 aug. 1855—*Fontes*, n. 932.

117 S. C. S. Off., 2 dec. 1840—*Fontes*, n. 844.

they could not be permitted to display their Masonic badges or banners.[118]

The "Odd Fellows" were included in the condemned societies according to a reply of the Holy Office to Bishop Fenwick of Philadelphia.[119]

The Sacred Congregation of the Propagation of the Faith in 1898 reiterated the inclusion of the Odd Fellows in its condemnations when it declared that they could not receive the Sacraments or Christian burial unless they withdrew from the society and sought absolution. If, however, they died suddenly, they could be granted Christian burial provided they had shown some previous signs of contrition and devotion. But all solemnity and pomp had to be avoided in their burial.[120]

There has not been any change in the legislation since that time and it has continued in force up to the present Code.

G. Anti-Clericals

Closely connected with the subject of Masonry was the question of the French anti-clericals, who were, in general, Masons. The Church of France suffered great harm at their hands in the early twentieth century and, as a result, they were subjected to ecclesiastical penalties, among which was the privation of Christian burial.

Relations between the Church and State in France had progressively grown worse from the first days of the Third Republic, the government of which was largely in the hands of Masonic anti-clericals. But it was only by the passage of the Law of Separation that the rupture between them became of the gravest nature. Promulgated in the Government's Journal on December 11, 1905, this law pretended to dissolve the religious Orders and to confiscate their properties, as well as

118 S. C. S. Off., instr. (ad Ordinarios Imperii Brasil.), 2 iul. 1878—*Fontes*, n. 1056.

119 S. C. S. Off., rescriptum circa Societates Secretas, 21 aug. 1850—*Concilii Plenarii Baltimorensis II, Acta et Decreta*, Appendix XV (p. 300) (Murphy: Baltimorae, 1894).

120 S. C. Prop. Fide, 10 maii 1898—*Fontes*, n. 4987.

a great quantity of other Church property throughout the country. The robbery was cloaked under the guise of a demand for certain reforms in the Orders, which reforms were obviously impossible and incompatible with the very nature of the Orders and with their allegiance to the Holy See. The law was severely condemned by Pope Pius X in two encyclicals to the French hierarchy, clergy and people.[121]

The members of Parliament who had voted the law were *ipso facto* excommunicated, according to the law of the Constitution *"Apostolicae Sedis,"* which had inflicted that penalty for any illegal alienation of Church property, no matter by whom made, as long as the permission of the Holy See had not been previously obtained. The same penalty applied to those who received property so alienated.[122]

Some difficulties immediately arose as to who were included in the excommunication. The Sacred Penitentiary, in a series of replies to questions from France, clarified this problem. In one reply it declared that mayors and civic officials whose duty it was to carry out the confiscatory decrees were not included in the penalty and were not to be denied Christian burial.[123] In another response excluded also those whose duty it was to take over the property for purposes of disposal in the name of the law. These liquidators could even receive their salaries from the stolen property. Only when they kept for themselves some of the immovables did they incur the censure and the privation of Christian burial.[124] But excommunication and the privation of Christian burial were *ipso facto* incurred by those who presumed to receive, or to buy, or to accept as a gift, the stolen religious property.[125]

Ignorance of the fact that they were obtaining Church property excused the buyers or receivers, for the word *"praesu-*

121 *"Vehementer nos,"* 21 febr. 1906—*Fontes*, n. 671; *"Une fois encore,"* 6 ian. 1907—*Fontes*, n. 677.

122 Sec. IV, n. 3—*Fontes*, n. 552.

123 S. Poenit. Ap., 3 ian. 1906—*ASS*, XL (1907), 249-250.

124 S. Poenit. Ap., 5 aug. 1907—*ASS*, XLI (1908), 680.

125 *Loc. cit.*

mentes" in the enacted excommunication required full liberty and deliberation before the penalty was incurred.[126] Thus, as far as the excommunication itself was concerned, it may be said to have fallen principally upon those who, by their vote, had made the law, and those who received the stolen goods; and no declaratory sentence was necessary for denying them Christian burial.[127]

Another difficulty arose on the point as to when the penalty was incurred: whether it was at the time of the voting or at the actual seizure of the Church property. Piat gives the two opinions in the controversy. The one held that the penalty was incurred only when the act was perfected, i.e., when the seizure had taken place,[128] while the other followed a new view that had arisen since the promulgation of the confiscatory laws of Belgium and of Italy, earlier in the century, namely, that the penalty was incurred when the law was promulgated, for it was at that moment that the act of usurpation and alienation was really constituted in its juridical existence. This later interpretation, according to Piat, reflected the more common opinion of the commentators of the Constitution "*Apostolicae Sedis.*"[129]

Regardless of whether the public officials administering the law were deprived of Christian burial by incurring the excommunication, they could be deprived of it under the heading of public sinners, if their attitude and actions in the performance of their duties constituted them as such. The decision as to when they fell under this category was left to the discretion of the bishops for individual cases.[130]

With regard to both those who were excommunicated and those who were considered public sinners even without being

126 Piat, *Commentarius*, pp. 240, (3); 248, (2); 232, (4).

127 S. Poenit. Ap., 17 sept. 1906—*ASS*, XL (1907), 254-255; 20 maii 1908—*ASS*, XLI (1908), 612-613.

128 Schmalzgrueber, lib. III, tit. 13, n. 165; Reiffenstuel, lib. III, tit. 13, n. 67.

129 *Commentarius*, pp. 248, 249.

130 S. Poenit. Ap., 17 maii, 1906—*ASS*, XL (1907), 254.

excommunicated, if it was a notorius fact that they died without signs of repentance for the wrongs that they had done the Church, they were to be deprived of Christian burial. If their repentance was doubtful, they were to be allowed Christian burial, but without any pomp or solemnity, i.e., with but a low Mass and the subsequent absolution.[131]

[131] S. Poenit. Ap., 20 maii, 1908—*ASS*, XLI (1908), 612-613. Mothon, *Institutions Canoniques*, II, 574.

HISTORICAL SUMMARY

The study of the sources of the legislation on the denial of Christian burial manifests for this canonical institute an impressive antiquity and a remarkable consistency. In the earliest period, before the peace of Constantine, evidence of the denial of Christian burial is deduced from the high degree of sanctity and holiness required of the members of Christ's Church, and the correspondingly great severity exercised toward those who proved unworthy of the gift of faith. Their exclusion from the Church was swift and complete, and they were not received back before showing signs of sincere repentance. To those who failed to evince any repentance, their utter cutting off from the Body of Christ and their consignment of the devil leave little room for doubt that they were excluded from finding a final resting place among the faithful.

The early part of the second period, from 300 to 1179 is outstanding because of the enduring definition given by Pope St. Leo I of the standard by which it was to be decided whether one was or was not to be given Christian burial: '*Quibus viventibus non communicavimus, nec mortuis communicare possumus.*" Other evidence of the denial is discovered, but none of a strictly legislative nature. Beginning with the Council of Braga, (561) a gradual increase is found in this type of legislation. Remarkable is the fact that at no period, either here or in the times earlier considered, did the penalty or the legislation of the denial of Christian burial appear as a novel or innovating departure from established and traditional discipline. This very lack of appearance of newness is an impressive indication of the antiquity of the penalty. During this period, while no change is apparent in the nature of the penalty from the time of its first apperance, there is a manifest increase in the number of offenses for which it was inflicted. Never as clear and determined as would be desirable, the seeds of the later development of the modern law are nevertheless discernible. This evidence becomes increasingly clearer toward the end of the period, especially in the II General Council of the Lateran in 1139.

In the decretal period the full development of the legislation on the denial of Christian burial may be said to be achieved. It was during this period that the law took the extent and form that it was to preserve until the Code of 1918. Here are enumerated in greater detail the offenses for which the penalty was incurred. But the element of mercy in the application and interpretation of the law is always apparent in the concern of the Legislator that the penalty be not inflicted so long as the dying one has made even the least redeeming gesture of sincere repentance. Evidence of this repentance is enough for the Church to desert the stern rôle of punisher and to adopt the attitude of a loving Mother who gives the last rites and honors to a prodigal son.

The one exception to this merciful tendency is discovered in regard to those who died in duels and other forbidden forms of combat. They were denied Christian burial regardless of how repentant they were. Severe though this descipline was, it eradicated an evil that was a menace to both the Church and State. With the decline of this crime the severity was relaxed and the new law permits the granting of Christian burial to repentant duelists.

The interpretation and application of the law as it substantially remained after the Ritual of Pope Paul V. in 1614 is the subject of the last chapter. Here is noted the continuation of the merciful tendency in the interpretation of the law. Here, also, was evolved an adjustment and adaptation to new conditions arising from modern events. The Protestant revolt had necessitated the taking of a large view by the Church of a form of cooperation with heretics in some places that approached closely to communion with them *in sacris*. This new situation arose mainly in countries whose populations emerged largely Protestant, where it often became necessary for Catholics and Protestants to share a common cemetery and church. While tolerating passively what could not be avoided, the Church at no time relaxed her determination that Catholics should rest in blessed and exclusively Catholic cemeteries. Nevertheless, the toleration that was necessitated resulted in a lowering among the faithful of the appreciation of Catholic burial. This was due to many influences of which a few may be named: the large number of people left without any religion by the Reformation, the disappearance in large part of the bitter anti-Catholic prejudice, the cooperation among Christians and the toleration and indifferentism among the various sects, the increase of the number of mixed marriages. All these conditions conspired to break down the Catholic's proper appreciation of burial in blessed ground. Concerned more with the essentials of religion, Catholics no longer beheld the lack of burial in a Catholic cemetery with the repugnance and shame that they formerly had.

In the midst of this situation it was asked whether it was not the lesser of two evils rather to admit for burial in blessed ground those who were not entitled to the privilege, than to encourage, by the refusal of Christian burial, the burial in non-sectarian cemeteries of the large number of Catholics in whose families there were non-Catholic members.

While passive toleration came as the result of necessity, the law remained unchanged. Moreover, its application remained strictly imperative in the cases of those whose disobedience and contempt for Church law placed them among the class of notorius public sinners.

It cannot be held, therefore, that the law has been modified. It remained the same in 1918 (before the Code) as it was in 1614. The necessary toleration remained temporary and expedient. However, in all instances of the denial of Christian burial, the later tendency has been not to deny it without the consultation of the bishop, with whom a large discretionary power was left by the Holy See, that he might act in accordance with the demands dictated by the conditions prevailing in his diocese.

PART TWO

THE CANONICAL COMMENTARY

INTRODUCTION

The title "Christian burial" was used throughout the historical part of this dissertation to translate the term *"sepultura ecclesiastica."* It will continue to be used in that signification in the canonical commentary.

Although the term "ecclesiastical burial" is sometimes used by authors who comment on the law in English, it is not so familiar or traditional a term as "Christian burial."

Woywod [1] uses the two terms "Christian burial" and "ecclesiastical burial" indifferently. Augustine [2] uses "Christian burial" entirely throughout his remarks on canons 2339, but uses "ecclesiastical burial" in his treatment of Title XII.[3]

Ayrinhac uses "Christian burial" in regard to canon 1204 and as a heading for Chapter II of Title XII.[4] But the same author entitles the whole of Title XII "Ecclesiastical Burial."[5] Ayrinhac-Lydon use "Christian burial" entirely in their treatment of canon 2339.[6]

Thus there seems to be no distinction made between the two English terms, for both are used to translate the Latin *"ecclesiastica sepultura"* as it is found in the various parts of the Code. Moreover, "Christian burial" in its Latin equivalent, *"sepultura Christianorum,"* is found in the ancient texts, in such works as a decree of Pope Eugene II (824 A.D.) [7] and in Thomassinus.[8]

1 *A Practical Commentary on the New Code of Canon Law* (3. ed., 2 vols., New York: J. F. Wagner, 1929), II, 489-90.

2 *A Commentary on Canon Law* (8 vols., St. Louis: Herder, 1931-1938), VIII (3. ed., 1931), p. 357.

3 *Op. cit.*, VI (3. ed., 1931), p. 102.

4 *Administrative Legislation in the New Code of Canon Law* (New York: Longmans, Green, 1930), pp. 60, 69.

5 *Loc. cit.*, p. 54.

6 *Penal Legislation in The New Code of Canon Law* (New York: Benziger Brothers, 1936), pp. 208, 209.

7 Mansi, XIV, 415.

8 *Vetus et Nova Ecclesiae Disciplina*, pars. III, lib. I, c. 68, n. 2.

Chapter I

DEFINITION OF CHRISTIAN BURIAL

It is a remarkable fact that nowhere in the old law is there a juridical definition of Christian burial.[1] This fact is all the more remarkable when it is recalled that there was a very general and commonly accepted traditional view of what Christian burial meant. This traditional concept of Christian burial consisted of two elements, according to D'Annibale, "de loco sacro (vel alio ad id destinato) et ritu catholico." [2] His definition is, in general, that which reflects the opinion of the accepted authorities, such as Reiffenstuel [3] and Wernz.[4]

But the primary element of the pre-Code notion was the burial in blessed ground, the *"locus sacer,"* or the place set aside by ecclesiastical authority for the burial of the faithful departed.[5] And it was this conception of the Christian burial that was considered throughout the first part of this dissertation.

The Code, however, has supplied for the defect of the old law and has defined Christian burial in canon 1204:

1 Ciprotti: " . . . deerat sepulturae ecclesiasticae definitio (c. 1204) . . . ," "De Consummatione Delicti"—*Apollinaris,* VIII (1935), 409, not. (3) ; Cappello: " . . . in iure antiquo legalis notio sepulturae ecclesiasticae deerat . . . ," *De Censuris* (3. ed. recognita et emendata, Romae: Marietti, 1933), n. 401.

2 *Summula Theologiae Moralis* (5. ed., 3 vol., Romae: 1908), I, 112.

3 *Ius Canonicum Universum,* lib. III, tit. 28, n. 2.

4 *Ius Decretalium,* III, 780.

5 Reiffenstuel. *loc. cit.;* Lehmkuhl, *Theologia Moralis* (11. ed., Friburgi Brisgoviae: 1910), II, 972; Santi-Leitner, *Praelectiones Iuris Canonici,* lib. III, tit. 28, n. 1; Sole supports this opinion by referring to c. 12, X, *de sepulturis,* III, 28, in which it is decreed that the bodies of those buried in blessed ground against the law are to be exhumed and "procul ab ecclesiastica sepultura iactari,"—*De Delictis et Poenis* (Romae, 1920), p. 156, not. (1) ; Maroto, "De axiomata 'ubi tumulus ibi funus' "—*Apollinaris,* I (1928), 25; Cippolini, *De Censuris* (Taurini, 1925), p. 181.

> Sepultura ecclesiastica consistit in cadaveris translatione ad ecclesiam, exsequiis super illud in eadem celebratis, illius depositione in loco legitime deputato fidelibus defunctis condendis.

It is not agreed, unfortunately, that this is a juridical defition, and hence an effort will be made to determine what is to be understood by the term "Christian burial" as it is used in the new law.

The investigation to follow is based mainly upon a study of the authors' interpretations of canons 1204, 1240 and 2339. Canon 1204 has already been seen; canon 1240 prohibits the granting of Christian burial to certain classes of people, while canon 2339 is the penal canon containing the sanction for canon 1240. Much of the subject matter to follow was discovered in the treatment of canon 2339, for, while the authors were either incomplete or ambiguous in their definition of Christian burial in their treatment of canons 1204 and 1240, they were clearly divided as to the meaning of the same term in canon 2339. Since canon 2339 refers explicitly to the prohibition of Christian burial contained in canon 1240 and penalizes the violation of that canon, it is entirely reasonable to conclude that the term should mean the same thing in both canons. Yet, it will be seen that in this there is not entire agreement for there are two schools of thought: the one, which holds that the meaning of Christian burial in the new law is identical with that of the old, and the other which holds that the new law has changed the meaning of the term.

To begin with the former, Wernz-Vidal claim that canon 1204 contains not a juridical definition but only a description of what a Christian *funeral* should be[6] In reference to canon 2339, they state that canon 1240, of which 2339 is the penal sanction, takes *"sepultura"* in the literal sense of the word, burial in blessed ground, and they support this contention by

[6] "Quo canone [1204] non habetur iuridica definitio sepulturae ecclesiasticae sed descriptio eorum quae ex lege Ecclesiae intervenire debent in funere fidelium . . . "—*Ius Canonicum,* VII, n. 451.

citing canon 1241 which, they hold, denies the *funeral rites* to those denied *burial* by canon 1240.[7]

Wernz-Vidal believe that Christian burial as belonging to the faithful, is the spiritual right of having their bodies interred in blessed ground, a right that is completed by the addition of the liturgical honors of the Church.[8] Denial of Christian burial therefore consists primarily in denying burial in blessed ground, and only secondarily in the refusal of the religious rites.[9]

According to Wernz-Vidal, then, Christian burial means in the new law just what it meant in the old; that is, it consists of two elements, the burial in blessed ground and the religious ceremonies surrounding that burial. But it is quite clear that they hold that fundamentally and essentially Christian burial is mere burial in blessed ground whether accompanied by the rites or not, for it this action, they maintain, that is punished by canon 2339, with or without the religious ceremonies.[10]

In this opinion Wernz-Vidal are supported by numerous authors, among whom are Sole;[11] Pighi,[12] Ciprotti[13] and Cip-

[7] " . . . ipse canon 1240, cuius sanctio habetur in nostro canone poenali [2339], *sepulturam* sumit in sensu inhumationis in loco sacro, nam *sepulturae* privato deneganda sunt officia funebria seu funus (can. 1241)."—*loc. cit.*

[8] "Ius sepulturae quo fideles patiuntur est ius spirituale competens fidelibus pie demortuis, ut condantur eorum corpora in loco sacro . . . ; quae depositio deinde ab Ecclesia honoratur honore liturgico praescriptis variis ritibus a ministro sacro ponendis."—*loc. cit.*

[9] Ergo directe exclusio fit inhumationis in loco sacro; cui autem hoc negatur, negandi sunt etiam . . . ritus sacri (can. 1241)."—*loc. cit.*

[10] "Quare, secundum declarationem veterum doctorum, censura incurritur si defunctus deponatur in loco sacro sive adhibito sive omisso praescripto ritu sacro . . . "—*loc. cit.*

[11] *De Delictis et Poenis* (Romae, 1920), n. 367.

[12] *Censurae Sententiae Latae* (Ed. altera, Verona: 1919), n. 81.

[13] " . . . ex can. 1240 (qui in can. 2339 revocatur) in quo ecclesiastica sepultura est inhumatio, ut ex cc. 1241, 1242 patet;"—"De consummatione delicti"—*Apollinaris* I (1928), 408-410; the same author makes an outright distinction between Christian burial as understood in canon 1204 and in canon 2339 when he states that in the latter it

polini, who holds that Christian burial is not the union of two essential elements, the *locus sacer* and the rites, but is mere burial in a blessed place.[14] Yet the latter author states that though canon 1240 treats of Christian burial in this limited sense—which conclusion he forms from a comparison with canon 1241—nevertheless he holds that *"ecclesiastica sepultura"* and *"officia funebria,"* as mentioned in canon 1241, are not to be understood in a disjunctive sense, for he insists that the privation of Christian burial includes both the denial of burial in blessed ground and the denial of the religious rites that accompany it.[15]

Thus he appears to hold one definition of Christian burial for canons 2339 and 1240 and another for canon 1241. This is the difficulty of all authors who try to carry into the interpretation of the new law the accepted definition of the old. To them Christian burial as understood in canons 1240 and 2339 means mere burial in blessed ground, while Christian burial as mentioned in canons 1204 and 1241 comprises both the burial and the accompanying religious rites.

Vermeersch-Creusen sum up well the case for those who hold to the pre-Code conception of Christian burial as burial in blessed ground. They contend that, *a,* the words of canon 2339 repeat entirely the old law in its more common acceptance, and therefore must be interpreted in the light of the old law: Christian burial means burial in blessed ground; *b,* they deny that the concept of Christian burial as stated in canon 1204 is new law and that it defines what is meant by *"tradere sepulturam ecclesiasticam;"* *c,* they hold that the distinction

means solely burial in a place legitimately designated, "although canon 1204 gives another definition of Christian burial": ". . . depositio in loco legitime deputato fidelium defunctorum cadaveribus condendis, quamvis c. 1204 aliam definitionem sepulturae ecclesiasticae tradat."—*loc. cit.*

14 "Ergo in sensu iuris sepultura ecclesiastica non est accipienda per modum unius cum ritu sacro nam hic ab illa distinguitur, sed pro simplici cadaveris repositione in loco sacro."—*De Censuris,* n. 85.

15 *Loc. cit.*

in canon 1241 between *"sepulturam ecclesiasticam"* and *"officia funebria"* supports their opinion; *d,* they argue that the purpose of the denial of Christian burial is to separate the unworthy from the faithful in their final resting place.[16]

Yet again the confusion of this school is manifest in the work of these authors when they state that the term always refers to the full process of Christian burial as stated in canon 1204.[17]

The views of the authors cited may be considered a sufficient example of the doctrine of that school which holds that the notion of Christian burial is the same in the new law as it was in the old; that though Christian burial may be considered in a broad sense as composed of two elements—the burial in blessed ground and the religious rites that accompany such burial—essentially it is solely the former; that though the denial of Christian burial implies the refusal of both elements, the penalty for the violation of such denial is incurred only when the essential act, the burial in blessed ground, is illegally performed.[18]

The authors of the second school hold strictly to the definition of canon 1204 as a juridical one that must be understood in its properly described sense wherever the term therein defined is encountered. Prominent among these authors is Cerato, who holds that the *"finis legis"* of the prohibition of Christian burial is not so much to separate the unworthy

16 *Epitome Iuris Canonici,* III, n. 538.

17 *Op. cit.,* II, 512.

18 Among the authors holding this view are most of the commentators on the Constitution "*Apostolicae Sedis*": Ballerini-Palmieri, *Opus theologicum morale* (Prati: 1889), VII, 322; Hollweck, *Die kirchliche Strafgezetze* (Mainz, 1899), n. 142; Bucceroni, *Commentarii* (Romae, 1899), n. 81; Pennacchi, *In Const. Apostolicae Sedis* (Romae, 1883), II, nn. 67-71); Piat, *Commentarius* (Paris, 1881), pp. 240, 241. Post-Code authors, besides those already quoted: Salucci, *Il diritto penale* (Subiaco, 1930), II, n. 224; Blat, *Commentarius Textus Iuris Canonici* (5 vols. in 7, 1921-1938, Romae: apud "Angelicum"), lib. V (1924), n. 180; Ayrinhac-Lydon, *Penal Legislation* (New York: Benziger Bros., 1936), n. 269.

from the faithful in their last resting place as it is to avoid the scandal that is bound to arise from the Church's associating herself, by her rites and honors, with those who do not deserve them. Thus he holds that canon 2339 punishes, not the compelling of the grant of burial in blessed ground to one who is unworthy, but the forcing of the performance of ecclesiastical rites, publicly and completely, over one who is refused Christian burial by the law.[19]

Typical of the opinions that hold canon 1204 to be a legal definition is this author's preoccupation solely with the *rites* of Christian burial. Omitting all reference to the mere burial in blessed ground as a cause for the penalty of canon 2339, he concerns himself with only two possibilities: is the penalty incurred in forcing a priest to assist at the grave, or is it incurred only in compelling a priest to grant all the three elements in which Christian burial consists according to the statement of canon 1204? He believes that the forced assistance of a priest at the grave, granted that the compulsion was known publicly, would occasion little if any basis for scandal, but that the granting amid constraint of all the elements enumerated in canon 1204 would almost invariably invite serious scandal.[20] Cerato does not believe that the forced assistance of a priest at the grave constitutes the granting of Christian burial in a legal sense, though it may be considered as such in a liturgical sense.[21] Such an act—the priest's assistance at the grave — may be and is a *part of* Christian burial; it is not the full canonical notion of Christian burial as stated in canon 1204; where the legislator defines the term and implicitly states what it is to mean thenceforth.[22]

19 *Censurae Vigentes* (2. ed., Patavii, 1921), n. 42.

20 *Loc. cit.*

21 "Etenim licet ex sola cadaveris depositione habeatur aliqua ecclesiastica sepultura, i. e., ecclesiastica sensu liturgico seu Christiano, non tamen exinde habeatur sepultura ecclesiastica sensu canonico."—*loc. cit.*

22 "Legislator canone 1204 implicite declarat quae sepultura exinde sit ecclesiastica, unde implicite interpretatur ex hac parte canonem 2339."—*Censurae vigentes*, n. 42.

According to this opinion, then, whenever and wherever it is possible to have the three elements of Christian burial as defined in canon 1204, they must be present to constitute that act in a legal sense.[23]

With regard to canon 2339's repeating the old law, and therefore being governed by the old law interpretation, Cerato distinguishes. This canon is partly new law and partly old; it is old law in regard to the penalty specified therein, but it is new law in regard to the crime punished: the illegal Christian burial. This newness is due to the new definition of canon 1204 which defines Christian burial as it is to be understood in the law. Therefore, canon 2339 is not to be interpreted according to canon 6, n. 2, as the opposing school would hold, but according to number three of the same canon.[24]

From this evidence it is clear that this author and those who follow him hold that the definition of Christian burial in canon 1204 is new law and therefore is not to be understood in the sense in which it was accepted by pre-Code authors or their followers among the commentators after the Code. Christian burial consists therefore, according to canon 1204, in the transfer of the body to the church, in the funeral services held therein, and in the depositing of the body in a place legitimately set aside for the burial of the faithful departed. It does not consist, as some would hold, in the mere burial of the body in blessed ground. This is the opinion of the second school. Cerato is supported by a large number of authors, of whom a few will be mentioned, such as, Cappello,[25]

[23] *Loc. cit.*

[24] " . . . in quo quidem vetus ius habetur quod attinet ad poenam, sed novum quod attinet ad delictum, cuius notio praefinitur. Unde c. 2339 non ad normam c. 6, n. 2 diiudicandus est sed potius ad normam c. 6, n. 3."—*Loc. cit.* Cappello: "Igitur c. 2339 interpretandus est ad norman c. 6, n. 3, *quia novum ius habetur quod attinet ad notionem sepulturae ecclesiasticae*, ac proinde ad delictum cuius conceptus praefinitur."—*De Censuris*, n. 101.

[25] This author declares that the legal definition given by the Code cannot be contracted to one or the other of its elements, and that all

Chelodi,[26] Beste,[27] Woywod,[28] DeMeester,[29] Coronata,[30] Cocchi,[31] Cavigioli,[32] Eichmann [33] and Pistocchi,[34]

An excellent summary of the opinion of this school is furnished in these words:

> "The question arises, are all three acts equally essential to the burial service, so that if one were omitted the penalty would not be incurred? It is an ancient controversy which act precisely was forbidden or intended by the penal law. The more common opinion accepted the burial place as intended by the Legislator, not the liturgical prayers and ceremonies. However, notwithstanding the fact that this was the common

three factors together constitute the object defined.—*De Censuris*, n. 401.

26 *Ius Poenale* (4 ed., Tridenti: Ardesi, 1935), n. 73.

27 *Introductio in Codicem* (Collegeville, Minn., St. John's Abbey Press, 1938), p. 603.

28 "It may therefore be said, with Chelodi, that ordinarily the three elements are necessary to constitute Christian burial . . . ,"—*Practical Commentary* (3. ed., 2 vols., New York: J. F. Wagner, 1929), II, 489, 490.

29 "Nomine sepulturae intelligitur non tantum inhumatio sed tota etiam pompa funeralis . . . levatio corporis eiusque delatio in ecclesiam, omnes preces et ritus qui in ecclesia, in deductione ad coemeterium et ad sepulcrum a ministris sacris peraguntur."—*Iuris Canonici Compendium* (3 toms. in 4 vols., Brugis, Desclée de Brouwer et Cie., 1921-1928), Tom. III, pars I, n. 1228.

30 In regard to canon 1240: "Hic nomine sepulturae ecclesiasticae veniunt omnes ritus sacri publice peragendi . . . necnon ipsius defuncti in loco sacro depositio."—*Institutiones Iuris Canonici* (5 vols., Taurini: Marietti, 1928-1936), II (1931), n. 813; "Mihi videntur hic (c. 2339) nomine sepulturae ecclesiasticae venire omnes tres actus canone 1204 recensiti."—*Institutiones Iuris Canonici*, IV (1935), n. 1966.

31 " . . . sensu codicis sepultura ecclesiastica tria importat"—*Commentarium in Codicem Iuris Canonici* (8 vols., Taurinorum Augustae: Marietti, 1931-1940), V (1932), n. 47. This author refers, in his outline of Title XII, to canon 1204 as furnishing a *canonical definition*—*op. cit.*, p. 89.

32 *De Censuris* (Taurini, 1918), p. 140.

33 *Das Strafrecht* (Paderborn, 1920), n. 46.

34 *I canoni penali del codice ecclesiastico* (Torino, 1925), p. 120.

opinion before the promulgation of the Code, it must now, we think, be abandoned. For canon 1204 is decidedly against such an interpretation and we *cannot depart from the significance of a term so clearly defined by the Legislator himself and then used without any further explanation.*" [35]

Lest the insistance that all three elements of canon 1204 be present in order to have Christian burial in a canonical sense appear too arbitrary, it should be noted that the authors allow for the interpretation of this definition in the light of circumstances. Thus Cappello says that all three elements should be present unless the first, the transfer of the body to the church, or the third, the burial in a legitimately designated place, be impossible of realization because of external circumstances, such as, for example, the prohibitions of civil law, epidemics of disease, death at sea, etc.[36] And Coronata declares that the second element listed in canon 1204—the services in the church—is quite sufficient of itself to constitute Christian burial, especially when the civil law forbids the procession to the church or to the cemetery, *for it is the essential part of Christian burial.*[37]

It is noteworthy that the Ritual itself makes allowances for the omission of various parts of even the church service, and

[35] Augustine, *A Commentary on Canon Law*, VIII, 359. Italics are inserted by the present writer.

[36] *De Censuris*, n. 401. Cf. also Chelodi, *Ius poenale*, n. 73. Woywod is of the same opinion and adds that custom in the United States has allowed the omission of the first element connected with Christian burial—the transfer of the body to the church—and has substituted for it the reception of the body at the church door.—*Practical Commentary*, II, 489-490.

[37] "Donare autem sepulturam ecclesiasticam possunt soli clerici quia hi soli ministri funerum seu rituum sacrorum, quibus essentialiter sepultura ecclesiastica constituitur, esse possunt."—*Institutiones Iuris Canonici*, IV, n. 1967; "Immo haberi videtur sepultura ecclesiastica sufficiens ad delictum de quo agimus (c. 2339) etiam in solis exsequiis factis in ecclesia . . . quia in his exsequiis constare videtur ritus sacer essentialis sepulturae ecclesiasticae."—*Op. cit.*, IV, n. 1966; Augustine. *A Commentary on Canon Law*, VIII, 360.

insists only on the absolution prayers; but it emphatically insists on these in two places.[38] It would appear, therefore, that the absolution prayers are the essential element, the *sine-qua-non,* of Christial burial.[39]

Lest it now be objected that the authors of the second school, by allowing these exceptions to their requirement of all three elements of canon 1204 for canonical Christian burial, ultimately arrive at the opinion of the first school, namely, that Christian burial implies, after all, nothing more than the burial of the body in blessed ground, it should be emphasized that the authors of the second school consider the third element of canon 1204 not in this exclusive and unrelated fashion, but rather as forming an integral part of the entire act and more comprehensive function at which the Church assists by means of all the liturgical prayers offered by her ministers.[40] There is, in fact, a wide divergence between the two schools on this point, and consequently it will not be out of place to digress here to consider this divergence.

Under the old law, burial in consecrated ground was the essence of Christian burial, as has been seen in the opinions of the authors of the first school. In the new law, the very lack of insistence on this point is so evident that it must not be allowed to go unnoticed. Not only does the *"locus sacer"* seem to have lost its primary importance in the notion of Christian burial as defined in the new law, but it is not even expressly mentioned in canon 1204, or, for that matter, throughout the

38 *Rit. Rom.*, tit. VI, c. III, nn. 14, 17.

39 Brys: "De Obligatione Ritus Sepulturae Sacrae," *Collationes Brugenses*, XXVI (1926), 320.

40 "Ut habeatur sepultura ecclesiastica ex sola depositione *cum ritu Catholico* requiritur ut locus sit legitime deputatus . . . " Coronata, *Institutiones Iuris canonici,* IV, n. 1966; Brys: "Nomine *exsequiarum* complectuntur tria: corporis elatio e domo et deductio ad ecclesiam; perfunctio sacri ritus in ecclesia, nempe, officium defunctorum, missa exsequialis et preces absolutionis; ipsa *sepultura* seu *deductio* cadaveris ab ecclesia ad locum sepulturae." *Collationes Brugenses*, XXVI (1926), 319. This definition of the *funeral* includes everything that is mentioned in canon 1204, which defines *Christian burial.*

whole Title XII of the Code, *"De sepultura ecclesiastica"* (canons 1203-1242), except for one place: in canon 1242, in reference to exhumation. Nor can it be maintained that consecrated or blessed ground is implied in the words of canon 1204, *"in loco legitime deputato,"* for there is considerable controversy over whether the place has to be consecrated.[41] Some authors hold that these words simply imply a place set aside for the burial of the faithful by the blessing of the bishop or his delegate.[42] Other authors believe that while such a designation is implied in the blessing by the bishop or his delegate, in reality the designation results fundamentally from an act of ecclesiastical jurisdiction, a juridical act of ecclesiastical authority.[43]

[41] This dispute dates from before the Code. Thus, D'Annibale stated that Christian burial consisted of burial in "loco sacro vel alio ad id destinato . . ."—*Summula*, I, n. 112; Many held "non sufficit ut deputatur (locus) auctoritate episcopi sed requiritur insuper ut sit rite benedictus, nec sufficit benedictio invocativa sed requiritur illa benedictio constitutiva"—*De Locis Sacris*, n. 223; for more on this dispute before the Code, consult the opinions given in Hollweck, *Die kirchliche Strafgezetze*, 142.

[42] Sole, *De Delictis et Poenis*, 367; Pighi, *Censurae Sententiae Latae*, n. 81; Cippolini, *De Censuris Latae Sententiae*, n. 84, Wernz-Vidal, *Ius Canonicum*, Tom. IV, vol. 1, n. 577.

[43] Cappello, *De Censuris*, n. 401; Cavigioli, *De censuris Latae sententiae*, n. 150; Cerato, *Censurae Vigentes*, n. 42; Eichmann, *Das Strafrecht*, p. 158; Salucci, *Il diritto penale*, n. 228; Cappello, Cerato and Cavigioli, in the texts already quoted, agree that it is not even necessary that the bishop actually decree the designation; it is sufficiently implied if a particular place, unblessed as a whole, has been used for the burial of the faithful over a long period of years, *"ex diurna consuetudine," "usu et consuetudine,"* for in such a case there is at least a tacit approval of the superior; Petroncelli writes: The essential note of this designation (deputatio) is the act of ecclesiastical jurisdiction; such an act is implied in the blessing by the bishop or his delegate, but fundamentally it is independent of the ritual and is a juridical act which may either exist alone or be understood as implied in the liturgical act. Thus one may have an ecclesiastical cemetery without its being blessed. An example of this is found in canon 1212 which sets aside an unblessed part of a Catholic cemetery for the burial of those who

Moreover, not only is a consecrated cemetery not essential to Christian burial, but the simple blessing of the grave by the priest celebrating the funeral is quite sufficient to constitute the designation required by the phrase *"loco legitime deputato"* contained in canon 1204.[44] According to this opinion, the possible existence of a Christian burial is in no way excluded or even impeded by the fact that the body is not interred in consecrated ground, but it may legally be had also when the body is interred in unconsecrated ground, provided that the place is legitimately designated by the ecclesiastical authority or is blessed by the ceremony given in the Ritual for the blessing of graves.

Such interpretations in no way detract from or abrogate the law that Catholics are to be buried in cemeteries that are blessed, but they do emphasize the fact that Christian burial, as a legal entity, does not depend upon the body's interment in consecrated ground. Therefore, those who by force of external circumstances, that is, in view of conditions which are beyond their control or that of the Church, must be buried in unconsecrated ground are not deprived of Christian burial by that fact. The alternative is entirely repugnant, for in that assumption there would be no Christian burial except in places where there were consecrated cemeteries. This would eliminate the population of whole nations from the benefit of this favor of the Church, nations in which it is impossible to have consecrated cemeteries because of the civil law prohibition,[45] and where cemeteries are public, open not only to Catholics, but also to people of any creed or of no creed.

may not be buried in blessed ground. The requirements for such an act of designation are simply the competency of the Ordinary and a just cause.—*La "deputatio ad cultum publicum,"* (Milano, 1937), reviewed in the *Apollinaris*, XI (1938), 593, by P. Felici.

[44] Cerato, *loc. cit.;* Cappello, *loc. cit.;* Coronata, *Inst. Iuris Can.*, IV, n. 1966.; Wernz-Vidal hold that such a blessing is of itself constitutive, i. e., is a consecration, and therefore renders the individual grave consecrated ground—*Ius Canonicum*, IV, 563.

[45] In France cemeteries may not be solemnly blessed.—*L'Ami du clergé*, XXXVII (1920), 192.

As will be seen later in regard to the legislation on funerals, the influence of these common cemeteries may be held accountable for a change in the old law in regard to the rigor of the requirement of the *"locus sacer"* for Christian burial. The place should be consecrated, if that can be done, but it does not have to be in order to have Christian burial in it.

It is precisely on this point that the authors who hold that the notion of Christian burial has not changed with the Code encounter their difficulty. They have to reconcile the definition of canon 1204, which does not mention consecrated ground and requires two other elements besides burial, with their pre-Code concept of Christian burial as essentially consisting in the interment of the body in consecrated ground.[46] They uniformly accept the wording of canon 1204 in its comprehensive meaning, except in the question of penalties, as in canon 2339, where they distinguish between what they consider the broad conception as given in canon 1204 and the narrower one of the old law, namely, that of interment in consecrated ground; they hold that the latter expresses the essential notion of Christian burial, and that there has been no change in the traditional definition of Christian burial.[47]

[46] Ayrinhac's words well reflect this difficulty which confronts those who hold the pre-Code view when he states: "Frequently by Christian burial is meant simply interment in consecrated ground even without any special religious rites. This is the sense in which it has been commonly taken . . . but canon 1204 requires three elements." *Penal legislation* (1920), n. 269. Lydon, in his edition of this work, omits the last part of this quotation and simply states that some require the three elements of canon 1204 for Christian burial, while others hold that the interment of the body in consecrated ground is in itself sufficient.—*Penal Legislation* (1936), n. 269.

[47] Vermeersch-Creusen: "funebria ipsi humationi accessoria sunt."—*Epitome* II, n. 550; "Negamus notionem sepulturae ecclesiasticae c. 1204 esse novam . . . "—*Epitome* III, n. 538; Ciprotti: " . . . ex can. 1204 (qui in can. 2339 revocatur) in quo sepultura ecclesiastica est inhumatio . . . "—"De Consummatione delicti,"—*Apollinaris* VIII (1935), p. 409, not. (3); Wernz-Vidal: " . . . nisi forte credatur codicem mutasse notionem sepulturae ecclesiasticae, quod verum non est."—*Ius Canonicum*, VII, n. 451, not. (22).

However, the majority of the post-Code authors, as has been noted, believe that canon 1204 is new law and introduces a legal definition of Christian burial which cannot be evaded, but must be understood wherever the term appears.

Since the two opinions in this controversy have been delineated, an effort will now be made to explain how the difference between the two schools of thought arose. Enough has been stated to show that both schools agree on the fact that Christian burial consists in two major elements, the religious rites and the interment in a place legitimately designated as a final resting place for the faithful departed. They disagree, however, as to which of these elements constitutes the essential one. The first school, Wernz-Vidal *et alii,* adhering to the old law notion, holds that the interment in consecrated ground is the essential element, while the second, Cerato *et alli,* holds that the essential element is the religious rites, the participation by the Church, through the liturgical functions and prayers of her ministers, in the last honors bestowed upon the departed. The former assert that canon 1204 does not change the old law conception since it prescribes the two major elements present in Christian burial from time immemorial; but when they treat the question of penalties, as in canon 2339, and when they must determine what *essentially* constitutes Christian burial, they cling to the pre-Code concept that it is mere burial in consecrated ground and that the other elements of canon 1204 are but accessories. The latter, aware that now, as always, Christian burial consists of the traditional two elements, insist that both should be present, as outlined in canon 1204, as far as possible; that is, there is no fully canonical Christian burial where one of the three parts of canon 1204 is omitted when it could be had. It is their opinion that Christian burial cannot mean one thing in one canon and another in others, when there is a juridical definition of the term and the term is thereafter used without any qualification. They admit that it may not always be possible to invoke all the elements of canon 1204 in a particular instance; for example, through force of circumstances beyond the control of the Church. In such a case, they hold, the essential element is the religious ceremonies, the rites, which of themselves constitute Christian burial. In reality the controversy narrows down to the question of whether the Code has changed the notion of Christian burial. Those who hold to the pre-Code conception of Christian burial claim that it has not; those who hold that the Code furnishes a juridical definition of its own insist that it has.

If the Code has introduced changes into the legislation of the old law on Christian burial, the interpretation of the new law will depend upon the meaning of the canons themselves, and not upon the doctrine of the pre-Code approved authors except insofar as the present legislation repeats the former law. But the Code does introduce changes into the legislation of the old law on Christian burial. Therefore the interpretation of the new will depend upon the significance of the canons themselves, except insofar as they restate the old law.[48]

The most obvious changes in the new law may be found in canon 1240 itself. Not only has the former specific mention of privation of Christian burial incurred by one's failure to make the "Easter Duty" been omitted, but several additions obtain: the addition of *"aliqua"* to the clause about the signs of repentance; the addition of *"post sententiam declaratoriam vel condemnatoriam"* to the provision relating to excommunication and interdict; the addition that in case of persisting doubt Christian burial is to be granted, provided that possible scandal is obviated.[49]

The next change to be noted is that the Code, unlike the old law, legislates separately for funerals and for burials, distinguishing clearly between the two, the *funus* and the *sepultura* or *inhumatio*, both when it considers the two subjects together in the same canon,[50] and also when it considers them

[48] Canon 6, n. 3.

[49] Cfr. *Rit. Rom.*, tit. VI, c. II, in the pre-Code and post-Code editions.

[50] Cc. 1218, § 2, § 3; 1224; 1226; 1227; 1232; 1233.

separately, as related to funerals in themselves [51] and to burial in itself.[52] Moreover, the use of the particle *aut,* as it appears in several of the canons which deal with both subjects, adds to the distinction between them.[53]

But not only does the Code treat these two elements of Christian burial separately. It treats funerals in such a prominent way that it clearly establishes the primary importance of this element in Christian burial. One illustration of this preeminence is to be found in chapter two of Title XII in the Third Book of the Code. This chapter is entitled: *"De cadaveris translatione ad ecclesiam, funere ac depositione."* It should not go unremarked that this title coincides almost exactly with the definition of Christian burial as given in canon 1204. Further, this chapter, the longest of the three of Title XII, not only treats of the three elements of Christian burial as defined in that canon, but it especially and principally is concerned with the funeral, the *funus,* the religious rites, and with other things only insofar as they are related to that and depend upon it.[54] It should not pass unnoticed that this chapter considers the third element of canon 1204, the burial itself, only at the very end and in a very brief manner.[55]

51 Cc. 1216; 1219; 1220; 1221.

52 Cc. 1208; 1209; 1228; 1229; 1231, § 2.

53 Cc. 1218, § 2; 1224; 1226; 1227; "vel" in c. 1232, § 1; "Codex enim plane distinguit ac distinctim recenset *funus* et *sepulturam,* quae pro loco sepulturae accipitur . . . ipse Codex, respiciens *funus* et *sepulturam* . . . eamdem iugiter retinet distinctionem, nec proferens verbum *sepultura,* extendit vim ipsius verbi ad complectendum etiam *funus.*"—Maroto, "De axiomata 'ubi tumulus ibi funus',"—*Apollinaris,* I (1928), 131.

54 " . . . deque funere, de ecclesia funerante ac de eius electione, de ministro funeris ceterisque ad funus spectantibus caput istum praecipue ac pro longiore parte agit; cetera autem ad ipsum funus ecclesiamque funerantem veluti refert tamquam quid a funere dependens." Maroto, *op. cit.,* pp. 278, 279.

55 Principally in canon 1231, indirectly in canons 1230, 1232, 1233; yet the chapter contains twenty-three canons. Maroto believes that

It may be objected in this connection that the legislator attends to the element which relates to the interment in chapter I of Title XII; and that since it is treated there ahead of chapter II which contains the legislation for the religious rites, its relatively greater importance is thus clearly established. This is not true, however, for the act or rite of burial and the place of burial are two distinct things, and it is the latter that is treated in chapter I, while the former, which is the third element in the definition of canon 1204, is treated only at the end of chapter two.[56]

Further change in the new law is to be found in chapter II in regard to the place of the funeral and the place of the interment. In the old law the place of the interment was the first thing to be considered in regard to Christian burial. Its choice determined the church of the funeral, the clergy, and the recipient of the offering; *"ubi tumulus, ibi funus"* was the principle that was followed.[57]

It is true that some post-Code authors have tried to support this principle in the new law,[58] and others have, though hesitatingly, retained it; [59] but still others, following a rising opinion, have not only denied this principle any juridical value

even canon 1231, which is the first to mention the element of burial, *ex professo*, emphasizes the primary importance of the religious rites over the burial, first by its very position—following the canons which define the funeral rites—and secondly from its very tenor, for it provides that only after the funeral has been carried out is the place of burial to be considered.—*op. cit.*, p. 274.

56 Cf. Cocchi, *Commentarium in Codicem Iuris Canonici*, V, n. 47.

57 Many states that this principle was supported by the constant jurisprudence of the Sacred Congregation of the Council and the Sacred Congregation of Rites.—*De Locis Sacris*, n. 190.

58 E.g., Coronata, in his early work, *De Locis et Temporibus sacris* (Augustae Taurinorum: Marietti, 1922), nn. 186, 202, 220; Vermeersch-Creusen, in an early edition of the *Epitome*, II (ed. alt., 1925), nn. 532, 538; DeMeester, *Compendium iuris canonici*, III (1926), nn. 1196, 1200; Cocchi, *Commentarium*, V (1932), n. 63.

59 Rossi, *La "sepultura ecclesiastica" e l' "ius funerum"* (Bergamo: Arnaldi, 1920), n. 60; Regatillo, in *Sal Terrae*, XIV (1925), 784-786; Vito, "La chiesa funerante" in *Palestra del Clero*, VI (1927), 485 ff.

in the new law, but have asserted that the reverse of the principle may now at times be followed, that is, the place of the funeral may dictate the place of the burial.[60] It should be understood, however, that this rule applies only when the place of the burial has not been chosen independently of the place of the funeral, as may be done in the new law, which provides for the complete separation and independence of those two acts.[61]

The legislation in regard to the place of the funeral is entirely new, for in the old law the funeral belonged to the church of the place of the burial, whereas now it belongs to the parish church of the deceased, unless he has chosen some other, regardless of the place of burial.[62] This is so complete a change from the old law that Maroto insists that it cannot be too emphatically repeated that today nowhere in the Code does the choice of the place of the burial determine absolutely the place of the funeral.[63] It is true that this choice is sub-

60 Vermeersch-Creusen, in reversing their earlier opinion, write: "Codicem illud principium deseruisse admittimus."—*Epitome*, II (3. ed., 1927), n. 527. These authors give the credit for the rise of this opinion to the work of H. Tondini, *De ecclesia funerante* (Forolini, Valbonesi, 1927), but Maroto states that this newer opinion had been taught in Rome from the date of the appearance of the Code.—*Apollinaris*, I (1928), p. 24, not. (63). That it was also taught early at Louvain is attested by E. Voosens, in *Ephemerides Theologicae Lovanienses*, III (1926), 405, and by J. Creusen in the *Nouvelle Revue Théologique*, LIV (1927), 783. Cf. also Claeys-Bouuaert-Simenon, *Manuale Iuris Canonici*, II (2. ed., Gandae et Leodii, 1924), nn. 43, 45; an unnamed author in *Ilustracion del Clero*, XVII (1928), n. 519, pp. 276-280; Maroto: "Nos tenemus novi canones quoad vetus axioma a iure veteri plane discrepare."—*loc. cit.*, p. 265.

61 Cf. canons 1216, 1226.

62 Nunc ut olim funus ecclesiis . . . sed adest diversitas in eo quod olim funus agnoscebatur ecclesiis mediante tumulo . . . ; nunc vero funus sic agnoscitur ecclesiis ut censeatur eis competere per se directe et immediate."—Maroto, *loc. cit.*, pp. 267, 268.

63 "Iuvat centies repetere ut nullibi in Codice hodie e iure coemeterii vel tumuli in aliquo loco fieri posse determinationem ecclesiae funerantis."—*loc. cit.*, p. 273.

ject to some moderation by the law,[64] but the important change to be noted here is that the law does directly provide, and provides independently of the consideration of the choice of the place of burial. It matters not at all whether the church chosen has a cemetery or not.[65]

The new legal right of the parish church to the funeral was confirmed by a reply to the Sacred Congregation of the Council to two questions proposed to it: Does the pastor have the exclusive right of the Christian burial of his parishioners who may have a grave in a common municipal cemetery? Does the same right belong to the same pastor if his parishioner chooses burial elsewhere? The reply to both questions was in the affirmative.[66]

Another change in the new law that is especially remarkable is in the use of the term *sepultura*. In the law of the Decretals that term was used to refer in general to all that pertained to the care and the cult of the dead,[67] and while the term was used mainly in the sense of the place of burial or of the right to burial in blessed ground,[68] it was also used with reference to the homage to be paid to the bodies of the faithful departed. This homage comprised both the act of the burial in consecrated ground and the funeral rites surrounding that act.[69]

In the Code, however, the word *sepultura*, when it is used

[64] That is, one may choose any church desired where a funeral may be held, according to canon 1226, and entirely irrespective of where the burial is to take place, or, in the failure of this, the law will determine the church, according to canons 1217-1225.

[65] Canon 1216 simply states that the church is to be the parish church, unless another is selected by the deceased.

[65] S. C. C., *Resolutio, Apuana*, 12 nov. 1927, AAS, XX (1928), 142.

[67] In X, lib. III, tit. XXVIII; in VI°, lib. III, tit. XII; in Clem., lib. III, tit. VII, in all of which the entire subject is treated under the title of *de sepulturis*.

[68] Santi-Leitner, lib. III, tit. 28, n. 1; Reiffenstuel, lib. III, tit. 28, n. 3; Schmalzgrueber, lib. III, tit. 28, n. 1.

[69] Reiffenstuel, *loc. cit.*, Wernz, *Ius Decretalium*, III, n. 773; c. 2 *de sepulturis*, III, 7 in Clem.; Many, *De Locis Sacris*, n. 100.

without the adjective *ecclesiastica,* usually designates only the place of burial.[70] Further evidence of this restricted use is contained in the constant use of *sepelire* as a synonym for *tumulare* or *inhumare* and vice versa.[71]

On the contrary, the term *sepultura ecclesiastica* is found used only in those canons in which the full meaning of Christian burial as defined in canon 1204 may be understood. Correspondingly, this term includes in its connotation both the burial rites and the actual burial itself.[72] "May be understood" is used advisedly, for, while Cappello [73] and Coronata [74] agree with Maroto that this term, wherever it is used, always involves the sense in which it is defined in 1204; others, like the

[70] Cf. cc. 1218, §§ 2, 3; 1223, 1224, 1226, etc.; also cc. 1172, § 1, n. 4; 1175; 1209, § 3; 1228; 1230, § 7; 1233, § 1; 1235, § 1; 1242; Maroto: "Igitur ius sepulturae simpliciter prolatum, prout ipsum verbum sepultura, referendum est ex se tantum ad locum sepulturae vel ad inhumationem cadaveris in aliquo loco;"—"De axiomata 'ubi tumulus ibi funus'," *Apollinaris* I (1928), 130; "Codex enim plane distinguit ac distinctim recenset *funus* et *sepulturam,* quae pro loco sepulturae accipitur . . . nec proferens verbum *sepulturae* extendit vim ipsius verbi ad complectendum etiam *funus,*"—*op. cit.,* p. 131; " . . . atque adeo de tumulatione aut de iure ad habendam tumulationem, haec designantur per verbum *sepulturam* . . . ," *op. cit.,* p. 132; Cf. also Coronata, *De Locis et Temporibus Sacris,* n. 186; Vermeersch-Creusen, *Epitome* II (5. ed., 1934), n. 512. The Code limits the use of *sepultura* to signify merely the place of the burial or the burial itself.—*Nouvelle Revue Théologique,* LIV (1927), 783.

[71] Cf. cc. 1173, § 1; 1202, § 2; 1203, § 1; 1205; 1213; 1215; 1229; 1231, § 1; 1232, § 2; 1235, § 2; 1237 §§ 1, 2; 1238; 2272, § 2.

[72] Cf. cc. 1212; 1214; 1239; 1240; 1241; 2260, § 2; 2275, § 4; 2277; 2339; " . . . adhibetur namque in inscriptione totius tituli, in c. 1204 et in aliis canonibus ubi praeter locum sepulturae seu inhumationis recte subaudiri queunt etiam officia funebria praemissa."—Maroto, *op. cit.,* p. 127; Vermeersch-Creusen; "verba *sepultura ecclesiastica* fere semper totum sepulturae processum significat (cf. can. 1204, 1239, 1240 etc.)"—*Epitome* II (5. ed., 1934), n. 512; Creusen lists canons 1239, 1240, 1241, 2339,—*Nouvelle Revue Théologique,* LIV (1927), 783.

[73] *Summa Iuris* (3 vols., Romae: Universitas Gregorianae, 1936-1939), II (3. ed., 1939), nn. 717, 762.

[74] *Institutiones Iuris Canonici,* II, nn. 794, 796, 813.

authors of the school that still holds to the old notion of Christian burial, do not agree that it has this meaning in all instances.[75]

The omission of the term *"locus sacer"* in so much of the legislation on Christian burial, which was considered above,[76] represents still another change in the new law, for it was a most commonly used term in the old. Again, in the old law the church with a family sepulchre therein had the right to conduct the funeral as well as the burial of the one to be buried there, even to the point of ruling out the deceased's choice of burial elsewhere.[77] But in the new law this is changed and that right has been abrogated; it is now provided that one is to be buried in such a family tomb if he has not chosen burial elsewhere. Moreover, there is no longer any mention of the right of that church to conduct the funeral.[78]

As has been stated, above, much of the change in the new law may be traced to the need of new legislation, a need that was caused in great part by the growth of the use of common or public cemeteries. According to Maroto, the Legislator has completely renovated the law on Christian burial in order to accomodate it to the new conditions of modern times.[79]

The very noticeable trend toward clemency that is apparent in the new law is likewise attributable in some measure to the increase of public cemeteries, a development that has given rise in some countries to a new evil, that of civil or lay

75 Thus some will accept Christian burial in one sense in certain canons, and in another in others. Cf. Blat, *Commentarium Textus Codicis Iuris Canonici*, lib. III, tit. 12, nn. 72, 74, 105; Vermeersch-Creusen, *Epitome*, II, nn. 522-524; Wernz-Vidal, *Ius Canonicum*, IV, nn. 570, 586; Ayrinhac, *Administrative Legislation*, nn. 58, 80.

76 Pp. 99-100.

77 Many, *De Locis Sacris*, nn. 226 ff.

78 C. 1229; Maroto: " . . . sed hodie ipsa legislatio ecclesiastica mutata est et non amplius ecclesiis agnoscit ius sepeliendi."—*Apollinaris*, I (1928), 135, not. (34).

79 *Op. cit.*, 278.

funerals devoid of any ecclesiastical association. The law on the denial of Christian burial has undoubtedly been mitigated with a view to discouraging these irreligious funerals, and also to avoid another modern evil: the demonstrations of hostility toward the Church and her ministers that have been known to take place on the occasion of the denial in places where the religious divisions of the modern times are sharply drawn and where anti-clericalism has developed.[80]

The new conditions which have caused the change are, first, the prohibition of all burials in churches by both the ecclesiastical and the civil law, and second, the fact that while formerly cemeteries belonged to a particular church, were usually contiguous to it, and, even when separated from it, were identified with it, now they are largely public and communal.[81]

The result has been a separation between funeral and burial, a separation that has brought about the change of emphasis from the place of burial to the funeral rite, so that while before the Code it was the former that was the primary concern, now the latter is the more important element of Christian burial.[82]

A similar explanation of the change in the law is given by Vermeersch, who notes that with the suppression of ecclesiastical cemeteries in many countries of Europe it is but natural

80 Brys: " . . . magis ad utendum stricta interpretatione impellimur, tum benigna mente Ecclesiae, quam eruere possumus ex multiplicibus mitigationibus iuri antiquo introductis, tum periculo vigente ne multiplicentur sic dictae civiles sepulturae et locum habeant manifestationes Ecclesiae hostiles." — "De Sepultura Ecclesiastica," — *Collationes Brugenses* XXV (1925), 161.

81 Maroto—*Apollinaris*, I (1928), 278, not. (43).

82 "Dein peculiariter nova ex integro ordinatio elucere videtur in capite secundo, ubi omnia decernuntur quae pertinent ad ritum sepulturae, seu obsequiae vel officium defunctis impendendum per omnes illos actus qui efficiunt sepulturam ecclesiasticam sensu formali in c. 1204 definitam. Porro ex iis omnibus actibus *primus qui inspicitur et accuratius ordinatur*, tamquam *primarium sepulturae ecclesiasticae elementum, est funus*,"—Maroto, *op. cit.*, 278.

that there should be much less concern about the place of burial.[83] In the light of the new legislation, he adds, the funeral and the burial are so separate that, without some other determining factor's intervention, the one cannot be determined by the other; rather, burial now is the natural complement of the funeral, and therefore of secondary importance to it.[84]

L'Ami du clergé reflects the preeminence of the ceremonial and religious element of Christian burial in its constant reference to Christian burial as *"sépulture religieuse."* [85]

Brys, likewise, uses *sepultura ecclesiastica* in the sense of religious rites, separate from the notion of the burial itself.[85] And Creusen, admitting that Christian burial may be considered under two aspects, that is, either as the ensemble of the liturgical functions or as the mere burial, maintains that the Code always uses the term *ecclesiastica* when implying the first sense, and limits itself to the word *sepultura* to signify the interment of the body in a cemetery.[87] *Funus* and *exsequiae,* he adds, *"désignent l'office célébré à l'église,"* which, as may be noted, comprises the second of the three elements listed in the definition of canon 1204.[88] That the conception of Christian burial which looks to the sum of the religious rites principally, and to the burial itself secondarily, is a new opinion since the appearance of the Code is fully admitted by Creusen, but, because of the increase of the number of those who are accepting it, he hopes that enough authors will, before long, have turned to it that the opinion of those holding to the pre-Code conception will no longer have even probability.[89]

83 " 'Ubi tumulus ibi funus': axioma?"—*Periodica,* XVI (1927), 65.

84 *Loc. cit.*

85 Cf. Vol. XL (1923), 308.

86 " . . . omnes et singuli fideles quatenus praedeterminare prohibentur ne sine sepultura ecclesiastica inhumentur."—*Collationes Brugenses,* XXVI (1926), 318.

87 *Nouvelle Revue Théologique,* LIV (1927), 783.

88 *Loc. cit.*

89 *Loc. cit.*

It has been demonstrated that the old law on Christian burial has been completely innovated in the Code with many and important changes. Since the new law does not repeat the old in its entirety, it need not depend upon the accepted interpretations of the old law for its meaning. But only insofar as it repeats the old will it be governed by those interpretations; and insofar as it reflects new law will it be interpreted in the light of the meaning of the canons themselves.[90]

To be classified as new law is the definition of Christian burial, the legal definition of canon 1204, of which there is no counterpart in the old law. Thus Christian burial is more than the mere fact of the body's interment in blessed ground; it is principally that assistance which the Church lends to the last honors paid the bodies of her faithful departed, through her participation in these honors by the prayers and rites performed by her authorized ministers. Amongst these various honors the interment in blessed ground constitutes but a single factor.

It is believed that in this interpretation a return is made to the most ancient view of what constituted Christian burial. For the earliest sources, in describing the funerals of the faithful, stress the ceremonial element of the action, asserting that Christians used to escort the bodies of the dead to the grave, singing psalms, reading the Scriptures and offering the Sacrifice.[91]

The original preëminence of the liturgical element seems

[90] Canon 6, 3°; Maroto: "Nec opponant adversarii in novo Codice generatim retineri veteram disciplinam de sepultura ecclesiastica et de re funeraria, et ideo novos canones ex veteris iuris auctoritate aestimandos esse. At id recte diceretur si constaret in novis canonibus ius vetus ex integro referri; constat autem e converso plurimas graviores que hac in re immutationes esse allatas; inde, prout habetur in c. 6, n. 3, canones qui ex parte tañtum cum veteri iure congruunt, qua congruunt, ex iure antiquo aestimandi sunt; qua discrepant, sunt ex sua ipsorum sententia diiudicandi."—*Apollinaris*, I (1928), 265.

[91] *Didascalia*, lib. VI, c. 22, n. 2—Funk, *Didascalia et Constitutiones Apostolorum*, I, 381.

further evident in the fact that the earliest Christians were buried not in cemeteries but in tombs along the Roman roads, as was the custom of the times, or in the gardens of the richer members of the congregation.[92] In fact the blessing of cemeteries cannot be traced beyond the sixth century, although that usage seems to have become established by that time.[93]

The antiquity of the use of rites and ceremonies is further witnessed by the Roman Ritual, which states that their use is founded on the most ancient tradition.[94]

Another indication of the liturgical nature of the act of Christian burial in the earliest days is found in the very early evidence of the denial of Christian burial. Coronata states that the refusal by the Church to receive the *oblationes,* the gift-offerings of the faithful for the benefit of the soul of the deceased, and the refusal of the customary escorting of the body to the grave, as referred to above, with the chanting of the psalms, the reading of the Scriptures and the offering of the Mass, constituted the refusal of Christian burial[95]

No less an authority than St. Augustine had to condemn the preoccupation of the faithful of his time to secure for themselves their burial in blessed ground. He reminded them that it is not so much the burial in blessed ground that benefits the dead as it is the circumstances of this burial, the prayers and religious rites, as well as the prayers of the people who visit such places and pray for the souls of those buried there[96]

Burial in blessed ground does not of itself benefit anyone; it is but a more honorable disposal of the body, a solace and a comfort to the living. It is the prayers and rites of the Church, asking the pardon of God, that benefit the soul. It seems only natural that these latter factors should involve the most im-

92 Fliche-Martin, *Histoire de l'Eglise,* I, 413; cf. p. 2 in the historical part of the present study.

93 Many, *De Locis Sacris,* n. 139.

94 *Tit.* VI, c. I, n. 1.

95 *Institutiones Iuris Canonici,* IV, n. 2018.

96 *De Cura pro Mortuis,* c. 4, n. 6—*MPL,* XL, 590.

portant element of Christian burial, for without them the burial of the body in blessed ground remains nothing more than a token of Christian honor.[97]

Moreover, in defining the penal nature of the refusal of Christian burial, Brys omits any reference to the debarment of burial in blessed ground as the particular evil of the penalty, but confines himself to stating that the privation is of a penal nature because it deprives the deceased of the *prayers* and *suffrages* of the Church and is a disgrace to him and his family.[98]

In the interpretation of the meaning of canon 1204, the writer of the present work will adhere to the opinion of that school of authors which believes that this canon affords a juridical definition of the term "Christian burial," which term, as used throughout the Code, must be understood as including the elements of that definition. In the light of the evidence presented, the notion of Christian burial which considers it primarily as implying a liturgical act rather than the actual interment in blessed ground will be adhered to. Therefor, the term "Christian burial" will be accepted in the sense of canon 1204,[99] as interpreted to mean principally the participation by the Church in the last honors paid the bodies of her faithful departed, a participation de-

[97] Tondini (*De ecclesia funerante ad normam novi Codicis*) justifies the greater importance of the religious rites when he asks if it is not right and proper to consider the prayers and the Mass to be of more profit to the souls of the dead than the burial of their bodies in blessed ground, especially in these days of common cemeteries in which people of various creeds, and even people of no creed, are buried indiscriminately—quoted by Creusen in *Nouvelle Revue Théologique*, LIV (1927), 783.

[98] "Defunctum privat enim precibus et suffragiis Ecclesiae, ipsique et familiae eius opprobrio est. In hac proinde explicanda, vi can. 19, stricta adhibenda est interpretatio."—"De Sepultura Ecclesiastica,"—*Collationes Brugenses*, XXV (1925), 161.

[99] " . . . *sepultura ecclesiastica* 'secundum propriam verborum significationem' ad normam can. 1204 . . . "—Blat, *Commentarium Textus*, lib. III, pars II, n. 103.

termined by the three acts of this canon, all of which imply her presence through the prayers and actions of her ministers.

Although canon 1204 prescribes the form in which this assistance should be rendered, it must not be understood to mean that all three elements associated with that form must of necessity always be present in order to constitute canonical Christian burial. It may well happen that, due to circumstances beyond her control, the Church cannot observe that form in its fulness. In such circumstances her participation to the extent that she can grant it will constitute Christian burial.

It is in such cases that the conception of Christian burial as implying primarily the sum of the liturgical acts, rather than just the actual interment in consecrated ground, is most helpful. Thus, relative to burial at sea, the deceased could be said to have received Christian burial if the priest were to invoke as many of the elements of canon 1204 as he could, possibly the functions preliminary to the actual burial in as far as the liturgical element of these functions is concerned. Also, in the matter of epidemics of disease, when processions and church services may be forbidden, the priest's assistance at the grave and the liturgical prayers would constitute Christian burial. The same would be true of countries whose civil law may prevent the bringing of the body to the church for services. In missions to which the priest can come but irregularly, the burial in ground set aside, either by legal delegation or by blessing, for the burial of the faithful, with the prayers supplied later by the priest, would constitute Christian burial for the people of that region, since it is as much as the Church could extend of her presence. When because of circumstances due to war or the difficulties of great distance, the act of the actual burial itself could not be carried out, then Christian burial may be said to have been accorded by the giving of the absolution and the celebration of a Mass, if possible, before the catafalque representing the remains of the one whose body is absent. In all these instances the

Church is granting as much of her participation as circumstances beyond her control allow.

The rigid demand that all of the three elements associated with the notion of Christian burial be present to constitute the act would deprive unknown numbers of their right. But, by understanding the interpretation of Christian burial as connoting the assistance of the Church through all the three acts delineated in canon 1204, or as many of them as she can confer, in the last respects paid to the bodies of the deceased, one practically obviates all difficulty in determining when Christian burial is had and when it is not had. It is had when the Church grants as much as she can of the function defined in canon 1204; it is not had when she refuses her rites and prayers, even though somehow one obtain burial in ground set aside for the burial of the faithful departed.

Thus the illegitimate burial of the body of an unworthy Christian in ground set aside for the burial of the faithful does not constitute Christian burial. The granting of burial in blessed ground to non-Catholics—a toleration that sometimes may be necessary to avoid greater evils—is not the granting of Christian burial. In both instances, by withholding her participation in these acts through her prayers and rites, the Church is withholding Christian burial. As Cerato well points out, such burial may be called a kind of Christian burial, but it is not a canonical Christian burial.

To hold otherwise is largely to remove from the control of the Church the granting of this right and to confer the power to grant it upon anyone capable of enforcing the interment in consecrated ground.

With this clarification of the meaning of the term "Christian burial," the definition of the denial of Christian burial is clear: it means the privation of all the acts prescribed by canon 1204 as the constitutive elements of that function in which the Church renders her final honors to her deceased faithful children. It therefore signifies the Church's authoritative refusal, in whole or in part, of the functions delineated in canon 1204. Substantially, this privation is in effect when these functions are denied, one or all together. Regarding this definition of the refusal or denial of Christian burial the authors in great number are in practical agreement.[100]

100 Wernz-Vidal: " . . . negat locum benedictum sacrosque ecclesiasticae sepulturae ritus . . . "—*Ius Canonicum,* IV, n. 585; "Nam sepulturae privato deneganda sunt officia funebria seu funus, ergo directe exclusio fit inhumationis in loco sacro; cui autem hoc negatur, negandi sunt etiam ritus sacri."—*op. cit.,* n. 451; " . . . sive in ritu sacro sive in loco sacro cum tali ritu connexo, . . . ,"—*op. cit.,* n. 565; cf. also Coronata, *Institutiones Iuris Canonici,* IV, n. 1966; II, 813; Cippolini: "Privatio sepulturae utrumque importat, loci nimirum et ritus sacri privationem."—*De Censuris,* n. 85; Vito, *Questioni Canoniche* (4 vols. in 1, Napoli, 1926), I, 8; Cerato, *Censurae Vigentes,* n. 42; Chelodi, *Ius Poenale,* n. 73; Beste, *Introductio in Codicem,* p. 603; DeMeester, *Iuris Canonici Compendium,* n. 1228; Sole, *De Delictis et Poenis,* p. 155, not. (4); Teodori, "Consultationes," *Apollinaris,* V (1937), 373; Brys, "De Sepultura Ecclesiastica,"—*Collationes Brugenses,* XXV (1925), 159; Ayrinhac, *Administrative Legislation,* n. 52; Haring, *Grundzuege des katholischen Kirchenrechts* (3. ed., Graz, 1924), p. 568.

Chapter II

THE PRINCIPLES OF THE PRIVATION OF CHRISTIAN BURIAL

INTRODUCTION

In Book III of the Code of Canon Law, Chapter III of Title XIII considers and determines those who are to be granted and those who are to be refused Christian burial. Since the present dissertation is mainly concerned with the privation of Christian burial, it will not consider the cases in which it is to be granted except under the aspect of non-refusal.

The fundamental principle underlying the privation of Christian burial was laid down by Pope St. Leo the Great (440-461), and was repeated by Innocent III (1198-1216) namely, that the Church, through a policy that is sanctioned both by the sacred canons and by custom, will not associate herself in death with those with whom she had no communion in life, or with those who, having been cut off or separated from her communion, have not been reconciled with her before death.[1]

Those who are refused Christian burial may therefore be divided into two groups: the unbaptized, who never had a right to it, and the baptized who have either lost the right to it or have incurred the penalty of its privation.

The principles that determine the refusal or the non-refusal of Christian burial are contained in canons 1239 and 1240. The classes of people who are to be denied it are listed in the same canons. The effects of the denial are treated in canon 1241, while canon 1242 is concerned with exhumation, which

1 "Sacris est canonibus institutum et consuetudine approbatum ut quibus non communicavimus vivis, non communicemus defunctis, et ut careant sepultura ecclesiastica qui prius erant ab ecclesiastica unitate praecisi, nec in articulo mortis Ecclesiae reconciliati fuerint."—c. 12, X, *de sepulturis*, III, 28; c. I, C. 24, q. 2.

is not a direct concern of this dissertation, but the effect of the illegal granting of burial to those to whom the law denies it.

This dissertation will be concerned mainly with canons 1239 and 1240, since it is they that are directly involved in the question of the denial of Christian burial.[2]

For the purposes of this work, the principles as contained in canons 1239, § 3 and 1240 will be treated first; consideration of the classes of people barred from Christian burial will follow in the next chapter.

Article I. The Principle Contained in Canon 1239, § 3

Canon 1239, § 3.—Omnes baptizati sepultura ecclesiastica donandi sunt, nisi eadem a iure expresse priventur.

No baptized person is to be refused Christian burial unless the law expressly denies it to him. Christian burial is therefore a right that belongs only to the baptized.[3]

Baptism is here considered in its canonical, not in its theological sense; that is, as a rite that gives *juridical capacity* to the one baptized.[4]

Therefore only those who are baptized with water are to be understood as included here; not those who are baptized with the baptism of desire or of blood, for while the latter may be quite sufficient to earn one eternal salvation, they do not confer the juridical capacity that is necessary to vindicate to the baptized the rights which the Church reserves for her members.[5]

[2] Coronata, *Institutiones Iuris Canonici*, IV, n. 1821, not. 7; Blat, *Commentarium Textus*, III, pars II, n. 102; Rossi, La "*Sepultura Ecclesiastica*" e l' "*Ius Funerum*," p. 29.

[3] Cappello: "Ius ad sepulturam ecclesiasticam oritur ex baptismo quo quis efficitur persona in Ecclesia Christi atque capax iurium et officiorum."—*Summa Iuris Canonici*, II, n. 759.

[4] Coronata: "Baptismus hic in suis iuridicis, non theologicis, effectibus consideratur, quatenus capacitatem iuridicam confert."—*Institutiones Iuris Canonici*, I, n. 119.

[5] Coronata, *Institutiones Iuris Canonici*, I, n. 119; Wernz, *Ius Decretalium*, I, nn. 81, 82.

Moreover, the mere fact of baptism itself does not give an inalienable right to Christian burial, for the canon adds that this right may be limited by the law. Therefore the law, but only the law, may deprive one of the right. The canon thus protects the baptized from an arbitrary imposition of this privation.[6]

Accordingly, the privation of Christian burial may not be extended to persons not covered by the law, nor applied to those who are deprived by law except under the conditions prescribed by the law itself.[7]

The privation of Christian burial is therefore a sanction the application of which the Legislator has reserved to Himself because of its gravity and because of the abuses that would arise if it were not governed by a uniform rule of public order.[8]

The law lists those who are to be deprived of Christian burial in canons 1239, § 1 (the unbaptized), 1240, § 1 (those who are penalized), and 87 (certain other disqualified persons). But before the classes of people who are denied Christian burial are considerel, it will not be beside the point to inquire whether Christian burial must be had. Is there an obligation to have Christian burial? May not one frustrate the law by declining the honor before it is denied? Or may his heirs do the same and spare themselves the shame of a refusal?

There appears to be no specific canon commanding that Christian burial must be had. Canon 1204 defines it; canon 1215 orders *a funeral;* canon 1203 commands *burial;* canon 1205 orders burial in blessed ground. But all these canons are concerned with other matters; canon 1203 forbids cremation; canon 1205 forbids burial in unblessed ground; canon 1215

6 Blat: "Competit hoc ius cuilibet fideli nisi iure canonico prohibeatur."—*Commentarium Textus,* III, pars II, 75; 102; 103.

7 Wernz, *Ius Decretalium,* III, n. 782.

8 *L'Ami du Clergé,* XL (1923), 309.

orders the funeral not to be omitted. There seems to be no formal precept commanding Christian burial.[9]

It may be objected than canon 1239 § 3 orders it; but that canon simply insists that it be not denied unless the law denies it. The words *"donandi sunt"* may mean that Christian burial is obligatory upon all, but they also may be just a command that it is not to be refused except, as the canon continues, when the law refuses it.

Regardless of this ambiguity, there is good and sufficient reason for the lack of formal command; namely, there is no one upon whom the law could lay the obligation. It cannot be commanded to the dead, and it is impossible to impose upon any particular person, to the exclusion of others, the care and the order of, and the moral responsibility for, the obsequies of another.[10]

However, the obligation clearly exists from custom, the authorized interpreter of the mind of the Church. Custom lays upon the survivors the duty to provide not only for burial, but also for the last prayers and suffrages of the Church for the repose of the soul of the deceased.

There is overwhelming evidence of this obligation in the opinions of both the pre-Code authors and those who write after the Code. Reiffenstuel answered the question of who may, and who must, be given Christian burial with the reply that only the baptized faithful *may and must* be given it. Whereas a comma separated the two verbal forms in the question, there is none between them in the answer.[11]

Wernz, in noting that one is not free to refuse Christian burial, declared that private choice in this matter may not change the public law which absolutely prescribed Christian burial for the faithful, unless they have rendered themselves

9 *L'Ami du Clergé*, XLII (1925), 814-815.

10 *Loc. cit.*

11 "Quaeritur, quinam in loco sacro sepeliri possint, ac debeant? Regula est: omnes et soli fideles baptizati in loco sacro sepeliri possunt et debent."—lib. III, tit. 28, n. 76.

unworthy of it.[12] This same author noted that any provision inserted in one's will that there should be no Christian burial is to be considered as not having been made. Moreover, the relatives or heirs have no right to refuse or impede the Christian burial of one of the faithful, even were he unworthy of it.[13]

That the spirit of the common law was not changed by the Code is amply clear from the opinions of the post-Code authors. Cappello asserts that Christian burial belongs to the public order and to public law, and that therefore no one may renounce it or be denied it by other than the ecclesiastical authorities.[14] Vermeersch-Creusen believe that Christian burial is gravely obligatory, not to an equal extent in all its elements, but as a whole.[15] Others note that Christian burial is prescribed by the Church for the honor and the repose of the dead, the comfort and edification of the living, and as a symbol of ecclesiastical communion and of religious truth. The last two reasons concern the public good. One is not free, therefore, to choose or to decline Christian burial.[16]

Finally, the reply of the Sacred Congregation of the Council to a question about canon 1239, § 3, seems to leave little doubt that Christian burial is obligatory. It stated that the provisions of canon 1239, § 3, are obligatory in the sense that one entitled under the law to religious burial may not exclude it at will, although he may forego the pomps and ceremonies that do not belong to the essence of the rites.[17]

12 *Ius Decretalium*, Tom. III, pars II, n. 780, p. 497, not. 35.

13 Wernz, *loc. cit.*

14 *Summa Iuris Canonici*, II, n. 705.

15 *Epitome*, II, n. 526.

16 Blat, *Commentarium Textus*, III, pars II, n. 102; Augustine, *A Commentary*, VI, 152; Mostaza, "Denegacion de Sepultura Ecclesiastica,"—*Sal Terrae*, XIX (1930), 332 ff., quoted in the *Ius Pontificium*, X (1930), 69, 70.

17 S. C. C., *Resolutio S. Severi*, 12 ian. 1924—*AAS*, XVI (1924), 188.

Article II. The Principles Contained in Canon 1240

Canon 1240, § 1.—Ecclesiastica sepultura privantur, nisi ante mortem aliqua dederint poenitentiae signa: . . .

Canon 1240, § 2.—Occurrente praedictis in casibus aliquo dubio, consulatur, si tempus sinat, Ordinarius; permanente dubio, cadaver sepulturae ecclesiasticae tradatur, ita tamen ut removeatur scandalum.

A. *The Nature of the Penalty*

It is now quite generally agreed that the privation of Christian burial, as it is legislated in canon 1240, § 1, is not merely the consequence of the incurring of other penalties, nor solely a provision of public order for the purpose of deterring Catholics from delinquencies, but is a true penalty in itself.[18]

In this canon therefore the Legislator punishes those who are guilty of crimes or delicts[19] against the faith: apostates and heretics; against the unity of the Church: schismatics; and those who offend against ecclesiastical authority: the members of Masonic and similar societies; those excommunicated

[18] C. 2291. 5°; Bernardini, "Privatio Sepulturae Ecclesiasticae."—*Il Diritto Ecclesiastico*, XL (1929), 473-479; Vermeersch-Creusen, *Epitome*, III, n. 492; Augustine, *A Commentary*, VI, 152; VIII, 357; Ayrinhac, *Administrative Legislation*, n. 77; Brys, "De Sepultura Ecclesiastica,"—*Collationes Brugenses*, XXV (1925), 161, 242; Coronata, *Institutiones Iuris Canonici*, II, n. 816; *De Locis et Temporibus Sacris*, n. 257; Buvée, *Ministère Paroissial* (Paris: Maison de la Bonne Presse, 1921), n. 815; Cappello, *Summa*, II, n. 761; Blat, *Commentarium Textus*, lib. V, n. 120; Wernz-Vidal, *Ius Canonicum*, VII, n. 342; Wernz, *Ius Decretalium*, VI, n. 141; Many, *De Locis Sacris*, n. 225.

[19] The Code uses the word delict in general for crime. Cf. Coronata, *Institutiones Iuris Canonici*, IV, n. 1639; Chelodi: " . . . unica exceptio: Titulus XV, 'De crimine falsi' "—*Ius Poenale*, n. 3. The same author clearly shows that *delict* and *sin* are not to be confused: " . . . aliud est delictum, aliud peccatum. Hoc multo latius patet. Primum est in ordine juridico, alterum in ordine morali," *op. cit.*, n. 2; Wernz-Vidal: "Quae distinctio inter peccatum et delictum semper fuit in Ecclesia observata."—*Ius Canonicum*, VII, 25.

or interdicted; suicides; duelists; those who have ordered their own cremation; and other public and manifested sinners.

To have a canonical delict it is necessary that there be an external and morally imputable violation of a law to which has been attached a canonical sanction.[20] Two conditions are therefore of necessity to be verified before a delict is established: the external objective fact of a violation of the law and the internal subjective element of moral imputability.[21]

Imputability is not quite the same as responsibility, though it sometimes is confused with it.[22] Imputability is rather that element in an act by which it is attributable to its agent as a free and voluntary cause.[23] If either element is absent, there is no delict.[24] However, once the external violation is a fact, moral imputability, the foundation of juridical imputability,[25] is presumed by the law, until the contrary is proved.[26]

Furthermore, the penalty of canon 1240, § 1 is a *latae sententiae* penalty, for it is incurred *ipso facto* by the deliquent and requires no declaratory sentence.[27]

20 Canon 2195.

21 Coronata: "Ad mentem Codicis ad delictum haec duo elementa illud (delictum) veluti in sua essentia constituentia requiruntur; nempe, imputabilitas moralis et factum externum;" *op. cit.*, IV, n. 1640; Wernz-Vidal: "externa actio auctori suo imputabilis," *op. cit.*, VII, n. 24; Chelodi, *op. cit.*, n. 2; Vermeersch-Creusen, *Epitome*, III, n. 383; Ayrinhac-Lydon, *Penal Legislation*, n. 201.

22 *Imputability* is a relation that exists between the act and the agent; *responsibility*, between the agent and his superior.—Roberti, *De Delictis et Poenis* (Editio altera emendata, Romae: Pontificium Institutum Utriusque Iuris, 1930), n. 62; Coronata, *loc. cit.*

23 Cf. Coronata, *op. cit.*, IV, n. 1640; Roberti, *op. cit.*, n. 61; Vermeersch-Creusen, *Epitome*, III, n. 387.

24 Coronata, *loc. cit.*, Cappello, *De Censuris*, n. 24; Chelodi, *Ius Poenale*, n. 2; Wernz, *Ius Decretalium*, VI, n. 13.

25 Chelodi, *op. cit.*, n. 5; Roberti, *De Delictis et Poenis*, n. 61.

26 Canon 2200, § 2.

27 Wernz-Vidal, *Ius Decretalium*, IV, Pars I, 141; Blat, *Commentarium Textus*, lib. V, n. 123; Cappello, *Summa* II, n. 761; Brys, *Collationes Brugenses*, XXV (1925), 163; Mostaza: "Nihil speciale requiritur in casibus manifestis ut non concedatur . . . sufficit administra-

It is not a penalty upon the dead but upon the living, for it is incurred as soon as the delict, as specified in canon 1240, § 1, is complete, whether that be a longer or a shorter time before the death of the delinquent.[28]

Bernardini explains that it is quite as possible to incur a penalty while one is living which is to be executed only after death as it is to possess during life a right that can be obtained after death, v.g., the right to burial in a particular family plot or vault.[29]

Moreover, Christian burial may necessarily be denied to one who is innocent of the delicts of canon 1240, § 1. This will be seen when the subjects of cremation and of Masonic societies are considered. The privation may not be due to any penalty which the deceased has incurred, but may be the result of the danger of scandal due to the circumstances surrounding the funeral, v.g., if the heirs have ordered cremation and scandal cannot be prevented, or if Masonic services or the displays of Masonic insignia are to be associated with the funeral, both of which are circumstances incompatible with the respect that is due to the Catholic faith.

It is sometimes alleged that the refusal of Christian burial is a useless penalty, since there is no hope of the reform of the deceased. But it should be recalled that it is a vindictive penalty and is therefore not intended directly for the reform of the delinquent. Its direct purpose is to repair the social order and to serve as a warning to others, who, when they see

tiva inquisitio."—"Denegacion de Sepultura Ecclesastica,"—*Sal Terrae*, XIX (1930), 322 ff., quoted in *Ius Pontificium*, X (1930), 69, 70; Coronata: " . . . patet ex ipsa natura poenae, quae si iudicialem Ordinarii sententiam requireret, pluribus in casibus effectu careret et inutilis evaderet."—*De Locis et Temporibus Sacris*, n. 257.

28 Bernardini: "Verum subiectum passivum poenae nequit esse homo mortuus. Est igitur poena vivis imposita." . . . "ergo privatio sepulturae afficit personam vivam et iam in poenis latae sententiae et in casu quo quis eum incurrat immediate ante mortem, quia statim ac incursa est, delinquentem tenet."—*Il Diritto Ecclesiastico*, XL (1929), 473, 479.

29 *Loc. cit.*

one denied the prayers of the Church and excluded from burial in blessed ground, may be moved to set their own affairs in order and seek reconciliation with the Church, lest they suffer a like misfortune.[30]

B. *Notoriety*

The element of notoriety is explicitly required in canon 1240, §1, 1° and implicity in Canon 1240, § 1, 2°: It will be seen, after the notion and force of notoriety have been examined, that notoriety is also implicitly required in the rest of the canon.

1. The Notion of Notoriety

A delict may be notorious by notoriety of law or by notoriety of fact. It is legally notorious when sentence has been pronounced by a competent judge in a trial,[31] or after the delict has been spontaneously confessed in a legal manner or in answer to a legitimate question by the judge.[32] It is factually notorious when it is publicly known and committed in such circumstances that it cannot be concealed by any subterfuge or excused by any legal principle.[33] Whether notoriety necessarily includes the idea of publicity, i.e., divulgation, as a prerequisite quality is disputed. The majority of the authors, however, hold that it does; that a notorious delict is one that is widely publicized, widely known, or certainly bound to become such,[34] to which is then added the element of notoriety, the fact of its being unconcealable and inexcusable.[35] Coron-

30 Gonzalez-Tellez, *Commentaria*, lib. III, tit. 28, c. 12, n. 7; Many, *De Locis Sacris*, nn. 217, 218.

31 Whether the trial is in a civil or in an ecclesiastical court—Coronata, *Institutiones Iuris Canonici*, IV, n. 1646.

32 ..Canon 2197, 2°; canon 1750; Ayrinhac-Lydon, *Penal Legislation*, n. 6.

33 Canon 2197, 3°; Ayrinhac-Lydon, *loc. cit.*

34 It includes, therefore, the notion of a public delict as defined in canon 2197, 1°.

35 Sole: "Notorietas aliquid addit publicitati seu divulgationi delicti,"—*De Delictis et Poenis* (Romae, 1920), p. 11; Vermeersch-Creusen, *Epitome*, III, n. 384; Blat, *Commentarium Textus Codicis Iuris Cano-*

ata[36] and Blat,[37] following Hollweck,[38] maintained that a notorious delict need not necessarily presuppose a delict public in the sense of canon 2197, 1°, i.e., by *divulgation,* for although it may include divulgation, it does not essentially require it. They believe therefore that public documents and legal and authentic records, as well as the irrefutable testimony of witnesses, all constitute, of themselves, sufficient public notice to meet the requirement of *"publice notum"* in the definition of notoriety; they consider that a delict is *"publice notum"* when it appears in such documents, regardless of whether the information is of common knowledge.[39]

Since, however, the opinion of the majority of the authors is more favorable to the delinquent, theirs will be understood here.[40] A notorious delict is, therefore, one that is not generally known or of common knowledge, or one that is bound to become such, but also one that is, as Vermeersch-Creusen so succinctly state it,[41] juridically certain and undeniable, whether the certitude is produced by a legal trial, by a juridical confession or by the number and quality of the witnesses.

Since notoriety is so important a condition for the application of the penalty now under consideration, it will be necessary to consider what notoriety contributes to the essential elements of a delict—external violation of the law and moral imputability—to differentiate it as a particular kind of delict.

In regard to the force of notoriety, Benedict XIV declared that notoriety produces the same moral certitude about a

nici, lib. V, n. 8; Wernz-Vidal: "Notorium publico aliquid superaddit," —*Ius Canonicum,* VII, n. 35; Cocchi: "*Publicum* est genus manifestationis, *notorium* est species *publici* quae huic aliquid addit . . . ,"—*Commentarium in Codicem Iuris Canonici,* VIII, n. 1; Ayrinhac-Lydon, *Penal Legislation,* n. 6; Chelodi, *Ius Poenale,* n. 4; Cerato, *Censurae Vigentes,* n. 2.

36 *Institutiones Iuris Canonici,* IV, nn. 1645, 1646, 1647.

37 *Commentarium Textus,* lib. V, n. 9.

38 *Die kirchlichen Strafgesetze,* § 5.

39 Coronata, *op. cit.,* IV, n. 1645, p. 3, not. 3 and 4.

40 In poenis benignior est interpretatio facienda.—Canon 2219, § 1.

41 *Epitome,* III, n. 384.

delinquent's guilt that a judge has when he pronounces sentence from the evidence produced in a trial.[42] This opinion is repeated in the Code itself when it legislates that notorious facts need no proof.[43] And Coronata states even more explicitly that notoriety permits the judge to pass sentence immediately without the need for a trial to establish guilt.[44]

The authors are quite agreed on this notion of notoriety as an element in a delict that makes it appear fully culpable; that makes most evident the intention of the delinquent to commit an act he knew was contrary to the law. Thus Vermeersch-Creusen declare that notoriety produces a jurdically certain knowledge of guilt that cannot be denied; that a delict is not notorious if any doubt remains of its imputability.[45] And Coronato states that notoriety produces *certain, absolute* and *public* knowledge of a delict; a knowledge which so proves the two elements of a delict that nothing can be alleged against either the fact of the violation or the law of its imputability.[46] Roberti, likewise holds that a notorious crime is one that is considered to be morally certain to all.[47] Cocchi adds that notoriety makes a delict so certain from either legal or factual

[42] Epist. "Ex omnibus," 16 oct. 1756—*Fontes*, n. 441; *De Synodo Dioecesana*, lib. VII, c. XI, n. VIII.

[43] Canon 1747, 1°.

[44] *Institutiones Iuris Canonici*, IV, n. 1645.

[45] "Notorietas est notitia rei quae juridice certa est, neque negari potest;" . . . "delictum non est notorium si de imputabilitate facti dubium moveri potest," *Epitome*, III, n. 384.

[46] " . . . et non quaevis notitia sed talis quae delicti duo elementa comprobare possit ita ut nequeat aliquid contra factum delictuosum aut contra eius imputabilitatem obiici; quae notitia *certa* et *absoluta* et *publica* ad delictum publicum non requiritur." *Institutiones Iuris Canonici*, IV, n. 1645; "Notorium dicitur illud quod ipsa evidentia rei ita certum est ut nulla tergiversatione celari possit. Quare delictum notorium est factum criminosum ipsa evidentia rei non solum ut factum sed etiam ut delictum ita certum ut nulla tergiversatione celari possit." —*De Locis et Temporibus Sacris*, n. 258.

[47] " . . . ut crimen moraliter omnibus constare censeatur."—*De Delictis et Poenis*, n. 44.

evidence that no further discussion of it is necessary.[48] Chelodi is perhaps most explicit when he notes that by notoriety the delict, both as to the act itself and as to the intention to act contrary to the law, is so plainly established before the people, that there cannot be even the slightest doubt about either." [49]

Moreover, in notorious delicts there is no room for the distinction which may be made in *public* delicts. Public delicts may be considered under a double aspect, as either *formal* or *material* delicts. A formal delict is one that is fully culpable. A material public delict is understood as one that stands in the external forum as a result of the fact of the external violation of the law and the presumption of guilt afforded by Canon 2200, § 2, but about the actual guilt of which there is no evidence. For example: a man kills another in a public place before witnesses, who, however, arrive only at the moment of the killing and who consequently have no way of knowing whether the killer acted in self-defense and was therefore innocent, or whether he was the unjust aggressor. The law, seeing the external act, presumes guilt and a *material* delict stands in the external forum, imputable to the killer until he proves his innocence.[50] When the guilt is proved there is established a *formal* public delict, one in which both the external violation of the law and the guilt are *known*.[51]

But notorious delicts cannot be so distinguished into material and formal delicts, for they are always so obviously fully

[48] "Ad notorietatem delicti in genere requiritur ut hoc vel in facto vel in iure ita certum est ut nulla amplius discussione egeat."—*Commentarium in Codicem Iuris Canonici*, VIII, n. 1.

[49] " . . . aliis verbis, si tum actio tum intentio mala ita aperte coram populo est probata, ut de utroque elemento delicti, obiectivo et subiectivo, ne levi quidem dubio locus est."—*Ius Poenale*, n. 4.

[50] "Posita externa legis violatione, dolus in foro externo praesumitur donec contrarium probetur."—canon 2200, § 2.

[51] Coronata, *Institutiones Iuris Canonici*, IV, nn. 1645, 1646; D'Annibale, *Summula Theologiae Moralis*, I, n. 242. However, a formal public delict is not in itself a notorious delict, for to be notorious, the formal delict must not only be public, but *so* publicly known that it is *unconcealable* and *inexcusable*—canon 2197, 3°.

imputable, from the nature of notoriety,[52] that they cannot escape always being considered formal delicts.[53] Thus a delict that is notorious can never be considered as only a material delict, but must always appear to be a formal one.[54] One who commits a notorious delict, therefore, is one who is popularly believed to have realized that he was acting contrary to the precept of the law and to have chosen to do so.[55] It is precisely

[52] This is true whether the notoriety be of law or of fact, for although the clause "nulla tergiversatione celari nulloque iuris suffragio excusari potest" appears only in the definition of notoriety of fact, it is equally applicable to notoriety of law. Coronata says: "Advertatur etiam pro casibus notorietatis iuris verificari clausulam quod delictum 'nulla tergiversatione celari possit aut excusari" . . . "—*op. cit.*, IV, n. 1646.

[53] Cocchi: " . . . notorium includit certam notitiam delicti et quidem *formaliter* sumpti, seu facti criminosi."—*Commentarium in Codicem,* VIII, n. 1; Roberti notes that the notions of both kinds of public delict, material and formal, are contained in the definition of notoriety: " . . . cum crimen in talibus adiuncts fuit commissum, vel ita notum est, ut nulla possit tergiversatione celari (materialiter) nulloque iuris suffragio excusari (formaliter)."—*De Delictis et Poenis*, n. 44.

[54] Coronata: " . . . et proinde non haberi posse delictum notorium notorietate iuris sicut nec notorium notorietate facti quod sit *notorium solum materialiter*, *formaliter* autem *occultum.*" — *Institutiones Iuris Canonici*, IV, n. 1646; "requiritur autem absolute ad delictum notorium ut constet non solum de delicti facto materiali sed etiam de dolo, culpa et non de defensione inculpatae tutelae, aut de casu fortuito. Quod si de his non possit constare, notorium delictum haberi non potest; circa quam notandum est multa dici notoria quae talia non sunt; unde multa cautela in hoc procedendum est."—*op. cit.*, IV, n. 1647; "Ut tale [delictum notorium] habeatur requiritur ut de eo iam certo constet et probationes habeantur non solum de facto sed etiam de imputabilitate."—*loc. cit.*, cf. Sole, *De Delictis et Poenis*, p. 11; Vermeersch-Creusen, *Epitome*, III, n. 384; Blat, *Commentarium Textus*, lib. V, n. 9; Chelodi, *Ius Poenale*, n. 4.

[55] Roberti: " . . . ut crimen moraliter omnibus constare censeatur."—*De Delictis et Poenis*, 44; Cocchi: "Notorietas inniti potest vel in actu judicialis sententiae contra quam nullum iuris remedium dari possit, aut in confessione iudiciali delinquentis; vel *in ipsa rei evidentia* contra quam nulla iuridica excusatio afferri possit ad auferendam delinquentis imputabilitatem."—*Commentarium in Codicem*, VIII, 1.

this element of inexcusability, which arises from the delinquent's apparent knowledge of the criminal character of his deed, that differentiates a *notorious* crime from one that is simply *public*.[56]

This distinction between notorius delicits and public delicts[57] must be born in mind, for, as Coronata well points out, a public delict only renders the delinquent liable to trial for his offence to determine his guilt, and to permit him to try to overthrow the presumption of law against him according to canon 2200, 2; a notorius delict permits sentence to be passed immediately without a trial, for the evidence of guilt is in the act itself, and to such an extent that there is no room left for doubt about it.[58]

The subject of the meaning of notoriety cannot be closed without the remark that notoriety of law is less forceful in its juridical effect than notoriety of fact, for a solid proof is more easily opposed to it. Thus a sentence or a juridical confession may be impugned with less difficulty than may a publicly known notorious fact.[59] Since, however, the canon does not distinguish the type of notoriety required, the presence of either is sufficient to constitute a notorious delicit.[60]

The determination of the existence of notoriety no longer depends upon the crime's having been committed before a major part of the community or upon the duration of time that it has

[56] Augustine, *A Commentary,* VIII, 17.

[57] The avoidance by the Legislator of repetition of the term "delictum publicum" in defining notoriety is remarked by Roberti. The latter substitutes the words "ita notum est" for the words "publice notum" of canon 2197, 3°, purposely, he adds, to differentiate a *notorious* crime from a *public* one.—*De Delictis et Poenis,* n. 44.

[58] *Institutiones Iuris Canonici,* IV, nn. 1646, 1647.

[59] Vermeersch-Creusen: "Contra notorietatem iuris non repugnat afferri solidam probationem; quare, per se, eius vis minor est quam notorietas facti"—*Epitome,* III, n. 384; Coronata, *De Locis et Temporibus Sacris,* n. 258; Wernz, *Ius Decretalium,* VI, n. 17.

[60] Coronata: "Quando in Codice sermo est de delictis notoriis, quaelibet notorietas sufficere censenda est, quia ubi lex non distinguit nec nos distinguere debemus."—*Institutiones Iuris Canonici,* IV, n. 1640.

existed. In the new law it is most conveniently left to the one who must decide the case to estimate the notoriety involved.[61]

2. The Extent of the Requirement of Notoriety

It was noted above[62] that notoriety is explicitly demanded in regard to the delicts mentioned in n. 1 of canon 1240 § 1, and implicitly required in n. 2. The latter follows from the fact that a judicial sentence is required in that number and a judicial sentence gives rise to notoriety of law.

It will now be seen that notoriety is required throughout the canon, for the rest of the canon is concerned with public and manifest sinners and "public" and "manifest" are terms that, taken together, mean substantially the same thing as "notorious."

Suicides, those killed in a duel and those who have willed their own cremation will be deprived of Christian burial only when they are also public and manifest sinners. This is quite evident from the Legislator's use of the term *"alii"* in number six of canon 1240, § 1.[63] In making the general provision that the law be extended to "other" public and manifest sinners, he clearly implies that the foregoing categories have been considered only in so far as they are also public and manifest sinners.[64]

[61] Roberti: "Hodie opportunissime notorietas arbitrio iudicis relinquitur aestimanda."—*De Delictis et Poenis*, n. 44.

[62] P. 134.

[63] "Alii peccatores publici et manifesti."

[64] Brys, *Collationes Brugenses*, XXV (1925), 162, 163, 245; Mostaza, *Sal Terrae*, XIX (1930), 332; Coronata: "Ius vetus, vi huius clausulae ["Manifestis et publicis peccatoribus, qui sine poenitentia perierunt"—*Rit. Rom. Paul. V., De Exsequiis,—Quibus non licet dare sepulturam ecclesiasticam*, cf. p. 58] plures comprehendebat qui nunc specifice in Codice determinantur ut sepultura ecclesiastica privati, ut adhaerentes sectae massonicae, duellantes, suicidas, etc."—*De Locis et Temporibus Sacris*, 262; Many likewise notes that many classes of delinquents were grouped together for the first time in the Ritual of Pope Paul V, and were deprived of Christian burial "ratione publici peccati."—*De Locis*

In the singling out of certain public delicts for special mention, the Legislator has merely emphasized their malice and their undoubted prohibition. Affiliation with Mansonry and the ordering one's own cremation are not new delicts with the Code. Persons guilty of these crimes were punished with the privation of Christian burial in the old law under the general heading of *public sinners*.[65]

But *public* and *manifest* sinners are in reality *notorious* sinners, for *manifest* adds to *public* that element of inexcusableness[66] which make a *public* sinner become a *notorious* one. This is made clearer when it is realized that one may appear to be a public sinner by repute, rumor, gossip and the like, for the word *public* requires only that the external fact of the breach of the law be commonly known or bound to become such. The addition of the term *manifest* to the term *public sinner* adds a note of obvious culpability, for by its definition *manifest* means *clear, evident, apparent.* Thus a public sinner is not a manifest sinner until his offense is provable by reliable witnesses who have certain knowledge of it and can testify to it.[67]

The remarks of the authors, in commenting on canon 1240, § 1, n. 6. confirm this opinion by their frequent use of the

Sacris, n. 220; one whose ordering his own cremation is publicly known is expressly referred to as a *public sinner* in *Periodica*, XIV (1925), 178; Wernz-Vidal, *Ius Canonicum*, IV, n. 586, not. (43); Brys, *Collationes Brugenses*, XXV (1925), 66. A suicide whose crime is publicly known is termed a *public sinner* in *L'Ami du Clergé*, XXXVIII (1925), 554.

65 Many, *De Locis Sacris*, n. 220.

66 Blat: " . . . et '*manifesti*' quia excusari nequent . . . "—*Commentarium Textus*, lib. III, pars II, n. 104.

67 Coronata: "Cum delictum *publicum* non est confundendum delictum *manifestum* quod exigit ut plures sint certi testes qui per scientiam certam et sensum corporeum rem cognoverint et desuper testimonium dare possint." *De Locis et Temporibus Sacris*, n. 263; Brys, "De Sepultura Ecclesiastica"—*Collationes Brugenses*, XXV (1925), 245; Wernz, *Ius Decretalium*, VI, n. 17.

term *notorious* in treating of the public and manifest sinners.[68]

Therefore it must be borne in mind throughout the discussion of the various delinquents mentioned in canon 1240, § 1, which will form the subject of the following chapter, that the element of notoriety must be understood as a requisite characteristic of their crimes, over and above the specific requirements mentioned in the various numbers of the canon.

The requirement that all the delinquents mentioned in canon

[68] Roberti: "Excommunicatus *notorius* de facto privatur non qua excommunicatus, sed qua publicus et manifestus peccator."—*De Delictis et Poenis*, n. 336; Coronata: "Possunt enumerari inter publicos peccatores et manifesti: . . . haeretici *notorii*, licet nulli sectae adhaeserint, itemque excommunicati etiam sine sententia si *notoria* sit eorum poena et delictum, per pluries annos paschalem communionem *notorie* omittentes, . . . si *notorius* sit status peccati."—*Institutiones Iuris Canonici*, II, n. 816; *L'Ami du Clergé* states that a sin is public and manifest when it "saute aux yeux de tous, avec une telle force d'évidence qu'il ne peut être discuté ou mise en doute par personne. *La notoriété* est une nuance d'accentuation qui renforce la note commune et ordinaire de publicité. Voice la publicité *notoire*, manifeste, requise par le canon 1240, § 1, n. 6."—XL (1923), 311; Blat: " . . . et *manifesti* quia excusari nequeunt."—*Commentarium Textus*, lib. III, pars II, n. 104; *Perfice Munus* expressly states that the *notoriety* required in canon 1240, § 1, n. 6, is that of canon 2197, 3°—VIII (1933), 356; Jullien, in a Rota Decision, explicitly refers to the *notoriety* required in canon 1240, § 1, n. 6, as not merely that which renders a delict provable, but that which also identifies it as commonly known.—*S. R. Rotae Decisiones, Decisio* LVI, XXII (1930), 627; Brys lists among public sinners those who "in *notorio* habitu concubinatus vivunt," and states that to be included under canon 1240, § 1, n. 6, a delict must be *notorious.*—*Collationes Brugenses*, XXV (1925), 245, 246; Cocchi notes that the public sinners referred to in this part of canon 1240 are those "qui excusari nequeunt."—*Commentarium in Codicem*, V, n. 71; Rossi defines as *manifesti* "those whose delict in indubitable both as to fact and to intention."—*La "Sepultura Ecclesiastica" e l' "Ius Funerum,"* p. 138; Mothon lists as public sinners in the sense of this canon those who live *notoriously* in mortal sin, e. g., *notorious* divorcees.—*Institutions Canoniques*, II, 574; Many, in reference to the same term in the old law: " . . . qui in *notorio* statu peccati vivunt . . . ita tamen ut mala fides certa sit et *notoria*, aliter enim non essent publici peccatores."—*De Locis Sacris*, n. 220.

1240, § 1, be notorious before they can be considered to have incurred the privation of Christian burial, is implicitly contained in the second paragraph of the same canon in which the Legislator orders that Christian burial is not to be denied if there is any persistent doubt as to a person's inclusion among the delinquents mentioned in the first paragraph.[69] It is only notoriety that leaves no room for doubt, for if there is any doubt about either the fact of the crime or the guilt of the delinquent, the delicit is not notorious[70]

C. *The Execution of the Penalty*

The process by which the penalty is declared to have been incurred is usually purely an administrative one, not a judicial one, and one that may be performed by the pastor of the deceased.[71] Schaaf states that it is for the pastor to judge each case,[72] and he notes that once the pastor of the deceased has decided the case, no other pastor has the right either to review the case or to give a decision contrary to that of the pastor of the deceased. The only recourse open to any other priest, who may feel that an injustice has been done is an appeal to the Ordinary.[73] But both Coronata[74] and Brys[75]

[69] "Occurrente praedictis in casibus aliquo dubio consulator Ordinarius, si tempus sinat; permanente dubio, cadaver sepulturae ecclesiasticae tradatur, ita tamen ut removeatur scandalum."

[70] *L'Ami du Clergé:* "If the crime is not notorious, there remains room for doubt and the Ordinary must be consulted; if the doubt persists, Christian burial must be granted, *remoto scandalo.*" XXXVIII (1921), 630, 631.

[71] Blat: " . . . sit exsequenda extraiudicialiter . . . "—*Commentarium Textus*, lib. V, n. 123; Mostaza . " . . . sufficit administrativa inquisitio ex parte illius qui sepulturam dare debet"—*Sal Terrae*, XIX (1930), 332; Icard, *Praelectiones Iuris Canonici*, II, 479.

[72] "Catholic Burial and Public Sinners,"—*The Ecclesiastical Review*, XCV (1936), 194.

[73] *Loc. cit.* Cf. *Dictionnaire de Droit Canonique*, "Sépulture," III, 503.

[74] *Institutiones Iuris Canonici*, II, n. 817; *De Locis et Temporibus Sacris*, n. 257.

[75] "De Sepultura Ecclesiastica"—*Collationes Brugenses*, XXV (1925), 162.

speak only in general of the minister of the funeral as the one who makes this decision. However, since the ordinary minister of funerals in the parish is the pastor,[76] their opinion would seem to agree ultimately with the opinion of Schaaf.

An investigation as to one's worthiness or unworthiness is obligatory. Buvée notes that a person is not to be considered entitled to Christian burial simply because he is not known to be unworthy of it. Christian burial should not therefore be granted to strangers without a reasonable certitude that they are entitled to it.[77]

D. *The Procedure in Doubtful Cases*

> **Occurrente in praedictis casibus aliquo dubio, consulatur, si tempus sinat, Ordinarius; permanente dubio, cadaver sepulturae ecclesiasticae tradatur . . . . 1240, § 2.**

The canon orders that in case of doubt the matter is to be referred to the Ordinary, if time allows.[78]

The power of priests is thus limited to those cases that are clear, those in which there is no doubt about the presence of all the conditions required by the law for the incurring of the penalty of the denial of Christian burial. The power to judge doubtful cases has been removed from them by the Legislator and given to the Ordinary, except in those cases in which the lack of time does not allow a referring of the matter to him.

The canon adds that if the doubt persists, the deceased is to be given Christian burial. This is an addition in the new law and indicates anew the increased clemency of the Code. For it gives the deceased a legal title to Christian burial on the basis of the doubt itself. He therefore has a *right* to Christian burial unless he is indubitably denied it by the law.[79]

76 Canon 462, 5°.

77 *Ministère Paroissial*, n. 819.

78 It is worth noting that this part of canon 1240 is not a penal law. Cf. canon 2291, 5°.

79 "Ce doute, s'il existe, est, d'après le droit lui-même, favorable au mort, et permet la sépulture ecclésiastique, bien plus, il lui donne droit à

This clause is equally applicable to the case in which the doubt persists even after the case has been referred to the Ordinary, and it is therefore binding upon him also. He is not to refuse Christian burial unless the deceased has been certainly denied it by the law.[80]

The Legislator has thus placed upon the Ordinary the duty of deciding doubtful cases, those that are not certainly evident to the pastor. This is an obligation that he can fulfill the better because of his wider experience, his knowledge of the general conditions of the diocese and his greater impartiality. These qualities permit him to reach a decision that is more suitable to the interests of the individual and of the general good of the Church.[81]

In practice, however, it is questionable whether recourse to the Ordinary will often be possible. Unless the pastor lives in or near the cathedral city, recourse by mail, the normal method,[82] will hardly be effective within the time that usually elapses between death and burial. It will therefore often devolve upon the pastor to decide doubtful cases. There seems no good reason, however, why recourse may not be made by telephone, although there is no obligation to make use of this means of communication.

la sépulture ecclésiastique."—*L'Ami du Clergé*, XXXVIII (1921), 630-631.

80 Brys: "Hoc praescripto canon normam tradit non tantum Ordinario, sed ministro funerum, si tempus recursum ad Ordinarium non sinat."—*Collationes Brugenses*, XXV (1925), 162; Coronata: "Datur in altera parte paragraphi norma quae tum Ordinarius, tum quilibet alius minister in casu dubii, si recursus fieri nequeat, dirigi tuto possunt."—*Institutiones Iuris Canonici*, II, n. 817; *De Locis et Temporibus Sacris*, n. 264.

81 S. C. S. Off., 19 maii 1886: "In casibus particularibus in quibus dubium vel difficultas oriatur, consulendus erit Ordinarius qui accurate perpensis omnibus adiunctis id dicernet quod magis expedire in Domino iudicaverit."—*Coll. S. C. P. F.*, n. 1657; Schaaf, "Catholic Burial and Public Sinners,"—*The Ecclesiastical Review*, XCV (1936), 192-194.

82 Cf. O'Reilly, *The General Norms of Dispensations*, The Catholic University of America Canon Law Studies, n. 119, Washington, D. C.: The Catholic University of America, p. 78.

Despite the fact that the law allows the pastor to deny Christian burial in those cases in which there is no doubt about the penalty's having been incurred, it will be often most prudent to consult the Ordinary even in such cases, because of the great margin of allowance that must be left for the influence of variable factors in the matter of the signs of repentance, scandal, doubts, and public opinion in a particular locality.[83] Moreover, particular law may at times require that all cases of the refusal of Christian burial be referred to the Ordinary, especially those in which difficulties are expected to arise from the execution of the privation.[84]

The doubt that may arise in an individual case may be one of law: about the existence or comprehensiveness of the law in this case; or of fact: whether the penalty has been incurred in the particular circumstances and conditions of the case.[85] It may also be about the fact or the notoriety of the delict, or about the sign of repentance, or about the fact of membership in, or the condemnation of, a sect.[86] The Code does not specify, and therefore *any* doubt that is sufficient to preclude certainty about the penalty's having been incurred would be sufficient to render the case a doubtful one.

The granting of the benefit of the doubt to the delinquent is entirely in accordance with the milder discipline of the times.[87] The more merciful course is therefore to be followed in doubtful cases. As Schaaf well states:

[83] Wernz-Vidal, *Ius Canonicum*, VII, n. 342.

[84] Brys, *Collationes Brugenses*, XXV (1925), 163; Mostaza, *Ius Pontificium*, X (1930), 69, 70; *Acta Episcopalia* of the Diocese of Bruges—*Collationes Brugenses*, XXXVI (1936), 261.

[85] Brys, "De Sepultura Ecclesiastica,"—*Collationes Brugenses*, XXV (1925), 162.

[86] Cappello, *Summa Iuris Canonici*, II, n. 761; *L'Ami du Clergé*, XXXVIII (1921), 630, 631; Brys, *Collationes Brugenses*, *loc. cit.*

[87] Brys: "Urgente necessitate et dubio permanente mitior et legitima interpretatio est sequenda in his legibus odiosis et poenalibus . . . "—*Collationes Brugenses*, XXV (1925), 161; Coronata, *Institutiones Iuris Canonici*, II, n. 817; Wernz-Vidal, *Ius Canonicum*, IV, n. 587; Wernz, *Ius Decretalium*, III, n. 782.

> In all such cases, it must be borne in mind that Holy Mother Church is solicitous for the dead, and, far from insisting on the rigorous course of the law, today practices the greatest forbearance and is ready to give the benefit of any reasonable doubt to the deceased.[88]

This giving of the benefit of the doubt does not include the granting of all the pomp and ceremony of the full rite of Christian burial. The authors agree that it is right and proper that the doubt in the mind of the Church about the worthiness of the deceased may be reflected in a curtailment of the usual honors paid to those to whose worthiness the Church renders testimony in her rite of ecclesiastical burial.

When the existence of the right to Christian burial is highly improbable, Brys confines the church service to a simple absolution without even a low Mass.[89] In this opinion he is supported by Augustine[90] and Vermeersch-Creusen.[91] But Coronata,[92] Rossi[93] and Schaaf[93] do not feel that the Mass should be omitted.[95] Since there seems to be no serious reason for omitting the Mass, or for depriving the deceased of its benefit, the church service may be limited to the low Mass and the absolution, without music, bells or the extra decorations and ceremonies that are sometimes added to the essential rites.[96]

88 "Catholic Burial and Public Sinners,"—*The Ecclesiastical Review*, XCV (1936), 191.

89 *Collationes Brugenses*, XXV (1925), 162. The same author states in another place that the absolution is the essential part of the Church service.—*Collationes Brugenses*, XXVI (1926), 320.

90 *A Commentary*, VI, 155.

91 *Epitome*, II, n. 549.

92 *Institutiones Iuris Canonici*, II, n. 817.

93 *La "Sepultura Ecclesiastica" e l' "Ius Funerum,"* p. 140.

94 *The Ecclesiastical Review*, XCV (1936), 193.

95 The Roman Ritual allows for the omission of the Mass if the funeral takes place at a time at which the Mass cannot be had, or for any other necessary reason.—*Rit. Rom.*, tit. VI, c. III, nn. 4, 18.

96 Wernz-Vidal, *Ius Canonicum*, IV, n. 587; Buvée, *Ministère Paroissial*, n. 818; Brys, *loc. cit.;* Coronata, *loc. cit.;* *Epitome, loc. cit.;*

E. *The Nature and the Effect of a Sign of Repentance*

Nisi ante mortem aliqua dederint poenitentiae signa.

Another condition that must be verified before the penalty is executed is that there be no sign of repentance on the part of the delinquent.

The new law has mitigated the old in two ways in this clause: it added *"aliqua"* and it extended the application of the clause to all the classes of people mentioned in the canon. Moreover, the new has clarified the old in the placing of this limitation in one clause at the head of the canon.[97]

Under the present law, all those who are mentioned in the canon are to be deprived of Christian burial only if they have not given any sign of repentance before death. The words could not be more general and they restore to the deceased a right to Christian burial even if he had lost it by the commission of the most notorious delicts that are listed.[98]

It is impossible to state just what will constitute *any* sign of repentance, for the external manifestation of regret can take place in a great variety of ways. Some, however, may be suggested: the kissing of a crucifix or of a religious image, an act of contrition, prayers and ejaculations, and other signs of piety.[99] Other signs may be: the sending for a priest or the

Mothon, *Institutions Canoniques*, II, 574; *Encyclopédie des Sciences Religieuses*, XI, 558.

[97] Some excerpts from the old law will bear this out: Christian burial was formerly forbidden to suicides "unless they gave signs of repentance before death"; to public sinners "who died without repentance"; to those who missed their Easter Duty and "who died without any sign of repentance"; to duelists "even if they gave signs of repentance before death." Cf. p. 58 above.

[98] Cappello: "Omnes . . . , si poenitentiae signa dederint, ius habent ad sepulturam ecclesiasticam, ideoque possunt ac debent sepeliri ritu sacro ex Codicis praescripto."—*Summa Iuris Canonici*, II, n. 761.

[99] Cappello, *Summa Iuris Canonici, loc. cit.;* Schaaf, *Ecclesiastical Review*, XCV (1936), 191; *Perfice Munus* (Vol. XI [1936], 591) mentions the case of a public sinner who was found dead with a crucifix

expression of a desire to see one, even if the priest does not arrive in time;[100] an expressed desire for the sacraments, or anything that shows regret for what the church disapproves of in one's life;[101] a promise to regularize one's situation as soon as possible; an expressed desire not to die without the sacraments; an expression of regret at having acted so as to be deprived of them.[102]

Schaaf notes that even such expressions as: "it might not be a bad idea to get back to the sacraments" may at times be sufficient, preferably with the Ordinary's approval. However, such signs may be rendered inefficacious because of the lapse of time between their utterance and the death, time in which they might have been realized but were not.[103] Such rather vague signs could be sufficient only in cases of doubt and with the consent of the bishop.[104]

The reception of the last sacraments would, of course, constitute a genuine sign of repentance. Even the presence of the priest with the sick one just before death, if it were publicly known, could be of sufficient weight to amount to a sign of repentance.[105] It is for this reason that priests are urged to visit the difficult cases alone. If public opinion concludes from his visit that the deceased repented, Christian burial may be granted, even though the priest may know privately that he refused the sacraments. Such a refusal would be considered formal only when it was made before witnesses other than the priest.[106]

It is easier to give the characteristics of the sign of repentance than the number of kinds. They must be clear, cer-

clasped in his hand. Unless suspicion of fraud were established, it held that such was a sufficient sign of repentance.

100 Coronata, *Institutiones Iuris Canonici*, II, n. 816.

101 Ayrinhac, *Administrative Legislation*, n. 78.

102 *L'Ami du Clergé*, XXXVIII (1921), 684.

103 "Catholic Burial and Public Sinners"—*The Ecclesiastical Review*, XCV (1936), 191.

104 *L'Ami du Clergé*, XXXVIII (1921), 684.

105 *L'Ami du Clergé*, *loc. cit.*

106 Duvée, *Ministère Paroissial*, n. 816.

tain, or at least probable.[107] They must be positive, but this does not mean that they must also be manifest or public; they need be only probable.[108] Thus the sign of repentance must be accepted in a very broad sense, especially *in articulo mortis*.[109] Moreover, they must be of sufficient weight to offset, when made public, the scandal and harm done by the deceased or that may arise from his being granted Christian burial.[110] This does not mean that they need be sufficient to satisfy the requirements for the reception of the sacraments; nor is there any necessity that they be sufficient to cover the need for reparation, satisfaction, restitution and the like.[111] However, a sign of repentance that was merely a presumed one would not suffice; for example, it might be maintained that there was no certitude of final impenitence and therefore the deceased may have repented in his last moments of life. The sign must be a positive one.[112] For the same reason, the reception of the sacraments *sub conditione* by an unconscious person is not a sign of repentance.[113] Nevertheless, a minimum is required; the canon states that *any* sign is sufficient. If there is doubt about the sufficiency of the sign of repentance, and the doubt is not resolved, it will of itself give the deceased the right to Christian burial, subject only to the condition that scandal must be obviated.

If the sign of repentance was not public, it must at least be capable of being publicized.[115] Moreover, the sign must have been witnessed by at least one witness who is worthy of credence.[116]

107 Ayrinhac, *Administrative Legislation*, n. 78.

108 Cappello, *Summa Iuris Canonici*, II, n. 761.

109 *L'Ami du Clergé*, XXXVIII (1921), 684.

110 *L'Ami du Clergé*, *loc. cit.*

111 *L'Ami du Clergé*, XL (1923), 310; Schaaf, *The Ecclesiastical Review*, XCV (1936), 191.

112 Brys, *Collationes Brugenses*, XXV (1925), 163.

113 Canestri, *Apollinaris*, IV (1931), 136.

114 Brys, *loc. cit.*

115 Wernz-Vidal, *Ius Canonicum*, IV, n. 586.

116 Cappello, *Summa Iuris Canonici*, II, n. 761; Buvée, *Ministère*

If the sign remains doubtful, Christian burial may be granted in the less solemn manner, that is, with a low Mass and absolution, without music, bells, and customary additions to the liturgical rites.[117]

F. *The Element of Scandal*

. . . ita tamen ut removeatur scandalum

The canon finally orders that scandal must be obviated. Brys notes that the Legislator uses the imperative,[118] but there is no need to look to the canon for justification of this sanction, for the avoidance of scandal is enjoined by the divine law itself.[119]

Scandal must be avoided not only in doubtful cases but in all cases. Christian burial must therefore be denied when it is prudently fore-seen that its concession will inevitably result in grave scandal for the faithful, regardless of the fact that the scandal is due to circumstances for which the deceased was not responsible. Thus it may happen that scandal is bound to rise from the fact that one is to be cremated, although he is innocent of the delict of having ordered it; or the heirs may have surrounded the funeral with conditions that are incompatible with the respect due the Catholic faith, v.g., the employment of Masonic services or insignia.[120] In such circumstances the considerations of public order override the right of the deceased, and if grave scandal cannot be obviated Christian burial is not to be granted.[121]

Paroissial, n. 818; Buvée declares that two witnesses would be required to prove impenitence.

117 Wernz-Vidal, *Ius Canonicum*, IV, n. 587.

118 *Collationes Brugenses*, XXV (1925), 162.

119 Blat, *Commentarium Textus*, Lib. III, Pars II, n. 104; Capello, *Summa Iuris Canonici*, II, n. 761.

120 Capello, *Summa Iuris Canonici*, II, n. 761; Coronata, *De Locis et Temporibus Sacris*, n. 264; Vermeersch-Creusen; "Bono enim privato salus et aedificatio multorum praeferri possunt."—*Epitome*, II, n. 335.

121 *L'Ami du Clergé*, XL (1923), 311. This was most emphatically stated in regard to cremation by the Instruction of the Holy Office, June 19, 1926.—*AAS*, (XVIII), 282.

One exception must be made, however, for it may happen that scandal is bound to arise from either the granting or the refusing of Christian burial. In this case, the course of action that will occasion the lesser scandal must be followed.[122]

When and how scandal will arise cannot be definitely determined, for it is a relative matter that depends much upon circumstances of times, places and people.[123]

Scandal may arise from too great leniency in applying the law as well as from too great severity.[124]

The measure of the obligation to obviate scandal will be in proportion to the amount of scandal which is already extant,[125] or which probably may be occasioned by the granting of Christian burial.[126] How great that may be will depend upon local public opinion.[127]

Thus one may be granted Christian burial without scandal in a large city of several parishes when in the same case he would necessarily be refused Christian burial in a small Catholic community because of the danger of grave scandal.[128]

L'Ami du Clergé suggests that the possibility of scandal and its degree may be ascertained, in regard to a specific case in a given community, by consulting the opinions of the better parishoners as to what effect they anticipate from the granting or the refusing of Christian burial. No doubt such a procedure would have to be surrounded with appropriate safeguards, but a prudent pastor knows his people and can quite easily and quickly gauge public opinion by taking counsel with

[122] *L'Ami du Clergé, XXXVIII* (1921), 685.

[123] *L'Ami du Clergé*, XXXVII (1920), 412; XXXVIII (1921), 29, 554, 685; XXXVI (1914-1919), 217.

[124] Wernz-Vidal, *Ius Canonicum*, IV, n. 587; Ayrinhac, *Administrative Legislation*, n. 79.

[125] *L'Ami du Clergé*, XXXVII (1920), 412.

[126] *L'Ami du Clergé*, XXXVIII (1921), 685.

[127] *Loc. cit.*

[128] *L'Ami du Clergé*, XXXVI (1914-1919), 217; XXXVIII (1921), 554, 685.

a few discreet members of the parish, whose opinions will reveal to him the attitude that will be taken by his people.[129]

Some factors that deserve to be taken into consideration in cases that possibly may involve scandal are: 1) public opinion. It is quite possible that one may be popularly considered as worthy of Christian burial who is not so in reality. *L'Ami du Clergé* believes that Christian burial must not be denied in such circumstances, for the existence of the public opinion of one's worthiness certainty precludes the possibility of his having committed a notorious delict.[130]

2) The danger of a lay or, *a fortiori,* of a Protestant funeral. Authors hold that the scandal to the faithful and the harm to religion caused by such funerals may often be much greater than would be caused by the granting of Christian burial to one not fully worthy of it.[131]

3) Consideration of the family. Christian burial is never to be denied to a person solely because of the faults of his family or granted to a notorious delinquent exclusively on the merits of his family.[132] However, it may possibly happen that whereas the solemn funeral of a person who is doubtfully worthy of Christian burial would be the source of scandal to the faithful and therefore prohibited, the less solemn or private funeral of the same person might be entirely without scandalous effects. Such a situation may arise when the deceased was the member of a family whose devotion to their religion is well known and who are, in the eyes of the people, deserving of special consideration. In such a case the privation of Christian burial may be construed as an unjust humiliation of the family and may cause more scandal than its concession.

129 *L'Ami du Clergé,* XXXVI (1914-1919), 217; XXXVIII (1921), 685; XL (1923), 311.

130 XL (1923), 311.

131 Wernz-Vidal, *Ius Canonicum,* IV, n. 587; Vermeersch-Creusen, *Epitome,* II, n. 549; Coronata, *Institutiones Iuris Canonici,* II, n. 817; *L'Ami du Clergé,* XXXVIII (1921), 584; Brys, *Collationes Brugenses,* XXV (1925), 161.

132 Vermeersch-Creusen, *Epitome,* III, n. 492; *L'Ami du Clergé, loc. cit.*

4) The circumstances of a sudden or accidental death. As in the last number, the probability of scandal may well determine when Christian burial is to be granted to a notorious delinquent who has met a sudden or accidental death. If there is any positive indication that the deceased had regretted his fault and had intended eventually to regularize his condition, v.g., his civil marriage and subsequent concubinage with its attendant scandal to the faithful, the circumstances of his death may well effect a benign interpretation of the law on the part of the ecclesiastical authorities. Such a sign of repentance, however vague and ordinarily inefficacious, may be increased in value as a symbol of contrition by the fact of the unexpected death. Popular opinion may quite possibly be scandalized by an arbitrary execution of the penalty of privation upon one who, if he had not been suddenly and unexpectedly overtaken by death, might have realized his good intentions. A less solemn funeral, or a private one without publicity, would seem to be in order in such circumstances and to obviate all scandal.[133]

It is a rare case in which any imminent scandal cannot be obviated by an announcement of the signs of repentance, made either publicly or in circles that assure its divulgation. This is the accepted and usual form of removing any extant scandal and of precluding future scandal.[134] Scandal may also be sufficiently prevented by the limiting or restricting of the pomp

[133] Woywod, *A Practical Commentary*, II, n. 1269; The Second Plenary Council of Baltimore: "In dubio vero, an sint a sepultura ecclesiastica arcendi, consulendus erit Ordinarius, cum id commode fieri poterit; secus autem, in partes lenitatis et misericordiae propendeat iudicium. *Quod praestandum consulimus praesertim, quandocumque defunctus morte subitanea correptus nullum habuit poenitendi tempus; cum iuxta regulam iuris, odia sint restringenda.*"—*Concilii Plenarii Baltimorensis II Decreta*, n. 889. [Italics in the quotation are supplied by the writer.]

[134] Vermeersch-Creusen, *Epitome*, II, n. 548; Wernz-Vidal, *Ius Canonicum*, IV, n. 587; Woywod, *Homiletic and Pastoral Review*, XXVI (1926), 855; Coronata, *Institutiones Iuris Canonici*, II, n. 817; *De Locis et Temporibus Sacris*, n. 264; Schaaf, *The Ecclesiastical Review*, XCV (1936), 192.

and solemnity of the service in the church to a low Mass and an absolution without music.[135]

Another step that is advisable at times is to prohibit the publication of the name of the Church or of the cemetery, under penalty of the refusal of Christian burial to one who is only dubiously entitled to it. The attendance of societies and confraternities may also be clearly out of order in the case of one whose life was a contradiction of their aims and ideals, but who was granted Christian burial because of a last-minute repentance. Again, a short talk by the officiating priest may be sufficient. He may explain the great mercy of the Church and of her reluctance to refuse Christian burial except in the cases in which one died in open hostility to God and to the Church; he may interpret the meaning of Christian burial: that it does not sanctify the one to whom it is granted, nor damn the one to whom it is denied, but is the act of the Church, commending the soul of one of her children to the mercy of God, provided that She has the slightest reason to hope that he has repented of his faults. He may also warn the faithful not to judge others whom the Church has judged, but to leave them to God's mercy and to pray for them.

The possibility and even probability that scandal will arise from the refusal of Christian burial with the result that a lay or Protestant funeral service will follow may sometimes be obviated. In many cases all that the survivors wish is that the deceased member of the family be not buried "like an animal." They may be of the best parishioners themselves and may be fully aware of the unworthiness of that member of the family to have the honors of Christian burial, but they ask only a minimum to save both the deceased and themselves from the ignominy occasioned by an irreligious burial. The situation calls for circumspect consideration, for at such times even the good parishioners are embittered by an arbitrary attitude on the part of the clergy. It is quite a different situation, how-

[135] Cfr. p. 147.

ever in which the threat of a civil or Protestant funeral is used as a means of demanding Christian burial. In the latter event, Christian burial could not be granted without contempt of the Church and of the law.

All the authors caution against the evil of lay or civil funerals and the scandal that they may cause. They warn that Christian burial must not be refused if the refusal is to result in an increase of this evil to the consequent decline of Catholic burial.[136]

In this delicate matter Schaaf has suggested a practical course. When Christian burial must be denied, it may be tolerated that the priest go to the funeral home or the family home to offer a few prayers under two conditions: the prayers must not be liturgical, and scandal must not arise from such an act. Therefore the prayers of the ritual could not be used. It would seem better that no book be used to avoid the appearance of any formality. The recitation of the *Our Father* the *Hail Mary* and a prayer for eternal rest would not be out of order.

Scandal must not result from this procedure. If this act by the priest were to be interpreted in any way as a flaunting of the law, even though he himself have no such idea in mind, he could not partake in such a service. Again, if his action were to be construed as an imitation funeral service, a mimicry of Protestant services, or a substitute ceremony to supply for the refusal of Catholic rites, he could not so act. All probable sources of scandal must be removed by prudent but adequate means to disabuse those present, and others, of any

136 Wernz-Vidal, *Ius Canonicum*, IV, n. 587; Coronata, *Institutiones Iuris Canonici*, II, n. 817; Vermeersch-Creusen (*Epitome*, II, n. 549): "Periculum scandali quod ex funere mere civili in quibusdam locis oritur potest a lege excusare vel in partes benigniores inclinare ubi aliquod dubium superest;" Brys, *Collationes Brugenses*, XXV (1925), 161; Many, *De Locis Sacris*, n. 221; *L'Ami du Clergé* (XXXVIII [1921], 584) states that the scandal caused by such funerals is quite as great as that caused by a life of public sin.

erroneous opinions that they may be suspected of even secretly holding.[137]

From the foregoing considerations of the principles that govern the privation of Christian burial, it becomes clear that the penalty is a measure of public order; is concerned with public delicts and public sanctions; is intended to prevent scandal that would or could be caused in a community by the rendering of public honors and religious suffrages to one who is generally known to be unworthy of them.[138]

It is a penalty that is not to be executed unless several conditions are verified:[139] 1) The penalty is not to be inflicted except upon those persons who have committed the delicts expressed in canon 1240, § 1; 2) It is to be inflicted on them only when the conditions required by law are present:

a. The delict must be certain in the external forum, that is, it must be clearly evident and not merely a matter of rumor or hearsay;
b. It must be known that no sign of repentance has been given;
c. There must be no doubt about the delict, its publicity, the lack of all signs of repentance;
d. Scandal must be avoided or, when that can not be accomplished, the least scandalous course must be followed.

From these facts the words of Wernz remain as true in the new law as they were in the old: the benign and legitimate interpretation is to be followed in these penal and burdensome laws, avoiding both extreme leniency and excessive rigor, lest

137 "Catholic Burial and Public Sinners," *The Ecclesiastical Review*, XCV (1936), 103, 104.

138 Brys, *Collationes Brugenses*, XXV (1925), 162; *L'Ami du Clergé*, XL (1923), 304, 309; XXXVII (1920), 412.

139 Wernz: "Quae negatio sepulturae ecclesiasticae nequit extendi ad alias personas in iure non expressas, neque applicari ipsis personis expressis nisi verificentur conditiones legibus ecclesiasticis determinatae." —*Ius Decretalium*, III, n. 782.

the faithful be scandalized and the Church held in contempt.[140]

The greatest difficulty will arise in those cases which remain doubtful, for then the deceased has a right by the law itself to Christian burial, a right that is limited however, by the obligation of divine law to avoid scandal. A practical rule suggested by *L'Ami du Clergé*[141] for such doubtful cases may be helpful:

> Christian burial will be granted when its denial will result in grave scandal to the faithful, whether that scandal arises from a Protestant or lay funeral, or from the fact that the deceased was popularly considered worthy of Christian burial, regardless of the pastor's private opinion. Obviously, he was not a notorious delinquent.
>
> Christian burial will be refused when its concession will give serious scandal because of the fact that public opinion holds the deceased unworthy of it, even though the pastor believes him worthy; or when the granting of it will be interpreted as a sign of moral weakness.

It must not be forgotten that an error in this matter has none of the consequences that would arise from a refusal of the sacraments. This law is purely one of the external forum, and the eternal state of the soul is in no way decided by it. Whereas the reception of the sacraments may mean the difference between eternal salvation or damnation, Christian burial cannot affect the eternal status of the soul which is already before God and beyond the power of the Church to save or to condemn.

Likewise, there are no occult cases; one is publicly worthy or publicly unworthy of Christian burial. Therefore those whose duty it is to decide whether the right has been lost in a particular case should not be unduly alarmed by the prospect of an error in their decision, serious though it be, or have scruples as to whether they have been too severe or too lax

140 *Ius Decretalium*, III, n. 782; Icard, *Praelectiones Iuris Canonici*, II, 479.

141 XL (1923), 311.

in the light of the objective reality of the facts. A wide margin of allowance must be left for the external and relative the local and social reasons motivating a refusal or a non-refusal of Christian burial. The privation of Christian burial is a grave sanction, but the gravity is external and relative.[142]

It is for these reasons also that the authors note that the law on the privation of Christian burial must yield at times to the force of necessity, when the evil that would be caused by its enforcement would be greater than that caused by its breach. Therefore, when, in a particular case, scandal, harm to the Church, the alienation of souls from the Church, injury to the peace of the faithful, or any other evil greater than the granting of Christian burial to one not worthy, is to be feared, it may be tolerated that Christian burial be conceded, in whole or in part, so long as there is involved no contempt of religion or of the Church.[143]

As *l'Ami du Clergé* well states, in the condition of the decadence of morals for which our times are noted, toleration in the matter of Christian burial may be necessary at times *ad vitanda maiora mala* and for the greater general good of the Christian society.[144]

142 *L'Ami du Clergé*, XL (1923), 309; *Dictionnaire Encyclopédique de la Théologie Catholique*, XXII, 4, 6; Schaaf, "*Catholic Burial and Public Sinners*"—*The Ecclesiastical Review*, XCV (1936), 191 ff.

143 Cocchi: "Quum leges ecclesiasticae cum gravi incommodo non urgeant quando ex denegatione sepulturae ecclesiasticae damnum tranquilitati fidelium merito timetur, tolerari potest ut sepultura ecclesiastica concedatur, dummodo absit contemptus religionis vel scandalum fidelium."—*Commentarium in Codicem*, V. n. 71; Beste: "Putamus in casu concreto ubi scandala, odia in Ecclesiam, alienationes animarum ab Ecclesia, perturbationes, aliaque gravia incommoda prudenter pertimescenda sint . . . cadaver defuncti licito inferri posse, namque ubi eadem est ratio eadem debet esse dispositio iuris."—*Introductio in Codicem*, p. 603; . . . secluso contemptu religionis, si ministro in aliqua casu immineat grave damnum vel malum ex denegatione sepulturae ecclesiasticae, licitum est aliquem ritum funebrem vel etiam totum ordinem exsequiarum peragere, quoniam lex ecclesiastica cum proportionate gravi incommodo non obligat, ex can. 2205, §§ 2 et 3."—*op. cit.*, p. 605; Vermeersch-Creusen, *Epitome*, II, n. 550; Many, *De Locis Sacris*, n. 221.

144 XXXVIII (1921), 554.

Chapter III

THOSE TO WHOM CHRISTIAN BURIAL IS DENIED

Canon 1239, § 1. Ad sepulturam ecclesiasticam non sunt admittendi qui sine baptismo decesserint.

Article 1.—The Exclusion of the Unbaptized

The Code forbids the granting of Christian burial to the unbaptized. There is no need to insist on this point for the Code is but repeating the ancient and universal law of the Church that she will have nothing to do in death with those with whom she had no communion in life,[1]

For the unbaptized, however, the privation of Christian burial is not a penalty, not the effect of personal culpability, but the result of a lack of a right. The unbaptized have no rights in the Church.[2]

The Legislator, nevertheless, expressed his solicitude for them by ordering that a special place be set aside for their burial in an unblessed portion of the cemetery.[3]

Since the doubtfully baptized, whether the doubt be of law or of fact, are not certainly unbaptized, they are allowed the benefit of the doubt about their baptism and are not denied Christian burial by this canon.[4] Therefore those who have been baptized conditionally while they were unconscious, as well as others whose baptism remains doubtful, may be granted Christian burial. This provision includes doubtfully baptized children who die before the sacrament can be administered absolutely.[5]

1 C. 1, C. 24, q. 2; c, 12, X, *de sepulturis*, III, 28.

2 Canon 87; *L'Ami du Clergé*, XL (1923), 309.

3 Canon 1212; Wernz-Vidal, *Ius Canonicum*, IV, n. 561, not. (16).

4 Cappello, *Summa Iuris Canonici*, I, n. 183; II, 759; Brys, "De Sepultura Ecclesiastica"—*Collationes Brugenses*, XXV (1925), 160; Coronata, *De Locis et Temporibus Sacris*, n. 256; *Palestro del Clero*, X (1931), 137.

5 Santi, *Praelectiones Iuris Canonici*, Lib. III, tit 28, n. 16.

Unbaptized infants of Catholic parents may not be granted Christian burial. The Code has made no allowance for them, as it has, for example, for catechumens, but retains the traditional prohibition.[6] If, however, they die in the mother's womb, and the mother dies also, the child may be granted Christian burial together with its mother.[7]

Brys holds that a growing practice is that of permitting an unbaptized child which died with its mother, though it actually be born, to be given Christian burial along with the Catholic mother, but only in a particular case and only to avoid greater difficulties, that could not otherwise be avoided.[8]

It is also held now that one who grants or compels the granting of Christian burial to unbaptized infants of Catholic parents does not thereby incur the penalties laid down in canon 2339 for the violation of the prohibition of Christian burial.[9]

Moreover, it is now the common opinion that the burial of an unbaptized infant does not violate the cemetery.[10]

Possibly the main reason for not granting Christian burial to unbaptized children is that it is of no avail to them. Canestri states that the prayers and rites of Christian burial are, by their nature, meant to assist the soul in purgatory;

6 Reiffenstuel, lib. III, tit. 28, n. 77; Wernz, *Ius Decretalium*, 781; Many, *De Locis Sacris*, 217.

7 Wernz-Vidal, *Ius Canonicum*, IV, 586; Brys, *Collationes Brugenses*, XXV (1925), 163; Cocchi, *Commentarium in Codicem*, V, 70; Coronata, *De Locis et Temporibus Sacris*, 256.

8 *Collationes Brugenses*, XXV (1925), 160, 161; Arregui, *Summarium Theologiae Moralis* (11. ed., Bilboa, 1930), n. 913; Ojetti, *Synopsis Rerum Moralium* (Romae, 1911-1914), n. 3702; Mahoney, "Burial of Unbaptized Infants"—*The Clergy Review*, XVIII (1940), 544, 546.

9 Coronata, *Institutiones Iuris Canonici*, IV, n. 1966; Cappello, *De Censuris*, n. 402.

10 Coronata, *Institutiones Iuris Canonici*, II, n. 748; Gasparri, *Tractatus de SS. Eucharistia* (2 vols., Parisiis, 1897), I, n. 253; Many, *De Locis Sacris*, n. 217; Vermeersch-Creusen, *Epitome*, II, n. 489; Augustine, *A Commentary*, VI, 38; contra: Ciprotti, "De consummatione Delicti"—*Apollinaris*, VIII (1935), 391.

thus the ceremony is fruitless when performed over those who will not go there in any event.[11] Further, Canestri detects a distinct danger and an abuse in the granting of Christian burial to unbaptized children. For, he states, it contradicts the dogma of the necessity of baptism to remove original sin; it is opposed to the doctrine that sanctification is acquired by individual effort and loyalty to Christ, not by heredity; parents will become careless and postpone Baptism if allowed to forget its vital necessity.[12]

Article II.—The Exception for Catechumens

Canon 1239, § 2. Catechumeni qui nulla sua culpa sine baptismo moriantur, baptizatis accensendi sunt.

The Code settled the ancient controversy over whether catechumens could be granted Christian burial. It states that those who die unbaptized through no fault of their own are to be treated as if they were baptized. If, however, they die unbaptized through their own negligence or fault, they are to be denied Christian burial.[13] Therefore a would-be convert who dies before he is baptized, if the lack of baptism is in no way due to his fault or negligence, is to be given Christian burial.[14]

Article III.—The Exclusion of Notorious Apostates

Canon 1240, § 1, 1°. Ecclesiastica sepultura privantur: notorii apostatae a christiana fide.

Apostasy from the faith, the first delict mentioned in canon 1240, is fittingly considered in the primary place, for it is a crime that is both most ancient and most reprehensible.[15]

11 "An concedenda sit sepultura ecclesiastica infantibus defunctis sine baptismo"—*Apollinaris*, IV (1931), 129, 130.

12 *Loc. cit.*

13 Vermeersch-Creusen, *Epitome*, II, n. 547; Blat, *Commentarium Textus*, Lib. III, Pars II, n. 103.

14 Augustine, *A Commentary*, VI, 152.

15 " . . . gravissimum crimen reputabatur et gravissimis poenis puniebatur . . . "—Coronata, *Institutiones Iuris Canonici*, IV, n. 1859.

An apostate is defined by the Code[16] as a baptized person who has completely abandoned[17] the Christian faith.[18] To fall under this category therefore one must desert or abandon the Christian faith as such.[19] It would not be sufficient to deny one or the other dogma, for that would constitute not apostasy but heresy. The two delicts differ, however, only in degree; both are of the same substance in that they denote a defection from the faith: the one an entire, the other a partial defection.[20]

The act of abandonment or desertion must be externally manifest, a condition necessary for the commission of a delict,[21] and moreover, it must be notorious,[22] that is, so publicly certain as to the fact and the guilt that it can in no way be concealed or excused, or, as Chelodi explains it, both the act and the wrong intention must be so apparent to the people that there is no room left for even a slight doubt about either.[23]

The element of notoriety thus limits greatly the number who will incur the penalty of the denial of Christian burial because

16 Canon 1325, § 2.

17 Regardless of the fact that he may still accept some truths that are Christian, if he does not believe them as a Christian.—Ciprotti, "De Consummatione Delicti," *Apollinaris*, VIII (1935), 231.

18 " . . . a christiana fide quae est divina et catholica . . . "—Blat, *Commentarium Textus*, Lib. V, n. 151; canon 1323, § 1.

19 "Totalis defectio a religione christiana per baptismum suscepta,"—Coronata, *op. cit.*, IV, n. 1856; " . . . a fide christiana recessio,"—St. Thomas, *Summa*, II-II, q. 12, a. 1; Suarez, *De Censuris*, disp. 21, sec. 2, n. 3.

20 Wernz-Vidal; " . . . apostasia et haeresis in sua temeritate substantialiter non differunt."—*Ius Canonicum*, VII, n. 382; Ciprotti, "De Consummatione Delicti,"—*Apollinaris*, VIII (1935), 231; Coronata, *Institutiones Iuris Canonici*, II, n. 911; IV, n. 1856.

21 Canon 2195, § 1; "Cogitationis poenam nemo patitur,"—c. 14, D. 1, *de poenitentia.*

22 Canon 1240, § 1, n. 1: "*Notorii* apostatae." The addition of the requirement of notoriety to the delicts mentioned in canon 1240, § 1, n. 1, is new in the Code; the old law did not require all of them to be notorious.—*Rit Rom. Paul V., De Exsequiis. Cf.* above p. 58.

23 " . . . aliis verbis si tum actio tum intentio mala ita aperte coram populo est probata, ut de utroque elemento delicti, obiectivo et subiectivo, ne levi quidem dubio locus est."—*Ius Poenale*, 4.

of the delict of apostasy, for it requires that the guilt of the delict be so obvious either *de iure* or *de facto* that it cannot be disputed.[24]

The margin of license is correspondingly lengthened by the same factor. Thus one may be guilty of the sin of apostasy by abandoning the faith in his mind, without committing a delict, for the penal law does not punish thoughts but acts, and requires an external manifestation of the internal sin to constitute a delict.[25] Further, one could be guilty of an external act of apostasy—therefore guilty of the delict—and be punished by the *ipso facto* excommunication that is inflicted upon that delict[26] without simultaneously incurring the penalty of the denial of Christian burial as a *notorious* apostate. The delict will not become notorious by the mere external manifestation of the sinful mind, but only when to all appearances the delinquent knew he was breaking the law and willed to do it.[27]

It is precisely this notoriety of the act, and not the mere fact of apostasy with the resultant excommunication, that canon 1240, § 1, n. 1, penalizes.[28] Thus it is the notorious external appearance of the delict that is punished by the denial of Christian burial, a fact which leaves some room, at least theoretically, for the law to operate inequitably. For example, some one may have publicly committed a deed which to all appearances implied beyond all doubt his internal denial of the faith, yet in his heart he may not at all have denied it. The law, given the external act, will presume the guilt to

24 Cocchi: "Ad notorietatem delicti in genere requiritur ut: hoc vel in facto vel in iure ita certum sit ut nulla amplius discussione ageat . . . "—*Commentarium in Codicem*, VIII, n. 1.

25 "Item qui animo a fide totaliter defecerit quin tamen id ullo modo manifestaverit, reus est peccati apostasiae; non est reus delicti apostasiae."—Coronata, *Institutiones Iuris Canonici*, IV, n. 1856; Vermeersch-Creusen, *Epitome*, III, n. 513.

26 Canon 2314, § 1, n. 1; Cappello, *De Censuris*, n. 208

27 Chelodi, *Ius Poenale*, n. 4.

28 Rossi, *La "Sepultura ecclesiastica" e l' "Ius Funerum,"* p. 131.

exist[29] and the delict is imputed to him until he proves his innocence. Since there was no internal consent, there is no excommunication, but there will be a denial of Christian burial if the external act appears notorius, i.e., so blameworthy that no one can doubt that he must have known that what he did was against the law and yet he chose to do it. Obviously, the possibility is almost negligible, but the fact remains that one may be punished under the penalty because of purely circumstantial evidence which is so strong in the external forum that it cannot be doubted.

It is quite immaterial whether the notorious apostate joins a sect, such as Judaism, Mohammedanism, or other non-Christian religious bodies, or whether he associates himself with quasi-religious or anti-religious societies, e.g., the deists, modernists, pantheists, indifferentists, materialists, free-thinkers or the like. He may not go over to any other belief or sect of unbelief but remain an atheist or unbeliever.[30]

Neglect of, or indifference towards, one's religious duties does not of itself, even if it extends over a considerable period of years, constitute apostasy or abandonment of the faith, according to the general opinion.[31] However, it does not seem improbable that in certain circumstances indifference or neglect could constitute the delict of apostasy, and result in a notorious apostasy. For according to the law[32] apostasy may

[29] Canon 2200, § 2.

[30] Brys, "De Sepultura Ecclesiastica,"—*Collationes Brugenses*, XXV (1925), 242; Coronata, *Institutiones Iuris Canonici*, IV, nn. 1856, 1862; Ciprotti: "De Consummatione Delicti,"—*Apollinaris*, VIII (1935), 281; Werns-Vidal, *Ius Canonicum*, VII, n. 380.

[31] "Ut apostatae non sunt habendi qui officia religionis penitus et a longo tempore negligunt."—Brys, "De Poenis Latae Sententiae,"—*Collationes Brugenses*, XXXIII (1933), 186; Idem, "De Sepultura Ecclesiastica,"—*op. cit.*, XXV (1925), 242; Vermeersch-Creusen, *Epitome*, II, n. 335; III, n. 513; Cocchi, *Commentarium*, VIII, n. 135; Coronata, *loc. cit.;* Cappello, *De Censuris*, n. 208; *L'Ami du Clergé*, XLII (1925), 816; Rossi, *op. cit.*, p. 131.

[32] Canon 1325, § 1.

be implied at times by the failure to profess one's faith.[33] It is therefore not always necessary that one actually have left the faith before one can *appear* to have left it. Canon 1325, § 1, clearly permits an implication of apostasy to arise from circumstances; i.e., whenever one's silence, subterfuge, or very manner of acting will be considered as an implied denial of the faith. It is noteworthy that one has no control over such a circumstantial obligation to make some demonstration of one's faith. The circumstances will dictate the obligation. The failure to respond to the demand of the law will permit the implication of the denial of faith to stand as a warranted assumption.

In the light of this legal obligation to profess one's faith when circumstances will reflect the failure to do so as equivalent to apostasy, it seems entirely possible that the neglect of one's religious duties, especially Sunday Mass and "Easter Duty" which are so strongly binding on all the faithful, could in certain conditions make one appear in the eyes of the public as an apostate, and even as a notorious apostate. Circumstances alone can determine when and where and how such neglect will imply the denial of faith in one community, while the same neglect will not do so in another. Thus in a community in which the practice of the faith is widely neglected by the people, it is not likely that one's neglect of even the severely sanctioned duties of religion would be considered by the community the result of his rejection or abandonment of the faith. On the contrary, in a community where the faith is devoutly cherished and practiced by all, one's continued absence from Mass and the sacraments, as observed by all, could easily give rise to the assumption by the community that the faith has been deserted.[34]

33 "Fideles Christi fidem aperte profiteri tenentur quoties eorum silentium, tergiversatio, aut ratio agendi secumferrent implicitam fidei negationem, contemptum religionis, iniuriam Dei vel scandalum proximi."—Canon 1325, § 1.

34 Teodori: "Non sunt veri apostatae qui religionis officia penitus negligunt, si a fide animo non defecerint: verum qui externe a fide

Such a one finds himself in the position wherein an obligation arises by law [35] to prove his faith, for his actions are being considered as an implied denial of it.

He would not be notorious, however, until it was publicly known that he realized that his manner of acting, that is, his neglect of his religious duties, constituted in the circumstances an implied denial of his faith, and he nevertheless had continued to neglect them. If he were known to have been warned by the priest of the need to counteract the public impression, and yet acted as if ignoring the warning, he could hardly escape being considered a notorious apostate.

It is not likely that the situation would arise in a larger community than the one taken as an example. For in a town or city where there are several parishes, it is difficult to know for certain whether one is habitually neglecting his religious duties; it is still more difficult to establish the neglect as being notorious. Nevertheless, in a closely organized parish anywhere it may happen that someone will be publicly known to have abandoned the practice of his religious duties for over a long period of time, despite the repeated efforts of his family, his pastor, and others to make him see the error of his ways. Once it is generally known that he realizes that his neglect is interpreted as abandonment of the faith and yet he gives no evidence of changing his manner of acting, he may quite easily appear to be a notorious apostate.

Apart from the question of when indifference in the practice of the faith will make a person appear to have incurred the penalty of the privation of Christian burial as a notorious apostate, the probability that the concession of Christian burial to one who has not practiced his faith over a long period of years will cause grave scandal to the faithful will dictate its refusal.

deficit, etiam interne defecisse praesumitur, et ita in foro externo ut apostata retinetur." *Apollinaris*, IV (1931), 432; Cappello, *De Censuris*, n. 208; Chelodi *Ius Poenale*, n. 57; Coronata, *Institut. Iuris Can.*, IV, n. 1856.

35 Canon 1325, § 1.

It must be remembered that circumstances have so much to do both with notoriety and with the obligation to publicly profess one's faith, that the case cannot be stated absolutely, but will vary with the circumstances of times, places and persons.

The case just considered is not to be confused with that in which there is no call for a profession of one's faith, where the non-profession of it or even the concealment of it may be justified by the fact that there is no appearance of having denied or abandoned it. Thus, one on a visit to Soviet Russia, or similar places, could conceal his Catholic faith without his action's being interpreted as a denial or desertion of the faith. But if there is a positive and generally-conceived appearance of abandonment, arising from the public reaction to one's manner of acting, then a demonstration of one's faith, especially by the return to one's religious duties, is called for by the law. To remain passive in the face of this circumstantially imposed legal demand is to appear deliberately to allow the implication of apostasy to stand. One who is known to realize that he is generally considered an apostate and who nevertheless makes no effort to dispel such an impression can hardly escape being considered a notorious apostate.

Apostasy may also be publicly and notoriously implied by the act of inserting in one's will a desire for a civil or non-religious funeral, if such an act were known to have been done deliberately by the deceased with full knowledge of what it implied. Any attempt to assume that such a serious and publicly known act of contempt is not notorious appears entirely unwarranted in view of the self-evident culpability of the act.[36]

Principles for practice: Christian burial is not to be refused to anyone merely because he is an apostate. He must be a *notorious apostate,* that is, one whose apostasy is publicly known, unconcealable and inexcusable. If there is any doubt about the apostasy, the notoriety of the apostasy, or the signs

[36] Buvée declares that one who dies after an unretracted public request for civil burial is to be denied Christian burial as a public sinner.—*Ministère Paroissial,* n. 818.

of repentance, let the case be referred to the local Ordinary if there is time. If the doubt persists, the Ordinary, or the priest, if the matter could not be referred to the Ordinary, is to grant Christian burial, taking all care to see that scandal is obviated.[37] If great scandal cannot be prevented, the divine law will overrule the benefit of the doubt which the positive ecclesiastical law has allowed, and Christian burial must be denied, for the good of souls and their edification must be preferred to an individual right.[38]

Scholion: Is one who was baptized a Catholic, but brought up in no religion whatever, an apostate? Although such a one may materially be considered as an apostate in view of canon 2200, § 2, he cannot be classified as a *notorious* apostate, i.e., as one who is publicly known to have realized that he did wrong in not practicing the faith, and to have abandoned it despite his possessing such a knowledge. If such is not the case, and it would very rarely be such in the case suggested, he is not to be considered as having incurred the penalty of the denial of Christian burial under canon 1240, § 1, 1°, as a notorious apostate. The fact that he has never been in external communion with the Church and the great probability of scandal in the parish, if he is granted Christian burial, would seem to preclude his being granted the honor. But since it is not certain that he has incurred the penalty, there seems to be no reason why he could not be given Christian burial in some place where he is not known, and where there would be no scandal.

Article IV.—The Exclusion of Notorious Members of Heretical Sects

Canon 1240. § 1, 1°: Ecclesiastica sepultura privantur: . . . sectae haereticae notorie addicti.

Christian burial is denied those who notoriously belonged to a heretical sect. This is a large departure from the old law

[37] Canon 1240, § 2.

[38] Vermeersch-Creusen: "Bono enim privato salus et aedificatio multorum praeferri debent."—*Epitome*, II, n. 335.

which refused Christian burial to all heretics.[39] The new law penalizes not heretics in general but such as notorioulý belong to a heretical sect.[40]

From its position between the terms *"apostatae"* and *"schismaticae,"* the term *"haereticae"* appears to refer to those religious societies that are composed of baptized people who are banded together in organized denominations independently of the Catholic Church, and who do not profess the whole Christian faith as it is revealed by God and defined by His Church.[41]

In regard to determining when or how one is considered to belong to a heretical sect, the authors allow a rather broad interpretation to be followed. Coronata observes that no special rite of admission can be set down as the determinant of such a fact, nor is any such determinant necessary to establish the delict.[42] A person may be considered to belong to such a sect when his name is inscribed in the membership registers—and this would seem the most conclusive evidence—or when he frequents their services and meetings, or even simply defends the heretical tenets of the sect.[43] Ciprotti believes that a person may be considered a member simply by his joining the sect, regardless of the form of affiliation, and by his appearing as a member of the congregation.[44] While Blat

[39] *Rit. Rom.*, tit, VI, c. 2; cf. Historical part, p. 58.

[40] Vermeersch-Creusen: "Nota peccatum haeresis a sepultura ecclesiastica non excludere, nisi notoriam apostasiam constituat vel *notoria ascriptione* sectae compleatur."—*Epitome*, II, n. 549; Brys: "Unde iam non solum delictum haeresis aut schismatis ut sic punitur privatione sepulturae ecclesiasticae, sed sola *notoria adscriptio* alicui sectae."—*Collationes Brugenses,* XXV (1925), 242; Coronata: "Non sufficit ad poenam professio haeresis aut schismatis etiam publica, sed requiritur *adscriptio* sectae haereticae vel schismaticae."—*Institutiones Iuris Canonici*, II, n. 816.

[41] Cfr. Blat, *Commentarium*, Lib. III, pars II, n.104; *Epitome*, III, n. 513; Cappello, *De Censuris*, n. 211; Coronata, *Institutiones Iuris Canonici*, nn. 1856, 1858; *The Catholic Encyclopedia,* XIII, 675.

[42] *Institutiones Iuris Canonici*, IV. n. 1947.

[43] Coronata, *op. cit.*, I, n. 570.

[44] "De Consummatione Delicti,"—*Apollinaris*, VIII (1935), 233.

explains *"addicti"* by simply adding *"ut socii,"* [45] Vermeersch-Creusen believe that a person becomes a member by the inscription of his name, or by repeated and public participation in the religious services of the sect, or by the public assertion of his affiliation with the denomination.[46]

But for the incurring of the penalty of the privation of Christian burial it is necessary that one be *notoriously* a member of the sect, that is, that he appear in the eyes of the people to have known that his adherence was forbidden by the Church and to have chosen to adhere to the sect nevertheless. His delict must appear so blameworthy that no doubt of it exists.[47]

According to the new law, therefore, two things must be evident before one can be considered to have incurred the privation of Christian burial for this offense; he must have committed a *delict*,[48] and the delict must be notorious.

The great mitigation in the new law in contrast to the severity of the old [49] is appreciated only when it is realized to what lengths the new law allows one to fall into errors in matters of faith before he is deprived of Christian burial.

Thus a person may unfortunately, not only think heretical thoughts, but openly profess them and thereby externalize his error; if he knows that what he is professing is contrary to the faith, he is guilty of the delict of heresy.[50] The delict is

[45] *Commentarium Textus*, Lib. III, pars II, n. 108.

[46] *Epitome*, III, n. 513.

[47] Cocchi: " . . . ita certum sit ut nulla amplius discussione egeat."—*Commentarium in Codicem*, VIII, n. 1.

[48] Canon 1240, § 1 states the conditions under which a person contracts a penalty, and therefore punishes only delicts: external and morally imputable violations of the law. Ayrinhac-Lydon: "The violation must have the conditions of knowledge and freedom to be morally imputable, for the Church does not intend to punish one who is not really guilty or a deed for which one is not responsible."—*Penal Legislation*, n. 2.

[49] "Omnes Haeretici"—*Rit. Rom.*, pre-Code ed., Tit. VI, c. 2.

[50] Canon 1325, § 2; Mac Kenzie: "The very essence of heresy is that it be a knowing, deliberate, presumptuous rebellion against the authority of God and the Church in the matter of religious belief or profession."

notorious if his guilt is publicly known and indisputable. Yet, he would not incur the penalty of canon 1240, § 1, 1°, for he has not joined a sect. If he is warned by the ecclesiastical authorities of his error and ordered to repent of it, and refuses to do so, he is guilty of another delict, that of obdurate heresy.[51] Even then he is not to be denied Christian burial by reason of the rule contained in canon 1240, § 1, 1°.[52] But when he becomes a notorious member of a heretical sect, no matter by what fact his affiliation is effected—it suffices that he publicly appear as such—he commits still another delict and the most serious of all.[53] He has, as Schmidt declares, committed formal contempt of the Catholic Church;[54] or, as Maroto states, his joining of a non-Catholic sect leaves no doubt of his defection from the faith.[55] Wernz-Vidal remark that the joining of a heretical sect simply aggravates the gravity of the delict of heresy and makes it notorious.[56]

In remarking that the act of becoming a member, or that the fact of being a member, of a heretical sect is *of itself* a notorious delict, Wernz-Vidal have assumed too much. But it must be admitted that the case of a Catholic's publicly adhering to a heretical sect without its appearing a notorious delict would be the exception. Any Catholic who knows his faith at all knows that such an act is forbidden.

Only after this final act of desertion is the penalty mentioned in canon 1240, § 1, 1° incurred *ipso facto* by the delin-

—*The Delict of Heresy*, p. 40; "It is only when the sin of heresy is externalized that the individual is guilty of a delict and subject to the external forum of the Church and punishable by the penalties contained in the penal legislation . . ."—*op. cit.*, p. 33.

51 Vermeersch-Creusen, *Epitome*, III, n. 513.

52 But if the fact is of public kowledge, he would in all probability be included in the category mentioned in canon 1240, § 1, 6°, namely under the heading of a public and manifest sinner.

53 "Si sectae acatholicae nomen dederint vel publice adhaeserint, ipso facto infames sunt . . ." canon 2314, § 1, 3°.

54 "De Vi Verborum Acatholicae, etc."—*Apollinaris*, V (1932), 80.

55 *Apollinaris*, III (1930), 614.

56 *Ius Canonicum*, VII, n. 389.

quent.[57] The great lengths to which the Legislator has gone in the new law to spare the Catholic this penalty—a fact that cannot but emphasize the severity of the sanction—is thus demonstrated.

The question now arises whether the law excludes from Christian burial those who belong to a heretical sect without knowing that they are acting against the law of the Church. Among these are included all those who were baptized in a heretical sect and have lived as non-Catholics in good faith or in inculpable ignorance, whether or not they have practiced the tenets of the sect. It may readily be granted that the case of their asking for Christian burial would be a rare one. It may likewise be conceded that the granting of Christian burial to them would in all probability occasion such unavoidable scandal among the faithful that on that score alone it would have to be denied them. The legal difficulty remains: if they ask it, on what legal ground are they to be refused it? It is not enough to show that they are considered heretics in the external forum, regardless of their good faith or ignorance. The canon refuses Christian burial only to those who *notoriously* belong to a heretical sect, and that means that they must appear both to know that what they do is against the law of the Church, and to will to do it nevertheless, and therefore be guilty of a formal delict. It has been seen above[58] that a notorious delict and a material delict are not to be confused, for the latter, by its nature, cannot have the qualities of the former. A delict cannot be considered notorious only in a material sense, for it must always appear formal, else it ceases to be notorious.

The old law included material heretics with formal heretics under the all-inclusive *"Omnes haeretici;"* the new law does not include material heretics when it mentions those who

[57] Since it is a *latae sententiae* penalty, there is no need for a condemnatory sentence, and the penalty is incurred at the moment the delict is completed.—Cappello, *De Censuris*, n. 4.

[58] Cf. Concept of notoriety, pp. 181 ff.

notoriously belong to a heretical sect. Moreover, canon 1239, § 3, declares that *all the baptized* are to be given Christian burial unless they are deprived of it by law.[59]

Has the Legislator, in granting such an extension of clemency in the new law, left a gap through which all heretics who do not notoriously belong to a heretical sect can enter to claim Christian burial? Such a conclusion can be drawn from the fact that there is a very great difference between the old and the new law in regard to the inflicting of this penalty on the grounds of heresy, and that the multitude of non-Catholics who may belong to a heretical sect in good faith or inculpable ignorance, or who are not even material heretics of any sect, seem to be exempt under the law that requires the delict to be *notorious*—which is but another term for its being, to all appearances and beyond a doubt, *formal*.

Canon 2200, § 2 is not of any assistance here. That canon but presumes guilt to be present in an external violation of the law sufficiently to render such a violation an imputable delict. But a *notorious* delict cannot be merely presumed to be such, for the assumed presence of guilt in a notorious delict is not based upon a presumption of law, but upon evidence in the act itself that is so certain, both as to the fact of the violation and as to the guilt of the delinquent, that there can be no doubt concerning either.[60] Therefore it cannot be maintained that the external adherence to a heretical sect, whether only through the fact of baptism, or through the constant practice of the heretical religion, constitutes a person as a *notorious* member of such a sect through the presumption of canon 2200, § 2. When the *delict* is *notorious,* there is no need for the presumption of canon 2200, § 2, for the evidence of the culpability and guilt of the delict is so clear that a judge could pass sentence immeditely on the strength of it without

[59] "Omnes baptizati sepultura ecclesiastica donandi sunt, nisi eadem a iure priventur."

[60] Chelodi: " . .. aliis versis si tum actio tum intentio mala ita aperte coram populo est probata ut de utroque elemento delicti, obiectivo et subiectivo, ne levi quidem dubio locus est."—*Ius Poenale,* n. 4.

any recourse to a judicial trial,[61] which action would certainly seem most presumptuous in the case in which the delict is only a material one, consisting in the external violation of the law and the presumption of canon 2200,§ 2, that is, a delict in which the actual guilt of the delinquent may be entirely unknown.

Does canon 1240, § 1, 6°, in reference to public sinners, apply? It seems not, for while it is very evident that Catholics who are publicly professing heresy would easily come under such a heading, because of the scandal and harm that their action would necessarily occasion for the faithful,[62] the same reasons do not hold for the external acts of non-Catholics. It seems an undue straining of the term "public sinner" to make it include the multitude of baptized non-Catholics who in ignorance of the fact that what they do is contrary to the law of the Church, and acting in good faith, adhere to a heretical sect, or who profess heretical beliefs, regardless of whether they claim a sect or not. In our country their action is not publicly scandalous or publicly sinful. As MacKenzie points out: "Even in our own nominally Christian country, there are many who belong to some non-Catholic sect or to no sect at all, . . . who hold erroneous tenets with *every evidence* [63] that they do so in entire good faith and honest acceptance of what seems to them the truth.[64] And Van Hove states that heretics who are such in blameless ignorance, or in good faith, are excused from formal sin.[65]

61 Coronata, *Inst. Iuris Can.* IV, n. 1564; Cocchi, *Commentarium in Codicem*, VIII, 1.

62 Cf. Cappello, *Summa Iuris Canonici*, II, n. 760; Coronata, *Institutiones Iuris Canonici*, II, n. 816; Brys, "De Sepultura Ecclesiastica"—*Collationes Brugenses*, XXV (1925), 212, 213.

63 The italics are inserted here by the writer.

64 *The Delict of Heresy*, p. 39; idem: "In our day as in St. Paul's, 'How shall they call on Him in Whom they have not believed? or how shall they believe Him of Whom they have not heard? and how shall they hear without a preacher?'—Romans, X: 14." " . . . this absence of personal guilt is not so much the exception as the rule."—*Loc. cit.*

65 *De Legibus Ecclesiasticis*, (Mechliniae: Dessain, 1930), p. 201.

How can such people be considered public sinners by a presumption of law in the face of such overwhelming evidence that they are not public sinners? Granted the external violation, the law presumes internal guilt until innocence is proved; but when the innocence is of public knowledge, it seems an entirely unjustified appeal to canon 2200, § 2 to hold that it still presumes the guilt. The purpose of that canon is to render a delict imputable and chargeable; the public knowledge of a person's innocence, in an individual case, should be more than sufficient to overthrow the presumption, which stands only in the absence of proof to the contrary.[66] Therefore it is only by a forced interpretation that material heretics can conceivably be considered canonically as public sinners.

The presentation of a practical case will serve to bring the difficulty out of the realm of speculation into the field of facts. Let it be supposed that a non-Catholic, baptized a Methodist, but never having practiced the tenets of that sect, or having abandoned it, marries a Catholic, *positis ponendis.* He is known in the community as a good husband and father. He educates his children in the Catholic school and supports the parish through his children's and his wife's contributions as well as through his own attendance at the parochial social functions. He may even be a frequent attendant at Mass with his family. At his death, his wife rightly or wrongly—and most probably because she does not want a Protestant or civil funeral—asks for Christian burial for her husband. On what legal ground is the pastor to refuse it? He knows that canon 1239, § 3, orders the granting of Christian burial to all the baptized unless they are denied it by law. He knows also that canon 1240, §1, lists the deliquents that are punished by law with the privation of Christian burial. Among them are mentioned two that possibly may apply to the case: notorious members of a heretical sect, and persons who live in a state of public sin.

[66] "Posita externa legis violatione, dolus in foro externo praesumitur, donec contrarium probetur."—Canon 2200, § 2.

But this man falls under neither of these two classifications. He cannot be considered a notorious member of a heretical sect, since it is not publicly known that he persisted in belonging to such a sect amid any realization that he was disobeying the law of the Church. Notoriety in any heretical affiliation connotes a formally heretical adherence to a sect and signalizes an unconcealable and inexcusable breach of the law. He is not a public sinner, for the whole community can testify that he was not living in sin, much less in public sin. To hold that the law, by canon 2200, § 2, will, despite clear evidence of innocence, continue to presume anyone to be either a notorious member of a heretical sect or a public sinner, or any other of the delinquents listed in canon 1240, is a distortion of legal reasoning. Presumptions yield to facts, and the law cannot be held to insist on presuming what the facts prove false. Moreover, such reasoning is in conflict with the obvious desire of the Legislator to apply this penalty only for the most grave offenses, a desire that is manifest in the many mitigations effected in the present law.[67]

The difficulty remains. Is the baptized non-Catholic entitled to Christian burial in the absence of certain evidence that he has incurred the penalty of its privation? The law orders that Christian burial must be given to *all the baptized* unless by law they are denied it. It has been demonstrated how unlikely it is that he has incurred the penalty of privation. The only solution of this difficulty lies in understanding the words *"omnes baptizati"* of canon 1239, § 3, as applying to Catholics alone. That such an interpretation is not unreasonable will now be demonstrated.

The first evidence that in the matter of Christian burial the Legislator had only Catholics in mind appears in the fact that throughout the whole of Title Twelve in the Third Book of the Code, which is concerned exclusively with Christian

67 "*Notorii* apostatae; excommunicati *post sententiam;* cum *aliqua* signa poenitentiae; *permanente dubio* . . . cadaver sepulturae tradatur." —cf. *Rit. Rom.*, tit. VI, c. 2, pre-Code and post-Code editions.

burial, there is no mention of any others than *the faithful.*[68]

The same preoccupation with only the faithful is evident in the comments of the authors. Blat declares that the right to Christian burial belongs to each of the *faithful,* unless canon law refuses it.[69] Wernz-Vidal states that Christian burial may, and must, be granted to all and to only the faithful.[70] The same authors declare that *Catholic* burial is a symbol of ecclesiastical communion which is not to be conceded to outsiders and to those who in life were freely separated from communion with the Church.[71] Brys likewise includes Christian burial among the rights that the Church owes to the *faithful.*[72] And in reference to the obligation of the liturgical rites of Christian burial, he notes that each and all of the *faithful* are bound to honor and respect these rights; no *Catholic* may refuse them.[73] Beste limits canon 1239, § 3, which grants Christian burial to all the baptized, to include only the *faithful.*[74]

The pre-Code authors also spoke of this right as one that belonged only to the faithful. Wernz declared that one of the meanings of Christian burial was simply that of interment in a place reserved for the burial of the *faithful* departed.[75] Reif-

68 "*Fidelium* corpora sepelienda sunt,"—canon, 1203; "Cadavera *fidelium* sepelienda sunt . . ."—canon 1205; " . . . cadavera *fidelium* . . ." —canon 1215; *Rit. Rom.:* "nemo Christianus in Communione *fidelium* defunctus . . .", tit. VI, c. 1, n. 24.

69 "Competit ius cuilibet fideli, nisi . . . " *Commentarium Textus,* Lib. III, Pars II, n. 102.

70 "Digna et legitima subiecta, quibus a ministris Ecclesiae licite sepultura ecclesiastica concedi potest et debet, generatim sunt omnes et soli fideles baptizati."—*Ius Canonicum,* IV, n. 585."

71 "At signa Communionis ecclesiasticae, in funeribus catholicorum consueta, non concedit extraneis et iis, qui dum viverent a communione Ecclesiae voluntarie se separarunt."—*Ius Canonicum,* IV, n. 565.

72 *Collationes Brugenses,* XXV (1925), 161.

73 *Op.cit.,* XXVI (1926), 318.

74 "Fideles igitur habent ius ad sepulturam et ideo enuntiatur regula in canone—'nisi eadem a iure expresse priventur' . . . "—*Introductio in Codicem,* p. 604.

75 *Ius Decretalium,* III, n. 780.

fenstuel laid down the rule that all and only the *faithful* may be buried in blessed ground,[76] and Santi even more specifically stated that Christian burial is the exclusive right of *Catholics*.[77]

Furthermore, the terminology of canon 1223, in the same Title XII, is quite as all-inclusive as that of 1239, § 3: "*Omnibus licet nisi expresse iure prohibeantur, eligere ecclesiam funeris aut coemeterium sepulturae.*" Yet the only exceptions thereafter mentioned in the law are in regard to cardinals, bishops, residential beneficiaries, religious, novices, etc. Obviously the Legislator has in mind only the faithful.

Further, it is entirely reasonable to suppose that, while the Legislator punishes notorious adherents to a heretical sect with the denial of Christian burial, he has such an act in mind not so much as a mere physical fact but rather as a consummate act of heresy, one that implies a preceding series of acts leading away from the true faith to notorious separation. This implication of a series of acts would indicate that persons born or baptized in heresy are not contemplated by canon 1240, § 1, 1°.

The commentators likewise stress in their discussion the evil of gradual *defection* from the faith, the partial *departing from*, or the *deserting*, or the partial *denial* of the faith that was once held, when they note that neither the sin of heresy nor the mere membership in a sect is sufficient to constitute the delict delineated in canon 1240, § 1, 1°, but that the delict must be completed by *notorious* membership.[78]

[76] Lib. III, tit. 28, n. 76.

[77] "Sepultura prout ius dicit est ius competens omnibus catholicis pie demortuis ut eorum cadavera in loco sacro et religioso sepeliantur."—*Praelectiones Iuris Canonici*, lib. III, tit. 28, n. 11; " . . . locus auctoritate episcopi benedictus in quo cadavera catholicorum sepeliuntur."—Ibidem, n. 1.

[78] Vermeersch-Creusen: "Nota *peccatum haeresis* non excludere a sepultura ecclesiastica nisi *notoriam apostasiam* constituit vel *notoria ascriptione sectae compleatur*."—*Epitome*, II, n. 549; Beste: "Ergo non sufficit solum peccatum vel delictum haeresis et schismatis neque merum factum adhaesionis sectae; sed requiritur ut *delictum compleatur ad-*

Another indication of the Legislator's sole preoccupation with those who have had the faith and have defected from it, is to be found in the reply of the Pontifical Commission for the Interpretation of the Code to a question submitted to it in regard to the meaning of the expression: "Those who belonged to a non-Catholic sect" in canon 542.[79] It was asked whether this adherence to a non-Catholic sect referred to those born and baptized in such a sect, or to Catholics who had fallen away from the faith and joined such sects. The reply was: in the negative to the first part; in the affirmative to the second part.[80] Although this reply was in regard to a particular canon and applies to that canon alone, the fact cannot be overlooked that in the use of the term the Legislator had only Catholics in mind.

Finally, if the Legislator had non-Catholics as well as Catholics in mind in canon 1240, § 1, 1°, there is no escaping the conclusion that the canon, applied to Catholics, would denote an increase of forbearance and a greater toleration of possible errors in faith than the old law allowed;[81] applied to non-Catholics, it would become a wide-open door for such of them as may not be included under *"notorie addicti sectae haereticae"* to lay claim to the right of Christian burial.

If the canon is considered as applicable only to Catholics, it offers little difficulty, both in regard to applying it to the individual Catholic, and in regard to its comprehensiveness as a measure that will include all those Catholics whose heresy

scriptione sectae coniuncta cum *notorietate.*"—*Introductio in Codicem,* p. 604; Mahoney, "Ecclesiastical Burial"—*The Clergy Review,* XVIII (1940), 547; Coronata, *Institutiones Iuris Canonici,* II, n. 816.

[79] "Invalide ad novitiatum admittuntur: Qui sectae acatholicae adhaeserunt."

[80] P.C.I., 16 oct. 1919—*AAS,* XI (1919), 477; "Pontificalis Commissio declaravit hos tantummodo, i.e., *a fide apostatas,* canonis verbis comprehendi."—anonymous commentator in *Ius Pontificum,* III (1923), 66.

[81] The old law punished *all heretics* with the privation; the new law greatly limits this to only those who notoriously belong to a heretical sect.

is public. For, as the authors state,[82] if they are not penalized by canon 1240, § 1, 1°, for having joined a heretical sect, their public heresy will very probably include them under canon 1240, § 1, 6°, as public sinners, whose actions are scandalous and harmful to society.

But if the new law were considered as applicable to baptized non-Catholics, it would offer great difficulty, both as regards including the individual non-Catholic under its penal provisions, and as regards the inexplicably broad gap between the all-inclusive old law—*"omnes haeretici"*—and the explicit and very considerable restriction of this in the new law—*"sectate haereticae notorie addicti"*—a disparity that would permit non-Catholics who are heretics only in a material sense, or who are members of no sect, to demand Christian burial as a right which is theirs by baptism.

Now, as to canon 1240, § 1, 6°, it is much more difficult to know when a baptized non-Catholic is guilty of a canonical delict than to know the same about a Catholic. The presumptions are usually in favor of the former's not knowing that he was breaking the law;[83] but they are also usually against the Catholic who may generally be supposed to have known that he was breaking the law. The Legislator has generously provided for cases that are doubtful by declaring that if the doubt persists the dubiously guilty person is to be granted Christian burial.[84] Here again the very provision that represents an act of clemency for Catholics would allow a breach through which all non-Catholics whose delict is dubiously dis-

[82] Cappello, *Summa Iuris Canonici*, II, n. 760; Coronata, *Institutiones Iuris Canonici*, II, n. 816; Brys, "De Sepultura Ecclesiastica,"—*Collationes Brugenses*, XXV (1925), 242-243.

[83] "These vindictive penalties may indeed be executed against any heretic whose *delict* can be *judicially proved.*" (italics added),—MacKenzie, *The Delict of Heresy*, p. 51.

[84] "Occurrente praedictis in casibus aliquo dubio, consulatur, si tempus sinat, Ordinarius; *permanente dubio*, cadaver sepulturae ecclesiasticae tradatur, . . . "—canon 1240, § 2.

cernible could enter in order to present their *title* and *claim* for Christian burial.

It is hard to believe that the Legislator intended so great an indulgence. Rather his concession of an increased clemency in regard to Christian burial was meant to be granted only to those who were baptized in the Catholic faith, and consequently the mitigations in the common law are equally to be referred to those so baptized.

The conclusion is inevitably reached that the Legislator did not have non-Catholics in mind in this legislation. Consequently, either they benefit from a *lacuna legis,* or they are quite adequately excluded elsewhere in the law. It will now be demonstrated that the Legislator did not overlook them or intend to include them in the mitigation of the law for the faithful, for they can be considered to be excluded under canon 87.

Their privation under canon 87 does not stand in opposition to the import of the final clause of canon 1239, § 3: *"nisi a iure priventur,"* for the privation of Christian burial according to canon 87 is incurred not as a penalty but suffered as a lack of a right. Canon 1240, § 1 is a penal canon that particularizes the meaning of the *last* part of canon 1239, § 3; canon 87 simply places a limitation on the words *"omnes baptizati"* which occur in the *first* part of canon 1239, § 3.

> **Canon 87: Baptismate homo constituitur in Ecclesia Christi persona cum omnibus Christianorum iuribus et officiis, nisi, ad iura quod attinet, obstet obex, ecclesiasticae communionis vinculum impediens, vel lata ab Ecclesia censura.**

By valid baptism one is made a person in the Church of Christ with all the rights and duties of Christians, unless, with regard to the rights, there intervenes an obstacle impeding the bond of ecclesiastical communion.

It must be remembered that baptism is considered in canon 87 in regard to its juridical, not its theological effects. It will be considered here also only in so far as it confers legal capacity upon the recipient, not in its conferring of grace and the infused virtues.[85]

By baptism, then, one does not necessarily inherit all the rights of a Christian, for the canon makes an exception in their regard. It states that they will not be received when there is an obstacle impeding the bond of ecclesiastical communion. Ecclesiastical communion may be defined as union with the faithful, the communion in one faith, the sharing in the same sacraments, the subjection to the same prelates, especially to the Roman Pontiff, who is the center of unity.[86]

It is in this lack of communion that baptized non-Catholics lose the rights of their baptism, for ecclesiastical communion arises from affiliation with the *visible* Church and from the external profession of the Catholic faith.[87] This affiliation with the visible Church does not necessarily flow from baptism, for one may be legally considered as baptized *outside* the Catholic Church.[88] Thus it may happen that persons may be validly baptized in the Church of Christ, yet, because of either their own intention, or that of their parents, or that of the minister of baptism,[89] they may lack full ecclesiastical communion with the faithful because of their having been affiliated with a non-Catholic sect in the very act of the conferring of their baptism.[90]

85 Coronata, *Institutiones Iuris Canonici*, I, n. 119.

86 Wernz-Vidal, *Ius Canonicum*, II, n. 1.

87 Cappello: " . . . [baptismus] baptizatum formaliter deputat *externae Ecclesiae catholicae communioni*."—*De Sacramentis*, vol. III, pars I, n. 411; Ayrinhac-Lydon: "The intention must be to make the baptized person a member of the visible Church."—*Marriage Legislation* (New, revised edition, New York: Benziger Bros., 1938), n. 133.

88 Cappello: "Unde triplex criterium seu fons assignari potest e quo desumitur utrum baptismus *in Ecclesia catholica* an *extra Ecclesiam catholicam* collatus censeri debeat: . . . " *loc. cit.*

89 Ayrinhac-Lydon: "Who are baptized in the Catholic Church? . . . The intention of the parents or guardians with reference to infants, or of adults in receiving baptism, or of the minister in conferring it, is the decisive norm. The intention must be to make the baptized person a member of the visible Church."—*Marriage Legislation*, n. 133.

90 Cappello: "Nisi contrarium constet, semper praesumitur ministrum

While such an affiliation will in no way detract from their incorporation into the Church of Christ, it will place an obstacle to their full communion with the faithful and to the reception of the rights that accompany this ecclesiastical communion. This loss of rights does not conflict with their being in the Church of Christ by baptism, because, although they have received juridical personality and capacity by valid baptism, they have lost the *exercise* of this personality or capacity; for a person may, indeed, remain a *subject* of the Church without being a *member* of it, for the connotation of *subjection* is more comprehensive than that of *membership*.[91]

It is precisely as non members of the visible Church that baptized non-Catholics lose the rights that arise from full communion with the faithful. As Ayrinhac states, this separation from ecclesiastical communion implies separation from the body of the Church and the loss of those rights and privileges which are attached to external membership, although it does not necessarily imply separation from the soul of the Church or the loss of all supernatural means of salvation.[92]

Moreover, the lack of communion may exist entirely without fault on the part of the one baptized. Blat compares the impediment to ecclesiastical communion as it exists in those who are baptized in a heretical or schismatical sect to that sustained by one who is deprived of receiving the sacrament

in baptismo conferendo habere intentionem aggregandi subiectum religioni quam ipse profitetur . . . . si parentes tradunt infantem baptizandum ministro acatholico aut cuidam laico cum expressa intentione illum aggregandi sectae acatholicae, filius habendus est baptizatus *extra Ecclesiam catholicam*. . . . in dubio de intentione parentum vel tutorum, si agitur de infante, *eorum religio catholica vel acatholica attendenda est*."—*loc. cit.*

91 Coronata: " . . . semel autem haec capacitas seu personalitas obtenta amitti nequit; *potest vero amitti ipsius personalitatis exercitium:* quo casu tamen homo baptizatus *subditus* Ecclesiae manet, licet forte *membrum* eius esse desinat; ex quo constat *notionem subditi latius quam notionem membri patere*."—*Institutiones Iuris Canonici*, I, n. 119.

92 *General Legislation* (New York, Bensiger Bros., 1923), 185.

of Matrimony, not through his own fault, but by even a maliciously inflicted dissability such as that of impotency suffered at the hands of an enemy.[93] Coronata, likewise, states that this separation from the body of the faithful may be entirely without personal fault.[94] Therefore, the same author continues, heretics and schismatics, (understanding those who are baptized in a heretical or schismatic sect), even though they are in good faith and escape the censures against heresy and schism, are bereft of many rights.[95] And Wernz-Vidal, in fixing the status of those who are baptized in a non-Catholic sect, declare that while they belong to the Church, they are, as sheep wandering from the fold, *de facto* separated from it.[96]

In the light of these considerations of the effect of the obstacle which is created by baptism in a non-Catholic sect upon the bond of ecclesiastical communion, it seems entirely reasonable to conclude, with Coronata, that one of the rights lost, or rather suspended, by such baptism is that of Christian burial.[97]

The loss of rights by non-Catholics because of canon 87 was strikingly emphasized by a reply of the Holy Office to a question as to whether non-Catholics may impugn the validity of their marriage in the Church court. The Holy Office replied

93 *Commentarium Textus*, II, n. 5.

94 "Obex tunc habetur cum impedimentum ex ipsa rei natura, independenter a iure positivo humano, vel ex separatione a corpore fidelium oritur . . . "—*Institutiones Iuris Canonici*, I, n. 119.

95 *Loc. cit.*

96 *Ius Canonicum*, II, n. 1.

97 "Potest tamen ipsum ius ad sepulturam ecclesiasticam ipso actu baptismatis suspendi, si nempe, baptisma ab haeretico haeretice recipiatur."—*De Locis et Temporibus Sacris*, 254; Reilly assumes the exclusion of non-Catholics from Christian burial as a manifest fact: "It is manifest that this right to ecclesiastical sepulture pertains only to Catholics. Heretics, even though they have been validly baptized in their own sect, have no claim to the services of the Church."—*Ecclesiastical Sepulture in The New Code of Canon Law*, The Catholic University of America, Canon Law Studies, no. 18, Washington: The Catholic University of America, 1923, p. 104.

that they could not and that the Code, especially canon 87, was to be observed.[98] Vermeersch, in commenting on this reply of the Holy Office, declared that the reference to canon 87 related to their incapacity due to their lack of ecclesiastical communion.[99] And an unsigned commentator in the *Ius Pontificium,* in regard to the same reply of the Holy Office, more explicitly explained that the *"obex,"* or impediment, always affects a non-Catholic by the very reason of his being a non-Catholic: *in acatholico ratione acatholicitatis,"* and that it flows implicitly from the common law, as the Holy Office expressly stated.[100]

It is significant that the reply of the Holy Office does not speak of the impediment as applying to only one right: that of impugning a marriage before the ecclesiastical court, but implies for non-Catholics a general incapacity to enjoy the rights that arises from the common law, especially from canon 87.

This incapacity for the enjoyment of the rights of the faithful seems confirmed also by the very nature and purpose of Christian burial. It is stated in the Roman Ritual that there should be retained the sacred ceremonies and rites with which the Church through immemorial custom has surrounded the obsequies of her faithful children. The Ritual points to these services as a *mystery of religion, a symbol of Christian piety* and a salutary aid to the *faithful departed.*[101]

It is therefore altogether equitable that non-Catholics should not be entitled to Christian burial, which is not only an honor and a privilege that the Church reserves for those of her children who have been faithful in their obedience and loyal in their communion with her, but also a source of edification to the faithful and, when refused, a warning to the delinquent.[102]

98 *AAS,* XX (1928), 75.

99 *Periodica, XVII-XVIII* (1928-1929), 55.

100 *Ius Pontificium,* VIII (1928), 9.

101 *Rituale Romanum,* tit. VI, c. I, *De Exequiis,* n. 1.

102 Santi: "Et quidem prohibitio sepulturae ecclesiaticae procedit ex duplici capite: scilicet, *quidam excluduntur ob defectum communionis*

This unworthiness of non-Catholics to receive Christian burial is thoroughly in accordance with tradition, beginning in the ancient times with the famous principle enunciated in the fifth century by Pope St. Leo the Great: *"Nos autem quibus viventibus non communicavimus, mortuis communicare non possumus,"*[103] incorporated in the decretal law by Innocent III in the thirteenth century,[104] and repeated in the nineteenth by Pope Gregory XVI, when he wrote to a bishop in Bavaria, protesting at the offering of a solmn funeral Mass for the late Protestant Queen, and declaring that it was entirely against "Catholic tradition" to grant such honors to one outside the fold.[105]

Conclusion

It is believed that canon 1240, § 1 is not to be considered as applicable to non-Catholics for the following reasons:

a. The canon is clear when applied to Catholics, but is extremely complicated when any effort is made to apply it to non-Catholics.
b. The use of *"fidelium"* in canons 1203, 1205, 1215, and its implication throughout Title XII argues the exclusion of non-Catholics.
c. Canon 1223, § 1, parallel in structure with canon 1239, § 3, allows all, unless they are expressly forbidden to do so by law, to select the church of their funeral and the cemetery of their burial. Yet nowhere there is no mention of the exclusion of non-Catholics in this matter.
d. The response of the Pontifical Commission in regard to canon 542, and the reply of the Holy Office with regard to the lack of right on the part of non-Catholics to be plaintiffs in an ecclesiastical court apply the same principle in relation to analogous cases.
e. Non-Catholics appear excluded by tradition.

ecclesiasticae; alii autem in poenam."—*Praelectiones Iuris Canonici, Lib.* III, tit. 28, n. 16.

[103] *Epist. CLXVII—MPL*, LIV, 1205, 1206.

[104] C. 12, X, *de sepulturis*, III, 28.

[105] Epist. "*Officium*," 16 febr. 1842—*Fontes*, n. 499.; cf. also *Analecta Iuris Pontificii*, IV (1860), 2390, 2391.

f. Non-Catholics appear excluded by the common law, especially canon 87.

Article V.—The Exclusion of Notorious Members of Schismatical Sects

Canon 1240, § 1, 1°. Ecclesiastica sepultura privantur: . . . sectae schismaticae notorie addicti.

Christian burial is denied to those who belong notoriously to a schismatical sect. A schismatic is anyone who, after receiving Baptism, and while retaining the name of Christian, refuses obedience to the Supreme Pontiff or refuses to communicate with the members of the Church who are subject to the Sovereign Pontiff as its head.[106] A schismatical sect is an organized religious body that is characterized by the same refusal of obedience and the same disavowal of communion.[107]

The commentary on members of heretical sects includes all that may be said about schismatics in regard to their inclusion in canon 1240. The canon penalizes Catholics who not only fall away from their obedience to the Supreme Pontiff as to the head of the Church, but formalize this error by joining, or by being publicly associated with, a schismatical sect. The association must be a notorious fact, that is, both unconcealable and inexcusable.

Article VI.—The Exclusion of Notorious Members of Masonic Sects and Similar Societies

Canon 1240, § 1, 1°. Ecclesiastica sepultura privantur: . . . sectae massonicae aliisve eiusdem generis societatibus notorie addicti.

Christian burial is denied those who are notorious members of Masonic sects or other societies of a like nature.

The Legislator repeats the term "sect," although it has already been used in this same number of canon 1240, § 1;[108] for, whereas there it meant religious bodies, here it refers to so-

106 Canon 1325, § 2.

107 Blat, *Commentarium Textus*, Lib. III, n. 104.

108 "Sectae haereticae aut schismaticae. . . ."

cieties that are not primarily religious. The use of both "sect" and "societies" eliminates any necessity of a strict differentiation between the two terms.[109]

Membership in a Masonic or kindred society may be established in many ways. Coronata states that it may be clearly evident from one's frequenting their meetings or gatherings, or even by publicly defending the tenets of the society.[110] He further notes that it is not the insertion of one's name but rather the public adherence to the sect that is of primary importance in the present consideration. Thus no special rite of induction into the membership of the society is necessary; it is sufficient that in the judgment of the public one be recognized as having membership in the society.[111] Ciprotti likewise declares that it is sufficient that one be publicly accounted as a member of the sect.[112]

The Holy Office decreed that a person cannot be considered as an occult Mason if he frequents Masonic meetings; if he wears their emblems and insignia publicily; and, in general, if he shows that he is a member of Masonry.[113] Therefore there need be no exact determination of how one became associated

109 Quigley writes: "Throughout the legislation concerning condemned societies, the Holy See uses indiscriminately the terms *societas* and *secta*."—*Condemned Societies*, p. 64. In the same tenor Cappello states that under the name of *sects* the pontifical constitutions have always understood *societies* or *aggregations*.—*De Censuris*, n. 297. Thus the distinction between *sect* and *society* that Coronata makes when he notes that a society is not necessarily a *sect*, is immaterial in the present discussion. He himself notes that others do not make the same exact distinction between the terms.—*Institutiones Iuris Canonici*, IV, n. 1948, p. 380, not. 8.

110 *Institutiones Iuris Canonici*, I, n. 570. IV, n. 1948; Schmidt, *Apollinaris*, IV (1931), 562, 563.

111 *Institutiones Iuris Canonici*, IV, n. 1947; Vermeersch-Creusen, *Epitome*, III, n. 513.

112 "De Consummatione Deliciti"—*Apollinaris*, VIII (1935), 233.

113 S.C.S. Off., 27 iun. 1838—*Coll. S.C.P.F.*, n. 868.

with the society, for in the matter of Christian burial it is the public appearance that counts.[114]

The Code, differing from the Constitution *"Apostolicae Sedis,"* [115] uses the term *Masonic* in a general sense, as a generic term, not as a proper name. It is also noteworthy that there is no mention of *condemned* Masonic sects.[116] It thus appears to be a presumption of law that all Masonic societies conspire against the Church and the State, and this presumption prevails until it is overthrown by evidence to the contrary. This presumption is evident from the generic use of the term "Masonic" without any qualification.[117] Therefore any sect that is Masonic is *ipso facto* included in canon 1240, § 1, 1°. Included also are women's organizations and auxiliaries which are affiliated with the men's socities, according to a decision of the Apostolic Delegation.[118]

As a consequence of this presumption there is no room for any distinction between Masonic sects, with regard to their malice or lack of malice, their harmful divisions and their harmless ones. As Pope Leo XIII pointed out, while it may readily be granted that some members of these societies may be entirely in good faith and without animosity toward the Church, it remains true that the evil of Naturalism is fostered and spread by the progress and growth of Masonry.[119]

114 For a discussion of when this point may be important, especially in regard to the incurring of censures for such affiliation, cf. Quigley, *Condemned Societies*, pp. 52-55.

115 12 oct. 1869—*Fontes*, n. 552.

116 Augustine, *A Commentary*, VI, 154. Condemned societies will be considered in connection with the treatment of "public sinners" in general, mentioned in number six of canon 1240, § 1.

117 Coronata: "Et praesumptio quidem iuris est quod quaelibet associatio, sive ordo, sive *logia* massonica, revera contra Ecclesiam vel Statum machinatur, cuiusvis ritus ea sit."—*Institutiones Iuris Canonici*, IV, n. 1948; Cappello, *De Censuris*, n. 298; Chelodi *Ius Poenale*, n. 71. Chelodi notes that affiliated sects are included.

118 Apostolic Delegation, Washington, D. C., Aug. 2, 1907; answer no. 15, 352-C. Cf. Quigley, *Condemned Societies*, p. 67; Fanning, "Secret Societies," *Catholic Encyclopedia*, XIV, 74.

119 Encycl. "*Humanum genus*," 20 apr. 1884—*Fontes*, n. 591.

And the Plenary Council of Latin America (1899), insisting that it but seconded the condemnations of Popes Pius IX and Leo XIII, condemned the proposition that Masonry may be harmless in one place and injurious in another, because of differences of beliefs, aims, and actions.[120] Therefore if the sect or society is Masonic, its members are thereby designated as delinquents in the sense of canon 1240, § 1, 1°.

Just what constitutes a society similar to Masonry is a matter of controversy. Some believe that two elements are essential: the secrecy by which the members or the leaders are bound, and the element of subversiveness according to which such societies plot and conspire against the Church or the State or both.[121]

Others believe that secrecy is not an essential element of the character of societies similar to Masonry, although it may be a *de facto* characteristic. According to this opinion, the one essential element is the working against the Church or the State. In support of this theory Quigley stresses the fact that the Holy See has declared that the societies condemned in the pontifical constitutions are to be understood as those which work against the Church or the State, regardless of whether their members are bound by an oath of secrecy.[122]

Any additional end of the society, be it a charitable, a philanthropic, or a cultural one, does not change this status. Nor need the pernicious end be a professed aim of the society. It suffices that *de facto* the society conspires against the ecclesiastical or the civil authority.[123]

Other societies may be condemned by various reasons, but unless they have this characteristic quality they are not to be

[120] Quoted by Wernz-Vidal, *Ius Canonicum*, VII, n. 448, p. 482, not. 12.

[121] Vermeersch-Creusen, *Epitome*, II, n. 535; Brys, *Collationes Brugenses*, XXV (1925), p. 243, not. (2).

[122] *Condemned Societies*, p. 56.

[123] Coronata, *Institutiones Iuris Canonici*, IV, n. 1949; Wernz-Vidal, *Ius Canonicum*, VII, n. 448; Cappello, *Summa*, III, n. 615; *De Censuris*, n. 297; Chelodi, *Ius Poenale*, n. 71.

considered as falling within the classification of Masonry.[124] Likewise, no matter how other societies may differ from Masonic sects in appearance, if they reflect this characteristic they are Masonic in the canonical sense of the term.[125]

The term "machinate," which is that commonly used to describe this subversive activity, means "to conspire," "to plot," "to work against," either formally, when following out an aim of the society, or *de facto,* when such an aim is not expressly professed or contained in the statutes of the sect. This opposition to lawful authority may be open or secret, by words, deeds, or writings.[126] Teodori [127] and Wernz-Vidal [128] add that the subversive acts of the individual members must be attributable to the society; the members must so act because of their affiliation with the sect. The activities of individuals who plot against the Church or State will not condemn a society unless these activities are part of a policy that is pursued by the society as such.

The scope of the activities that are to be included under the term "to work against" or "to oppose" the Church is very broad. Most authors agree that it includes all activities against the teaching, the authority, the constitution, the rights and prerogatives of the Church and against ecclesiastical persons in their official status, but not as private individuals.[129]

124 Coronata, *loc. cit.*

125 Teodori, "Secta Massonica"—*Apollinaris,* IV (1935), 580.

126 Cappello, *De Censuris,* n. 300; Wernz-Vidal, *Ius Canonicum,* VII, n. 448; Teodori, *loc. cit.;* Coronata, *Institutiones Iuris Canonici,* IV, n. 1950; Augustine, *A Commentary,* VIII, 342.

127 *Loc. cit.*

128 *Ius Canonicum,* IV, n. 586.

129 Coronata declares that such a society is any society which arouses opposition to the doctrines, the authority, the power, the constitution, the rights and privileges of the Church, or towards ecclesiastical persons as such, *even by open political opposition* as well as by secret machination.—*Institutiones Iuris Canonici,* IV, nn. 1949, 1950; Cappello, *De Censuris,* n. 209; Teodori, *loc. cit.;* Sole, *De Delictis et Poenis,* p. 269; Wernz-Vidal, *Ius Canonicum,* VII, n. 448; Cipollini, *De Censuris,* n. 140; Cerato disagrees with those who believe that attacks on the Church's

Quigley[130] notes that the Holy See gave a very definite idea of the broad scope intended to be included in its condemnations when it declared that Masonic sects included all those societies that act *in any way* against the Church.[131] Likewise, the scope of those societies that must be considered Masonic in character because of their efforts to undermine the State is acknowledged to be just as broad, according to the wording of the same decree of the Holy Office.

Only the legitimate authority, however, is to be understood, for a government that is not legitimately the ruler of the people has no claim to support since it has no right to rule. Nevertheless, a *de facto* government, a usurper, may have the right to a limited obedience, because the common good may best be served by rendering such obedience.[132]

Under the heading of Masonic sects there are certainly included all those societies which work to overthrow the existing legal government in simple persuance of their avowed policy of opposition to all forms of organized government, such as the nihilists, anarchists, bolshevists, and communists in the strict sense.[133] Included also are those societies which propose revolutionary ideas under the guise of cultural aims even as apart from political action. As Coronata points out, their *cultural* aim is to prepare future *political* leaders who will enforce their subversive ideas.[134] This technique has been proved to be that of some so-called "liberal" societies which mask their

doctrine and on ecclesiastical persons are included.—*Censurae Vigentes*, n. 109.

130 *Condemned Societies*, p. 65.

131 ". . . eae omnes intelliguntur quae adversus Ecclesiam vel Gubernium sibi *aliquid* proponunt . . ."—S.C.S. Off., 5 aug. 1846—*Fontes*, n. 889.

132 Cappello, *De Censuris*, n. 299; Teodori, *Apollinaris*, IV (1931), 580; Ciprotti, *Apollinaris*, VIII (1935), 402; Pastoral Letter of the Bishops of Belgium, Oct., 1940—N.C.W.C. News Release, 2/10/41-M.

133 Coronata, *Institutiones Iuris Canonici*, IV, n. 1950; Chelodi, *Ius Poenale*, n. 70.

134 *Loc. cit.*; Pistocchi, *I Canoni Penali*, n. 103.

true purposes behind the screen of purely theoretical discussions. In reality they often are subversive groups, composed of a revolutionary and ruling minority that uses the prominence and reputation of so-called "intellectuals" as a front.

Not to be included, however, are those societies that openly and legitimately propose and work for a change in the form of government, e.g., royalist societies in a democracy, and republican societies in a monarchy. So long as they are not conspiratory in character, use only legal means to attain their ends, and work openly and legitimately for only a change in the form of rule and government, they cannot be included among those societies which work against the State.[135]

Some difficulty may be experienced in determining when socialistic societies will be included among Masonic societies. Chelodi believes that they certainly are not included if they seek simply a legitimate change of government and pursue their aims within legal bounds.[136] Cappello points out that many who join socialistic societies do so in the belief that they are joining purely political movements. In practice it will have to be determined in the individual case whether a real society exists, that is one with leaders and an organization; whether over and above the social improvement of the working classes the society also works for the overthrow of the Church or State.[137]

The requirement of the canon that one *notoriously* belong to a Masonic or similar society will eliminate most of the difficulty in regard to determining, in an individual case, the granting or the refusing of Christian burial. For if there is any doubt about the nature of the society, the doubt operates in favor of the deceased. Moreover, public opinion may quite easily determine whether the society is considered inimical to the Church or the State, so that the element of scandal may determine the course to be adopted.

135 Coronata, *loc. cit.;* Cappello, *De Censuris*, n. 299; Chelodi, *Ius Poenale*, n. 71.

136 *Loc. cit.*

137 *De Censuris*, n. 298; Brys, *Collationes Brugenses*, XXV (1925), 243.

The distinction must always be borne in mind that only Masonic or similar societies are included in canon 1240, § 1, 1°. Other condemned societies are not here considered; their notorious members will be considered under the general classification of public sinners in canon 1240, § 1, 6°.

Besides the sects nominally Masonic, or those that enroll only Masons, Quigley includes only the Knights Templars among the societies that are of Masonic type. He holds that the Knights of Pythias and the Odd Fellows, though they are condemned societies, are not condemned as Masonic.[138]

It is not certain, therefore, how many or exactly what societies are Masonic in type; nor need it be in order to determine whether Christian burial is to be granted or denied. Because of the requirement of notoriety, any doubt whether the society is Masonic or of Masonic character, or any doubt whether the deceased was known to have belonged to such a society and to have known that he was so affiliated contrary to the law of the Church, will render his affiliation non-notorious and *entitle* him to Christian burial, if the doubt persists and all likely scandal is precluded.[139] Moreover, any sign of repentance will suffice to entitle him to Christian burial.[140] The probability of ensuing scandal will play a large part in determining the course to be followed in a doubtful case. Public opinion in a parish will have its own conception of the nature of the society in question, namely whether it is inimical to the Church or to the State.

Christian burial must be denied to even a repentent Mason if Masonic insignia or emblems are to be displayed at the

138 *Condemned Societies*, p. 66. His opinion is also that of Ayrinhac-Lydon, *Penal Legislation*, n. 258; Coronata, *Institutiones Iuris Canonici*, IV, n. 1951.

139 Chelodi: A delict is notorious " . . . aliis verbis, si tum actio, tum intentio ita aperte coram populo est probata ut de utroque elemento delicti, obiectivo et subiectivo, ne levi quidem dubio locus sit."—*Ius Poenale*, n. 4.

140 Canon 1240, § 1.

funeral or upon the body.[141] This prohibition applies regardless of whether the deceased or his relatives are to blame for their display.[142] Christian burial is likewise denied if a Masonic service is to be held. No delegation of Masons with their emblems is allowed. If they assist as individuals, no flaunting of their insignia may be tolerated.[143]

It may be tolerated to have Masons act as pall-bearers, provided that the prohibition against the wearing of emblems and the display of insignia is duly observed.[144]

Article VII.—The Exclusion of the Excommunicated and the Interdicted, After a Declaratory or Condemnatory Sentence

Canon 1240, § 1, 2. Ecclesiastica sepultura privantur . . . excommunicati vel interdicti post sententiam condemnatoriam vel declaratoriam.

The old law refused Christian burial to those who were publicly excommunicated with the major excommunication and to those who were interdicted by name, or who were in an interdicted place, so long as the interdict lasted.[145]

The Code has terminated many controversies regarding the circumstances in which Christian burial is to be denied because of excommunication or interdict. It is denied only to those whose excommunication or interdict has been proclaimed in a sentence by a judge,[146] who therein either inflicts the penalty or declares it to have been already incurred.[147] This is equivalent to an excommunication or interdict *by name.*

Excommunication or interdict by name is more than merely

141 S.C.S. Off., 2 dec. 1840—*Fontes*, n. 844.

142 *Loc. cit.*

143 S. C. S. Off., 5 iul. 1878—*Fontes*, n. 1056.

144 S.C.S. Off., 1 aug. 1855—*Coll. S.C.P.F.*, n. 1116.

145 *Rit Rom. Pauli V, De Exsequiis;* cf. Historical synopsis, p. 58.

146 Blat states that the sentence is to be a judicial one "*proprie dicta.*" —*Commentarium Textus*, Lib. III, n. 104.

147 Those who have incurred a *latae sententiae* excommunication or interdict are therefore not included. Lydon, *Ready Answers in Canon Law* (New York: Benziger Brothers, 1934), p. 98.

a *personal* penalty, for while the latter may be incurred *ipso facto delicti,* the former must always be the result of a sentence or a decree.[148]

Therefore there is no longer any difficulty as to when one is to be denied Christian burial because he has been excommunicated or interdicted. Unless a sentence or decree naming both the delinquent and the penalty has been passed, it cannot be said that the delinquent has incurred the penalty of the privation of Christian burial according to canon 1240, § 1, n. 2. It may be added that such a sentence occurs quite rarely in modern times.[149]

Since notoriety of law is an obviously required characteristic of these cases, it may well be asked whether one who is excommunicated or interdicted without such a sentence, but whose penal status is notorious *de facto,* retains his right to Christian burial. Forfeiture of this right seems altogether likely, for even though such a person would not be denied Christian burial on the grounds of his excommunication or interdict, he cannot but be classified as a public sinner whose contempt for his excommunication, demonstrated by his lack of effort to remove it, is a scandal to the faithful.[150]

A difficulty that is new with the Code is the question of whether only a part of Christian burial is denied by the incurring of the interdict *ab ingressu ecclesiae.* Wernz-Vidal feel that the interdict *ab ingressu ecclesiae,* by its very nature, prevents only that part of Christian burial that is to be performed in a *church.*[151] The opinion of these authors represents

148 Coronata, *Institutiones Iuris Canonici,* IV, n. 1796.

149 Brys, *Collationes Brugenses,* XXV (1925), 244; Chelodi, *Ius Poenale,* n. 36.

150 Coronata, *Institutiones Iuris Canonici,* II, n. 816; Cappello, *Summa,* II, n. 760; Roberti, *De Delictis et Poenis,* n. 336; Blat, *Commentarium Textus,* Lib. III, Pars III, n. 173; *L'Ami du Clergé,* XXXVII (1920), 447; Conran, *The Interdict,* p. 133.

151 *Ius Canonicum,* VII, n. 308; also, Ayrinhac-Lydon, *Penal Legislation,* n. 141.

a change from the pre-Code view that held that this type of interdict prevented Christian burial, as a whole.[152]

The correct opinion, however, as stated by Roberti, holds that one who has incurred this type of interdict is denied Christian burial in the same way as one who is interdicted personally,[153] that is, according to canons 2275, 4° and 1240, § 1, 2°, only after a condemnatory or declaratory sentence.[154] Moreover, Roberti adds, while some may try to limit or restrict the prohibition of Christian burial, as provided in this interdict, to the church ceremony alone, this cannot be done, for Christian burial is defined in canon 1204 [155] and must be understood in that sense whenever thereafter the term is employed.[156]

Roberti's opinion is supported by the text of the canon itself which clearly states that three separate rights are denied: the celebration of the divine offices in a church, the assistance at them and Christian burial.[157] Further, this opinion is entirely in agreement with the pre-Code notion of the complete denial of Christian burial, as a separate effect of the interdict ab *ingressu ecclesiae*.[158] Finally, the authors are agreed that

152 Wernz-Vidal note that this was commonly admitted.—*loc. cit.*

153 The interdict *ab ingressu ecclesiae* is a form of personal interdict: Cappello, *De Censuris*, n. 472; Chelodi, *Ius Poenale*, n. 41; Vermeersch-Creusen, *Epitome, III*, n. 478; Roberti, *De Delictis et Poenis*, n. 368; and also Wernz-Vidal, *Ius Canonicum*, VII, n. 308.

154 Roberti *De Delictis et Poenis*, n. 369; Coronata, *Institutiones Iuris Canonici*, IV, n. 1797; Conran: "Hence if one who is under personal interdict dies, he is not to be deprived of Christian burial by reason of his censure of interdict so long as no sentence has been issued against him."*The Interdict*, p. 133.

155 Blat, in reference to canon 2277: " 'aut ecclesiaticam sepulturam' secundum quod consistit ex can. 1204 . . . "—*Commentarium Textus*, Lib. V, n. 105.

156 *De Delictis et Poenis*, n. 369; Coronata: "Sepultura ecclesiastica hic intelligenda est de toto ritu sacro . . . "—*Institutiones Iuris Canonici*, IV, n. 1797.

157 Canon 2277.

158 Wernz-Vidal note this, declaring that formerly by this type of interdict Christian burial was denied both in the church and in the

the denial of Christian burial always includes the privation of both the rites and the burial in blessed ground.[159] Therefore there is no justification for trying to separate it in this matter alone, i.e., to allow burial in blessed ground and the rites at the grave, but to deny the church ceremony.

The reason for the difficulty of Wernz-Vidal is clear. They are among the authors who have retained the pre-Code conception of Christian burial as implying essentially the burial in blessed ground.[160] It is understandable, therefore, that they would distinguish between the church rites and the burial when they consider the former to be only an accompaniment of the latter. Their difficulty further arises from the change in the law in regard to cemeteries, which are now independent of the parish church, whereas formerly they were considered a part of it.[161] In conformity with this change, they have consistently modified what they admit was the pre-Code notion to the effect of the interdict *ab ingressu ecclesiae* in regard to Christian burial, namely, the full privation, to divide Christian burial, as they understand it, into two parts: the essential and the accidental. They believe that the essential part may still be had in view of the separation in the Code of the law on cemeteries from that on churches, while the accidental part—the church service—is denied.

Their error results from their recognizing one change in the new law, namely that in regard to cemeteries, while denying another, namely the legal definition of Christian burial. Those who have recognized both changes find that the denial of Christian burial is as complete in the new law as it was in the old in the matter of interdict *ab ingressu ecclesiae.*

cemetery.—*Ius Canonicum*, VII, n. 308. The Congregation of Bishops and Regulars likewise distinguished between the denial of Christian burial and the other two effects of the interdict *ab ingressu ecclesiae.*—"Neapolitana," 9 martii 1855—*Fontes*, n. 1971.

159 Cf. above, p. 125.

160 *Ius Canonicum*, VII, n. 451.

161 Maroto, *Apollinaris*, I (1928), 278; Roberti, *De Delictis et Poenis*, n. 357.

Therefore, although canon 2277 does not contain the qualifying clause: "ad normam can. 1240, § 1, 2°,"[162] it specifies the privation of *ecclesiastica sepultura,* and according to canon 1204 that is legally defined as consisting in both the liturgical rites and the burial in blessed ground.

Roberti's opinion that the privation of full Christian burial results from an interdict *ab ingressu ecclesiae* in the same way that it results from a personal interdict, of which the former is but a type, seems therefore correct. This opinion is further strengthened by the contradiction in the opinions of Wernz-Vidal who admit that the privation of Christian burial always includes the denial of all rites and ceremonies as well as the interment in blessed ground,[163] but who also wish to grant the interment and deny the church ceremonies in the matter of the privation of Christian burial as provided in the interdict *ab ingressu ecclesiae.*[164]

The new law has omitted the provision of the old for the denial of Christian burial to those who are in a place that is under interdict, so long as it may last.[165] The Code has, however, limited the solemnity of Christian burial during local interdicts. In a locality which is under interdict Christian burial may be had from any parish church, even if it is interdicted, or from the only church in a town, even if it is not a parish church, with the exclusion, however, of all external solemnity. There must be no music, chant, playing of the organ or ringing of the bells.[166] If, however, the interdict is laid upon a particular chapel of a church, no ecclesiastical rites, or actual burial, may take place therein.[167] The same

162 The clause appears in canon 2260, with regard to the effect of excommunication, and in can. 2275, with regard to the effect of personal interdict.

163 *Ius Canonicum* IV, n. 585.

164 *Op. cit.* VII, n. 308.

165 "Negatur sepultura ecclesiastica . . . iis qui sunt in lcoo interdicto, eo durante."—*Rit. Rom. Pauli V, De Exsequiis,* cf. above p. 58.

166 Canon 2271, 2°.

167 Canon 2272, § 1.

provision holds for an interdicted church that is neither a parish church, nor a cathedral, nor the only church in the place.[168]

If the cemetery is interdicted, full Christian burial in its three elements may be held, with this exception: in the cemetery itself there may be no ecclesiastical rites of any kind.[169] There is here a distinct curtailment of the substance of the notion of Christian burial, which, besides the rites at the house and at the church, provides for the rites at the grave.[170] There seems no reason, however, why the rites at the grave, which were forbidden during the interdict of the cemetery, could not be supplied after the raising of the interdict.[171]

There is a difference of opinion as to the exact nature of the "ecclesiastical rites" that are prohibited. According to Blat [172] and Coronata [173] this term denotes the omission of all *sacred* rites, that is, the prayers and ceremonies that are prescribed by the liturgy. It seems significant, however, that the Legislator uses the word *ecclesiastical* in canon 2272, § 2, where he is treating of the prohibition of the rites in the interdicted cemetery, while he uses the word *sacred* in the two canons immediately preceding and in the first part of the same canon. Roberti believes that this change of terms is not accidental but is a prohibition not only of the liturgical rites, but also of any prayers by the minister, any use of holy water, of candles, bells, incense, or even of the coverlet for the coffin.[174]

Article VIII.—The Exclusion of Suicides

Canon 1240, § 1, 3°. Ecclesiastica sepultura privantur . . . qui se ipsi occiderint deliberato consilio.

168 Canon 2272, § 3.

169 Canon 2272, § 2.

170 "Expletis in ecclesia exsequiis, cadaver tumulandum est ad norman librorum liturgicorum in coemeterio . . . "—canon 1231, § 1.

171 Augustine, *A Commentary*, VIII, 207.

172 *Commentarium Textus*, Lib. V, n. 100.

173 *Institutiones Iuris Canonici*, IV, n. 1701.

174 *De Delictis et Poenis*, n. 357.

At this point it must be recalled that it has already been established[175] that the following delicts listed in canon 1240, § 1, namely: suicide, dueling and cremation, are in effect to be understood as *notorious* delicts in view of the fact that the perpetrators of the delicts are implicitly included under the classification of *public and manifest sinners*.[176]

Therefore, over and above the requirements of the specific part of canon 1240, § 1, that treats of each, there is the additional requirement of notoriety. The delict will not be punishable with the privation of Christian burial unless it is notorious, that is, unless the delinquent was publicly known to have realized that he was breaking the law and was also publicly known to be fully responsible for the breach, to such an extent that there remains no doubt about either element of his act, the fact of the violation of the law or the guilt inherent in it. In the matter about to be considered, therefore, the act of suicide must be a notorious delict. The consequence of this is that no matter how culpable the suicide may be, if it is not publicly known that the deceased was fully responsible for his deed, he is not to be denied Christian burial. Therefore, if only a few discreet persons know of the fact that the suicide was clearly a deliberate act, and if they can be depended upon to conceal the fact, Christian burial is not to be denied.[177]

Suicide is defined in the Code as the laying of hands on one's self with the result that death follows.[178] The commen-

[175] Cf. above, pp. 140-142.

[176] The use of the word *alii* in canon 1240, 1, 6°, implies that those guilty of the aforementioned delicts are also public and manifest sinners.—Brys, *Collationes Brugenses*, XXV (1925) 163, 245; Coronata: "Ius vetus, vi huius clausulae (peccatores publici et manifesti) plures comprehendebat qui nunc specifice in Codice determinantur: adhaerentes sectae massonicae, duellantes, suicidas, etc."—*De Locis et Temporibus Sacris*, n. 263.

[177] Claeys Bouuaert-Simenon: "Si suicidium licet culpabile non sit notum nisi membris familiae, curandum est ut non fiat publicum et sepultura ecclesiastica concedi potest."—*Manuale Iuris Canonici*, n. 815, p. 487, not. (6).

[178] "Qui in seipsos manus intulerint, si quidem mors secuta sit, sepul-

tators note that this expression of the laying of hands on one's self is not restricted to its literal meaning, but is to be understood in the sense of taking one's life.[179]

The Code is more explicit in canon 1240, § 1, 3°: "Those who have killed themselves deliberately." Thus suicide may be committed not only by the use of the hands, but also apart from such a use, for example, by throwing one's self from a height, by drowning, and in innumerable other ways by which a positive and gravely culpable act is placed that ends one's life.[180]

Blat specifically excludes from the category of suicide the so-called hunger-strike.[181] Since the hunger-strike is a controversial issue among moralists, his opinion may be accepted; moreover, unless such an act is publicly and indubitably culpable, it is not notorious and it does not occasion for the deceased the privation of Christian burial under the rule of canon 1240, § 1, 3°.

The old law punished with this penalty those who killed themselves out of desperation or in rage.[182] The Code has changed this to "full deliberation,"[183] which is not to be presumed but to be proved.[184] When full deliberation is not evident, Christian burial is not to be denied on the grounds of culpable suicide.[185]

tura ecclesiastica priventur ad normam can. 1240, § 1, n. 3";—can. 2350, § 2.

179 Coronata, *Institutiones Iuris Canonici*, IV, n. 2018; Wernz-Vidal: "dolosa occisio sui ipsius"—*Ius Canonicum*, VII, n. 474; Ayrinhac-Lydon: "Self-destruction"—*Penal Legislation*, n. 306.

180 Blat, *Commentarium Textus*, Lib. V, n. 192.

181 *Loc. cit.*

182 "Siepsos occidentibus ob desperationem vel iracundiam."—*Rit Rom. Pauli V, De Exsequiis*, Cf. above, p. 58.

183 Roberti: "Adest deliberatio cum quis aequo animo crimen patrandum statuit."—*De Delictis et Poenis*, n. 64.

184 Cocchi, *Commentarium in Codicem*, V, n. 71; Buvée, *Ministère Paroissial*, n. 818.

185 Vermeersch-Creusen. "Cum lex strictae interpretationis sit, ubi de consilio defuncti non constat, benigna interpretatio praevalebit."—

One of the factors that would ordinarily preclude the presence of full deliberation is intoxication. *L'Ami du Clergé* gives a thorough résumé of the possible effects of drunkenness upon the element of deliberation, and of its relation to Christian burial. In principle, the act of suicide in the state of intoxication is not properly an object of the penal law, for full advertance is not present, and consequently there also is not present the sufficient moral responsibility which alone can justify the privation of Christian burial.

It is not impossible, however, that the probability of scandal will dictate the refusal of Christian burial in such cases, not as a penalty for the delict of suicide, but as a measure of public order for the common good. For it may be generally known that the intoxication was not of a sufficient degree to excuse the act, or it may be known that the deceased intentionally became intoxicated in order to take his life.

In the first supposition the pastor, when he is face to face with the doubt raised by the fact of intoxication and when no time remains for consultation with the Ordinary, will be guided by the principle which requires the avoidance of grave scandal. He will accordingly adopt a severe or an indulgent course, as the circumstances dictate.

In the second, if it is notorious that the deceased planned to become intoxicated in order to kill himself, the general social consciousness of his guilt may be sufficient to require the privation of Christian burial because of scandal. The proof of antecedent intent, however, must be strong to destroy the reasonable doubt of culpability that rises from the state of intoxication at the time of the act.[186]

The presence of insanity is very often alleged as proof for the lack of full deliberation. However, insanity must be

Epitome, II, n. 549; Coronata: "Cum loquatur de deliberato consilio, quaelibet diminutio responsibilitatis . . . ab hac severissima poena excusare videtur."—*Institutiones Iuris Canonici*, II, n. 816; Fanfani, *De Iure Parochorum* (Taurini-Romae: Marietti, 1924), n. 349

186 XXXVI (1914-1919), 398.

proved, not presumed.[187] Insanity is not to be presumed even in doubtful cases, that is, when it is not certain whether insanity was the cause of the act.[188] However, in these cases as well as in those in which the doubt is concerned with whether the death was suicide or an accident, the doubt itself favors the deceased.[189] The necessity of proving insanity arises from the law, for once the act is established as suicide, it is guilt, and not insanity, that must be presumed.[190] In cases of doubt as to the insanity, however, the ecclesiastical authorities do not require strong evidence of mental derangement, but easily accept any positive signs of its presence from the testimony of doctors, or of the relatives, or of those who are qualified to give such evidence..[191]

There is ordinarily little danger of scandal in the granting of Christian burial to a suicide, since most people at present consider suicide itself a sign of mental disorder.[192] This is es-

187 Cappello, *Summa*, II, n. 760; Wernz-Vidal, *Ius Canonicum*, VII, n. 474.

188 Coronata, *Institutiones Iuris Canonici*, IV, n. 2018.

189 Canon 1240, § 2; Coronata, *loc. cit.*

190 Canon 2200, § 2.

191 Coronata: "Verum facile in hoc re deferendum est iudicio medicorum et etiam consanguineorum qui affirmant suicidam sanae mentis non fuisse." *loc. cit.;* Buvée urges the pastor to obtain from the doctor or coroner a certificate of insanity which will constitute at least a doubt and therefore permit Christian burial.—*Ministère Paroissial*, n. 818; Ayrinhac notes that "in such cases the Church would not require very strong evidence and in all cases of doubt would permit at least a private funeral."—*Administrative Legislation*, n. 79, This was also the opinion of the Congregation of Bishops and Regulars when it stated that the pastor should accept readily the testimony of the doctors when there was no reason to doubt their impartiality.—*Coll. S. C. Ep. et Reg.*, pp. 54-58; Brys: "Quidquid tollit voluntarium vel deliberationem rationis ut actio non sit graviter mala, tollit enim poenam. Sufficiente deliberatione carent omnes ii qui gravibus infirmitatibus nervorum laborant."—*Collationes Brugenses*, XXV (1925), 244; Mostaza, *Sal Terrae*, XIX (1930), 332.

192 Ayrinhac, *Administrative Legislation*, n. 79; Vermeersch-Creusen, *Epitome*, III, n. 552.

pecially true where the deceased had led a pious life previous to the act.[193]

No purpose is served by considering the various types of insanity or the degrees of its manifestation. The canon requires that the act of suicide be notorious; consequently any doubt about either the full advertance to the act of self-murder, or of the guilt, would destroy notoriety.[194]

L'Ami du Clergé notes that some who say that suicide is always a sign of insanity will conclude that therefore Christian burial is never to be denied to a suicide.[195] But it refutes this objection by pointing out that, according to the law, suicide must be established as a *mortal sin* in order to incur the privation. In the absence of the certitude of this mortal sin, Christian burial may not be denied. Moreover, in reference to the objection that doctors may be too lenient or unscrupulous in declaring the presence of insanity, *L'Ami du Clergé* adds that the Church should not be blamed for their faults.

Therefore, in practice, the following conditions should be ascertained as present before Christian burial is denied to a suicide:

a. The act of suicide must be *certain*. One who is found dead should not be presumed a suicide.
b. The act of suicide must be *notorious*. If either the act or the culpability in the act is known only to the family, to the doctor, to the priest, or to others who can be depended upon to conceal it, Christian burial may be granted.
c. The act of suicide must be *deliberate*. Nervous ailments, mental derangements, mental strain, all militate against full deliberation and easily overthrow the presumption of law that the act of suicide is imputable as a delict.

[193] *Coll. S.C. Ep. et Reg., loc. cit.*

[194] Coronata: "Cum Codex loquatur de deliberato consilio, quaelibet diminutio responsibilitatis, *quae in morbis mentalibus verificatur*, ab hac severissima poena excusare videtur." *Institutiones Iuris Canonici*, II, n. 816.

[195] XXXVIII (1921), 554.

Article IX.—The Exclusion of Duelists

Canon 1240, § 1, 4°. Ecclesiastica sepultura privantur: . . . mortui in duello aut ex vulnere inde relato.

Christian burial is denied to those who have died in a duel or from a wound received therein.

The authors are not entirely agreed on the definition of a duel, although they are in agreement on some of its elements. A duel is a prearranged[196] combat staged with deadly weapons[197] between two[198] or more persons on private responsibility.[199] The authors are also agreed that both the time and place of the duel must be determined in the preliminary arrangements, but they disagree as to whether the choice of weapons must also be pre-arranged. The majority holds that the pre-arranged choice of weapons is essential to the constitution of the duel, that is there is no duel unless all three elements: the time, the place and the weapons, are decided upon before the occasion of the duel itself.[200] But Coronata maintains that the weapons need not be chosen until immediately

196 Coronata insists on the lapse of time between the agreement to duel and the actual duel. Otherwise, he states, only a quarrel is had, not a duel in the canonical sense. Therefore if the parties meet by chance and the challenge is made and accepted and they fight at once, or repair immediately to a place agreed upon, there is no duel.—*Institutiones Iuris Canonici*, IV, 2020. The element of deliberation is necessary to distinguish a duel from a quarrel, which is impulsive and thoughtless whereas a duel is deliberately planned and executed.

197 It must necessarily therefore involve the danger of death or of a grave wound.—Ayrinhac-Lydon, *Penal Legislation*, n. 307.

198 Both must be active. An encounter is not a duel when one party remains entirely passive.

199 It must be a private quarrel.—Ayrinhac-Lydon, *Penal Legislation*, n. 307. It is thus opposed to that combat which is undertaken under military obedience.—Cocchi, *Commentarium in Codicem*, V, n. 203; Coronata, *Institutiones Iuris Canonici*, IV, n. 2022.

200 Ayrinhac-Lydon, *loc. cit.;* Blat, *Commentarium Textus*, lib. III. n. 104; Cappello, *De Censuris*, n. 345; Brys, *Collationes Brugenses*, XXV (1925), 245; Wernz-Vidal, *Ius Canonicum*, IV, n. 475; Cocchi, *Commentarium in Codicem*, V, n. 203; Chelodi, *Ius Poenale*, n. 80.

before the combat.[201] And Chelodi admits Coronata's contention that the authorities who support the latter's opinion are of sufficient weight to cause a doubt to exist as to the exact definition of a duel.[202] The opinion which favors the delinquent is that which requires the more; therefore, unless the three elements are present, the encounter cannot certainly be called a duel in a canonical sense.

The requirement that the weapons be capable of inflicting death or grave harm is likewise essential; otherwise there is not a duel, even if death were inflicted by the use of other weapons that normally are considered not to be deadly.[203] Consequently, neither pugilism nor fencing[204] will constitute a duel.[205]

When all the other conditions are present, that is, the prearranged time, the chosen place and the selected weapons, then no agreement that the affair will be terminated at "first blood," or after a specific wound, will in the least alter the criminal nature of the duel.[206] Consequently if some one is killed *unintentionally* in a combat of the nature of a duel, there is no escaping the fact that he died in a duel.

Similarly, the lack of the usual formalities in no way detracts from the character of the encounter, provided that the essential elements of a duel are present. Thus any absence of

[201] *Institutiones Iuris Canonici*, IV, n. 2020. Coronata cites in support of his contention: Genicot-Salsmans, *Institutiones Theologiae Moralis* (Bruxellis, 1922), I, 379; Ballerini-Palmieri, *Opus Theologicum Morali* (Prati, 1889), II, 923, 925, and the words of Pope Gregory XIII: " . . . statuto tempore et loco."—*Const.* "Ad tollendum," 5 dec. 1582—*Fontes*, n. 149.

[202] *Ius Poenale*, n. 80.

[203] Blat, *Commentarium Textus*, lib. V, n. 193; Coronata, *Institutiones Iuris Canonici*, IV, n. 2020; Wernz-Vidal, *Ius Canonicum*, IV, n. 475.

[204] An exception with regarding to fencing will be considered below.

[205] Cappello, *De Censuris*, n. 345.

[206] Clement VIII, *Const.* "Illius vices," 17 aug. 1592—*Fontes*, n. 176, § 5; Coronata, *Institutiones Iuris Canonici*, IV, n. 2023.

the customary acts of provocation, of the exchange of cards, of the appointment of "seconds," etc., is immaterial.[207]

Benedict XIV,[208] in his sweeping condemnation of duels, eliminated almost every possible reason that could be alleged in defense of the act, so that there was no probability that there could be a *legitimate duel.* The authors, likewise, are agreed that every duel is of its nature a delict.[209]

The wound which is inflicted in a duel must be fatal in character if the death which later ensues is to be considered as caused by the infliction of this wound.[210] Therefore, if the death which followed a duel was caused by a heart attack, or by disease which was incidentally occasioned by a wound which of its nature was not fatal, such a death would not be considered as the result of the wound or of the duel.

The Code has made only one change in the old law with regard to duels: it has revoked the provision that Christian burial was to be denied even after signs of repentance had been manifested by the duelist. This delict is now included under the general provision of canon 1240, § 1, that any sign of repentance will suffice to permit the granting of Christian burial.

Moreover, as for all the cases listed in this canon, the element of a prerequisite notoriety will render easy the determination of those cases which involve a privation of Christian burial because of death in a duel. Unless the delict is so publicly known, both as to the fact of the duel and as to the guilt of the deceased, that it is both unconcealable and inexcusable, it is not a notorious delict and the deceased has not

207 Coronata, *Institutiones Iuris Canonici*, IV, n. 2020; Chelodi, *Ius Poenale*, n. 80.

208 *Const.* "Detestabilem," 10 nov. 1752—*Fontes*, n. 422.

209 Coronata: "Duellum privata auctoritate initum est semper delictum, nihil refert qua de causa initum sit."—*Institutiones Iuris Canonici*, IV, n. 2022; Wernz-Vidal, *Ius Canonicum*, IV, n. 475; Vermeersch-Creusen, *Epitome*, III, n. 432; Cappello, *De Censuris*, n. 340.

210 Blat, *Commentarium Textus*, lib. III, n. 104; Brys, *Collationes Brugenses*, XXV (1925), 245.

incurred the penalty of the privation of Christian burial under canon 1240, § 1, 4°. With this principle in view, it is not difficult to assert that the cases wherein this penalty is incurred will be, in the present times at least, rare.

Exception must always be made, however, for the possibility that an imminint danger of scandal may effect the privation, not indeed as a penalty inflicted upon the deceased, but as a measure of public order for the common good. The public does not always know the legal facts and it may happen that one is generally, although erroneously, believed to have died in a duel or from a wound received in a duel. It will then be for the pastor, unless he has time to refer his doubts to the Ordinary, to decide whether probable scandal can be effectively obviated by announcement of the facts, or whether only the privation of Christian burial will suffice to prevent grave scandal.

The exception alluded to above in reference to fencing[211] is that of the so-called *Studentenmensuren,* the form of dueling that is common among German university students. The uncertainty that existed concerning these affairs was occasioned by the fact that, although these encounters had all the essential elements of a duel: previous agreement as to the time, place and the deadly weapon to be used in the encounter, such precautions were taken that not only the possibility of death, but even that of a grave wound, was rendered extremely unlikely. Therefore they seemed to lack a requisite for a duel properly so-called, for despite the fact that deadly weapons, usually heavy sabres, were used, there was present no intention on the part of the participants, nor was there serious probability, of inflicting either death or grave wounds.

A controversy over the question of the inclusion of these affairs in the delict of dueling lasted from 1890 until recent years. Although they were condemned by the Sacred Congregation of the Council in 1890,[212] the controversy continued, and

[211] Cf. above, p. 208, note 204.

[212] 9 aug. 1890—*Fontes,* n. 4281.

it did not cease even with the promulgation of the Code. These *Mensuren* were again condemned in 1923, in reply to a question whether the condemnation of 1890 had survived the Code and was still in effect.[213] Notwithstanding this reply, the controversy was still waged until it was clearly and unmistakably settled in 1925, when the question was again submitted to the Holy See. The point at issue was: whether the lack of intent to kill or mutilate did not remove these contests from the classification of duels. The Sacred Congregation of the Council decided that, while these encounters may lack the malice and evil intent that is associated with a duel, they are in reality but the preparation for later duels in the strict sense, according to the code of honor of the students themselves and that of many European, especially German, armies, and that as the proximate occasions of duels in the full sense they are condemned under the same penalties.[214] These affairs have therefore been clearly condemned and have been assimilated to duels so that there should be no further doubt about their prohibition.

That this reply has not changed the traditional concept of the duel,[215] however, is held by Coronata, because of the specific character of the condemnation. It has determined that the *"Studentenmensuren"* of the German university students are to be considered and punished as duels. It does not determine whether intent to kill or maim is essential to a duel.[216]

213 S. C. C., *Resolutio*, 10 feb. 1923—*AAS*, XV, 154.

214 *Resolutio*, "Ratisbonen," 4 apr., 13 iun. 1925—*AAS*, 132.

215 Vermeersch-Creusen note that the common opinion is that intent to kill or to gravely wound is usually considered a characteristic of a duel: "Plerique enim scriptores duellum periculo gravis vulneris definiunt."—*Epitome*, III, n. 553; Vermeersch, *Periodica*, XIII (1923), 181; XIV (1924), 39, 148.

216 *Institutiones Iuris Canonici*, IV, n. 2021; Vermeersch-Creusen believe that the Sacred Congregation intended to condemn the student duel because of the type of weapons used and the danger of grave scandal, rather than to give an interpretation of the term *duel*.—*Epitome*, III, n. 553; Vermeersch gives the same reasons as Coronata for the condemnation.—*Periodica*, XV (1926), 49.

Article X.—The Exclusion of Those Who Ordered Their Own Cremation

Canon 1240, § 1, 5°. Ecclesiastica sepultura privantur: . . . qui mandaverint suum corpus cremationi tradi.

By cremation is meant the deliberate destruction of the human body by means of fire.[217]

Cremation in its modern revival appeared among the by-products of the French Revolution. By the middle of the nineteenth century it had become a rapidly growing evil, fostered mainly by Masons, anti-clerical elements, and materialists, as a symbol of the mortality of man and as a contradiction of the immortality of the soul.

It should be understood, however, that cremation is not in itself totally evil and that it may at times be tolerated as a necessity, v.g., in times of war or pestilence.[218] Even in these circumstances, however, it is repugnant to human nature, a fact that was demonstarted during the World War when it was not adopted in any general way.[219] As adopted and advocated by the avowed enemies of religion to symbolize their false principles, it is entirely reprehensible. It is quite largely because of the impious purpose and the perverse character of its proponents that the Church has so severely forbidden it.[220]

With regard to the penalty of the privation of Christian burial, it should be made clear at once that cremation itself is not punished by canon 1240, § 1, 5°; it is the *will to be cremated,* as manifested in an express act or word, that is

217 Coronata, *De Locis et Temporibus Sacris,* n. 130; Cappello, *Summa,* II, n. 707.

218 Coronata, *De Locis et Temporibus Sacris,* n. 129; Wernz-Vidal, *Ius Canonicum,* IV, n. 574.

219 Cappello, *Summa,* II, n. 707; Brys, *Collationes Brugenses,* XXV (1925), 43.

220 Canon 1203; Wernz-Vidal, *Ius Canonicum,* IV, nn. 572, 574; Brys, *Collationes Brugenses, loc. cit.;* Prümmer, *Theologisch-praktische Quartalschrift,* LXXXI (1928), 539-546; "De Crematione Praesens Quaestio," *Periodica,* VIII (1929), 62.

penalized.[221] The Pontifical Commission for the Interpretation of the Code left no doubt of this will of the Legislator to punish the intention, not the fact of cremation, when it declared that the penalty provided in canon 1240, § 1, 5° is incurred even when cremation does not actually take place.[222] Therefore cremation itself is not prohibited under penalty of the denial of Christian burial; it is the *ordering* of one's own cremation that is the delict that gives rise to the penalization.[223]

The command or order must also be notorious. The privation will not be incurred as a penalty unless both the act of ordering the cremation and the guilt of the delinquent are unquestionably public and certain.[224]

221 Blat: " . . . 'mandaverint,' i.e. expresserint voce aut scripto propriam huiusmodi voluntatem."—*Commentarium Textus,* lib. III, n. 104.

222 "An vi canonis 1240, § 1, 5° ecclesiastica sepultura priventur qui mandaverint suum corpus cremationi tradi et in hac voluntate permanserint usque ad mortem, etiamsi crematio ad normam canonis 1203, § 2, non sequatur?"

R. "Affirmative."—10 nov. 1925—*AAS,* XVII (1925), 583; cf. Dalpiaz, *Apollinaris,* VII (1934), 249.

223 Thus one could even join a cremation society, or vote for laws that favor cremation without having given a command that he be cremated himself. Although such a one would not incur the penalty of privation under canon 1240, § 1, 5°, it seems likely that he would incur it as a public sinner, under canon 1240, § 1, 6°. Cf. Brys, *Collationes Brugenses,* XXV (1925), 67.

224 In the light of this requirement, the pastor was not justified in denying Christian burial in the following case. He refused it to a deceased convert upon whose death it was discovered that he had inserted a clause in his will, made previous to his conversion, that his body be cremated after his death. The convert did not have the publicly known perverse will necessary to constitute notoriety when he made the will, for at that time he either did not know of the prohibition or did not know that it applied to himself. Even when his desire to be cremated became public knowledge, there was no evidence that the deceased knew that he was acting contrary to the law of the Church. It cannot be said that his act became notorious after his death, because of the absence of all evidence of public and certain knowledge of guilt. Moreover, his non-Catholic relatives testified that

The pre-Code legislation was emphatically re-stated by the Instruction of the Holy Office in 1926.[225] It recalled that, although the decree of 1886 [226] did not forbid the granting of the rites and suffrages of the Church in the case of those persons who were cremated, not at their own request, but at the order of others, nevertheless, by the express terms of the same decree, the rule applies only in so far as scandal can be prevented. "It is beyond doubt that the privation of Christian burial remains in full force even in this case, if the circumstances do not afford sufficient grounds for the hope that scandal will be prevented." [227]

The Holy Office further insisted that no presumption of repentance is sufficient to constitute a release from the penalty. Nor does the fact that the deceased practiced some religious act in life or might have repented at the last moment, suffice to constitute a positive sign of repentance for the notorious will to be cremated. "For since nothing can be known for

his conversion had been so complete that had he known of the prohibition, or adverted to his will, he would have, they were sure, revoked the clause. The absence of notoriety necessitates a decision that he did not incur the penalty, even though the fact of the will to be cremated became public.

In this case, scandal would hardly have prevented the granting of Christian burial, because the convert could easily have been presumed not to know of the prohibition or not to have adverted to the clause in his will, made quite some time before the conversion. A simple announcement of the fact would, in ordinary circumstances, suffice to obviate any possible scandal, especially if all publicity about the fact of cremation, the place and time, etc. were carefully avoided. If, on the contrary, circumstances were such that scandal could not be prevented, Christian burial would have to be denied for the public good.

225 19 iun.—*AAS*, XVIII (1926), 282; Wernz-Vidal: "Solemnitas peculiaris huius documenti et rei momentum indicat et confirmationem continet praecedentium S. Officii decretorum."—*Ius Canonicum*, IV, n. 573.

226 S. C. S. Off., 15 dec.—*Coll. S. C. P. F.*, n. 1665.

227 Instruction of 1926, *AAS*, XVIII (1926), 282. The privation, in the circumstances specified, is not a penalty, but a measure of public order for the common good.—Dalpiaz, *Apollinaris*, VII (1934), 249.

certain regarding this supposed retractation, it is obvious that no consideration can be given to it in the exterior forum."[228] It is clearly evident, therefore, that "any sign of repentance," as specified in canon 1240, § 1, must be a positive sign, and one that is relevant to the crime for which privation of Christian burial was incurred.[229] Such a positive sign may be explicit or implicit, that is, there is no necessity for a formal retractation, if only some evidence is present that the perverse will has been retracted, that is to say, an evidence, no matter how small, that will be acceptable in the external forum as a positive sign.[230]

The conditional conferring of the sacraments upon an unconscious person who is known to have deliberately and perversely ordered his own cremation is not a sign of repentance. All that is present is the hope that he may have repented before his last breath, although there are no signs of his having done so before losing consciousness. Much more is required for the granting of Christian burial to one who has incurred the penalty of the privation than is needed for the administration conditionally of the last sacraments of Penance and Extreme Unction. Conditional administration of the sacraments upon

228 Instruction of 1926, *loc. cit.* An act of piety or a good reputation is not sufficient to amount to a positive sign of repentance for the perverse will to be cremated.—Vito, *Quistioni Canoniche*, II, pp. 67-72.

229 "Ut detur sepultura ecclesiastica, retractatio illius pravae voluntatis, et quidem explicita, haberi debet; retractatio implicita seu per coniecturam supposita, nihil efficere potest adversus illam voluntatem contrariam de qua positive constat."—Dalpiaz, *Apollinaris*, VII (1934). 249. Dalpiaz does not exclude signs of repentence that are implicit in the sense that they denote a retraction of the perverse will made by a nod, a gesture, or any other means that will be an indication of a positive intention on the part of the one who cannot speak. His use of the term "implicit" is in the sense of conjecture or supposition that has no foundation except in hope.

230 Coronata: "Poena non incurritur si mandatum implicite saltem aliquo poenitentiae signo revocatum sit."—*Institutiones Iuris Canonici*, II, n. 816; Brys, *Collationes Brugenses*, XXV (1925), 66; Vito, *Quistioni Canoniche*, II, p. 72, not. 1.

an unconscious person is valueless as evidence of a change of heart by the deceased.[231]

On the contrary, the reception of the last sacraments by one who is conscious easily forms the basis, if publicly known, for a presumption that the delinquent repented of all his faults, including his notorious will to be cremated. The presumption would stand even if it were known that he did not actually advert to this fault of his life, and therefore did not expressly retract it.[232] The notoriety that is required for the incurring of the penalty disappears in the face of such a public opinion of the repentance of the deceased and he is no longer a public and manifest sinner in a canonical sense.[233] Similarly, notoriety would have disappeared if the disposition to be cremated were publicly known to have been made some years before death, but to have since been either explicitly or implicitly retracted.[234]

With regard to the absence of notoriety due to the reception of the last sacraments, it is conceivable that one could be publicly considered worthy of Christian burial who was in reality unworthy. This could happen were a public sinner known to have sent for the priest and to have been alone with him for some time. The presumption that he arranged his affairs of conscience would easily gain ground in such circumstances; yet, in reality, he may have refused to retract his perverse will to be cremated. It would not be for the priest to publicize the sinner's recalcitrance. Thus he could know privately that the deceased was unworthy of Christian burial; but he would be correct in following public opinion in the case and granting it.

231 Dalpias, *loc. cit.;* Prümmer, *Theologisch-praktische Quartalschrift,* LXXXI (1928), 539-546.

232 Brys, *Collationes Brugenses,* XXV (1925), 66; Coronata, *Institutiones Iuris Canonici,* II, n. 816; Salsmans, *Nouvelle Revue Théologique,* XLIII (1926), 618.

233 Vermeersch-Creusen, *Epitome,* II, n. 549; Brys, *Collationes Brugenses, loc. cit.*

234 Salsmans: "La disposition peut-être vieille de plusieurs années n'est pas un obstacle à lui accorder les rites ecclésiastiques."—*loc. cit.*

It could also happen that the confessor, noting that the penitent who was about to die had ordered cremation in good faith,[235] although he was popularly considered to be guilty of the act, might decide to leave him in his good faith, and in following the principles of moral theology give him final absolution. The publicity of the absolution would remove the possibility of scandal and he could be given Christian burial, without his ever having retracted his will to be cremated.[236]

In either of the cases considered, or in any case wherein the priest's information of the unworthiness of the deceased is of a private nature, it is not for him to reveal it. The priest is usually the judge in these cases, not the witness. Moreover, untold possibilities of harm to religion would result from his publicizing the unworthines of one who was publicly considered worthy. Where such a situation exists, there is obviously no notoriety, and therefore the penalty has not been incurred. The priest is fully justified in disregarding his own private opinion and in granting Christian burial.[237]

In no case is the penalty of Christian burial ever incurred by the fact of cremation. However, the necessity to avoid

[235] One who wills cremation in good faith does not incur the penalty, but the good faith must be proved.—Coronata: "Item illa poena non afficit illos qui forte cremationem bona fide mandaverint, illamque non retractaverint; quia privatio sepulturae ecclesiasticae poena est ad quam incurrendam culpa requiritur moralis. Attamen illa bona fides probanda est, non praesumenda."—*De Locis et Temporibus Sacris*, n. 132.

[236] Blat, *Commentarium Textus*, lib. III, n. 104; Brys, *Collationes Brugenses*, XXV (1925), 67.

[237] *Periodica*, in reply to a question whether it was necessary to divulge the fact, not publicly known, that one had willed his own cremation, replied that it was neither necessary nor desirable. The scandal caused by such a revelation is entirely to be avoided. Christian burial is denied to one who has ordered his own cremation only in so far as he is a notorious sinner; if his perverse will is not known, he is not such. Therefore neither by the positive nor by the natural law is the revelation necessary or even to be recommended.—XIV (1925), 178.

scandal may sometimes dictate the refusal. It is then a measure of public order, and not a penalty.

Catholics should be warned that not only is there no obligation upon them to carry out the will of one who has ordered his own cremation,[238] but they themselves become liable to the privation of Christian burial under the classification of public sinners [239] if they carry it out, or order the cremation of another. They should likewise be warned that they may not cooperate in any formal way with the carrying out of cremation, or in making or observing the civil laws that favor it.[240] Material or passive cooperation may at times be necessary, v.g., in times of war or disease, or, in hospitals, with regard to the disposal of amputated organs or parts of the human body.[241]

Article XI.—The Exclusion of Other Public and Manifest Sinners

Canon 1240, § 1, 6°. Ecclesiastica sepultura privantur: . . . alii peccatores publici et manifesti.

It has already been demonstrated that *public* and *manifest*, considered together, have the force of *notorious*.[242] This conclusion is corroborated by the words of the canon itself, for it is provided in canon 1240, § 2, that Christian burial is not to be denied if there remains *any* doubt that the penalty of canon 1240, § 1,[243] has been incurred.[244] Only when a delict is notori-

238 Canon 1203, § 2. Such a provision is legally considered as not having been made.

239 Wernz-Vidal, *Ius Canonicum*, IV, n. 583, not. (43) ; Coronata, *De Locis et Temporibus Sacris*, n. 131.

240 Coronata, *loc. cit.*

241 The Holy Office decreed that the Sisters in a hospital may "silently" comply with the orders of doctors that such parts be burned. —S. C. S. Off., 3 aug. 1897—*Coll. S. C. P. F.*, n. 1975. However, where it is possible, a portion of the hospital grounds should be set aside and blessed as a burial ground for amputated parts of the bodies of the faithful.—S. C. S. Off., 3 aug 1897—*loc. cit.*

242 Cf. above, pp. 140-142.

243 Only part 1 of canon 1240 is a penal law.—canon 2291, 5°.

244 "Occurrente praedictis in casibus aliquo dubio, consulatur, si

ous is there no room for even a slight doubt concerning it.[245]

It remains to determine what is to be understood by *alii peccatores.* The word *"alii"* is an addition in the new law.[246] According to Vermeersch-Creusen, it has the force of *"ceteri."* [247] It has been noted above [248] that its use indicates that the preceding delicts delineated in canon 1240 give rise to the penalty only when they are public and manifest sins.

Considerable difficulty arises at this point because of the fact that the Legislator does not define what is meant in law by a *public sinner.*[249] Recourse to the old law shows that a quite comprehensive notion prevailed before the Code as to who were public sinners in law. They were, as Many states,[250] first, those specifically mentioned in the law as such; suicides, duelists, those who failed to make their Easter duty, usurers, and secondly, "public and manifest sinners" in general. The common opinion of the doctors, he asserts, was that the latter comprehended all those who died *publicly impenitent,*[251] and those who lived in a state of notorious [252] sin and died without

tempus sinat, Ordinarius; permanente dubio, cadaver sepulturae ecclesiasticae tradatur . . . "

245 Chelodi: "ne levi quidem dubio locus est."—*Ius Poenale,* n. 4; Cocchi: " . . . ita certum est ut nulla amplius discussione egeat."—*Commentarium in Codicem,* VIII, n. 1; Vermeersch-Creusen: " . . . delictum non est notorium si de imputabilitate facti dubium moveri potest."—*Epitome,* III, n. 384.

246 "Negatur igitur ecclesiastica sepultura . . . manifestis et publicis peccatoribus qui sine poenitentia perierunt."—*Rit. Rom. Pauli V, De Exsequiis—Quibus non licet dare sepulturam ecclesiasticam;* cf. above, p. 58.

247 *Epitome,* III, n. 553.

248 Pp. 140-142.

249 Coronata: "Quinam autem sint dicendi publici peccatores non determinat Codex."—*De Locis et Temporibus Sacris,* n. 203; *Institutiones Iuris Canonici,* II, n. 816.

250 *De Locis Sacris,* n. 220.

251 *Rit. Rom. Pauli V:* "qui sine poenitentia perierunt."—*De Exsequiis,* cf. above, p. 58; c. 11, *de sepulturis,* 111, 28; cf. also gloss at the word "communicabatur": "constat eos in peccato mortali decessisse."

252 Many considers *public sinners* in the sense of *notorious sinners,* whether the sin be notorious by law or by fact.—*loc. cit.*

signs of repentance, e.g., those who lived in a state of notorious concubinage or prostitution, those whose work or duty could not be performed without their committing sin, members of condemned societies.[253] Furthermore, notoriety was an essential note in all cases.[254]

Whether this interpretation of the term *public sinner* can be considered to have been carried over into the new law is not clear. The difficulty arises from the fact that the penal law punishes *delicts,* not *sins.*[255] Canon 1240, § 1, as a penal canon, inflicts a penalty that is incurred *ipso facto* by the commission of certain *delicts.*[256] But a delict is essentially the external and morally imputable violation of a law to which a sanction, at least an indeterminate one, has been attached.[557] Therefore there is no delict when no legally sanctioned law has been externally and culpably violated.[258] Thus there is a possibility that what is a sin may not be a delict. As Chelodi [259] and Coronata [260] point out, *sin* and *delict* are not synonomous in the new law. The former connotes a much broader concept

[253] *De Locis Sacris, loc. cit.*

[254] Many: " . . . ita tamen ut mala fides sit certa et *notoria,* aliter enim non essent *publici peccatores.*"—*loc. cit.*

[255] Chelodi notes that the penal law was made to protect the juridical order, and that it does not punish all actions which break the divine law or which are *intrinsically* evil, nor even all those acts which are forbidden by human law, but only those which endanger the social order.—*Ius Poenale,* n. 2.

[256] Authors speak quite generally of the *delicts* treated in this canon; among them are: Chelodi (*Ius Poenale,* n. 2), Coronata (*De Locis et Temporibus Sacris,* n. 263), (*Institutiones Iuris Canonici,* II, n. 816), Schaaf, (*The Ecclesiastical Review,* XCV (1936), 191), Augustine (*A Commentary,* VI, 156), Wernz-Vidal (*Ius Canonicum,* IV, n. 585), Rossi (*La "Sepultura Ecclesiastica" e l' "Ius Funerum"* p. 138), Brys (*Collationes Brugenses,* XXV [1925], 162, 163, 245) and the unnamed writer in *L'Ami du Clergé* (XXXVIII [1921], 109).

[257] Can. 2195, § 1.

[258] Chelodi states that the principle: *nullum crimen, nulla poena sine lege* is now incorporated in the Code.—*Ius Poenale,* n. 2.

[259] *Loc. cit.*

[260] *Institutiones Iuris Canonici,* IV, n. 1641.

than the latter.[261] For whereas every delict is a sin, not every sin is a delict.[262] Moreover, as Chelodi notes, it would not be possible, or even prudent, for the law to punish all sins, *even public ones*.[263]

It is therefore quite possible that one may commit a *public sin* that is not also a *public delict*. The two are not necessarily the same, though in a specific case they may be, i.e., one may be a notorious sinner in a *literal* or in a *canonical sense*, or in both.[264] In the literal sense, a notorious sinner is one who has notoriously violated the law of nature, of God or of the Church; one whose consequent unworthiness is commonly known to the faithful of the place.[265] Such violations may take place in innumerable ways, especially in respect to the laws of justice, charity, temperance, piety, etc. In a canonical sense, a notorious sinner, or a delinquent, is one who has committed a notorious delict, such as any of those which are specified in canon 1240, § 1, nn. 3, 4, 5, or any other canonical delict.[266]

The question therefore is: does canon 1240, § 1, 6° punish public *sinners* or only public *delinquents?* May one incur the penalty of the privation of Christian burial by the commission of a notorious fault that is not prohibited by a penally sanctioned law?

The extent of the punitive power of the law was not clearly limited even in the old law. Thus D'annibale[267] and Holl-

261 Chelodi: "Aliud est *delictum*, aliud *peccatum*. Hoc multo latius patet."—*Ius Poenale*, n. 2.

262 Coronata: "Quodlibet delictum est peccatum; non item e contra quodlibet peccatum est delictum".—*Institutiones Iuris Canonici*, IV, n. 1641.

263 "Omnia autem peccata, esti publica, auctoritate sociali punire neque possibilis neque prudens res esset."—*Ius Poenale*, n. 2.

264 *L'Ami du Clergé*, XL (1923), 300.

265 Brys, *Collationes Brugenses*, XXVIII (1928), 378.

266 Coronata: "Ad publicum pecatorem constituendum non sufficit quodlibet pecatum sed publicum requiritur delictum."—*Institutiones Iuris Canonici*, II, n. 816.

267 *Summula*, I, n. 296.

weck[268] maintained that there is no delict, and therefore no penalty, unless there is an external and culpable violation of a penal law. Wernz[269] and Lega,[270] on the contrary, extended the punitive power of the penal law, at least in the abstract, to a point which comprehended all external sins. They held that the penal law was not so strictly determined that it was impossible to punish evil acts which were forbidden by no positive law, especially when such acts upset the social order. They believed that *guilt* and *damage* suffice by natural law to constitute a *delict.*

That controversy seems now to be settled by the Code through its incorporation of the opinion of D'Annibale into canon 2195, § 1,[271] so that only those acts are punishable by penal law that are delicts in the sense of that canon: external and morally imputable violations of a law with a canonical sanction, at least indeterminate.

However, new doubts have arisen because of canon 2222, § 1, which permits the infliction of penalties for other evil acts than those specifically prohibited under explicit penal sanction by the positive law. The problem of reconciling canons 2195, § 1 and 2222, § 1 is not to be treated here, but it is sufficiently serious to throw doubt upon the question at issue: is an evil act a delict only when it satisfies the specifications of canon 2195, § 1?[272]

Because of the difference of opinion caused by the controversy over these two canons, the definition of *public sinner* cannot be absolutely stated. It certainly includes those who are guilty of notorious *delicts;* whether it also includes literally notorious *sinners,* who may not have committed a canonical delict according to the definition in canon 2195, § 1, is doubtful.

268 *Die Kirchliche Strafgezetze,* § 1.

269 *Ius Decretalium,* VI, n. 16.

270 *Praelectiones de Iudiciis Ecclesiasticis,* III (1896), n. 16.

271 Roberti, *De Delictis et Poenis,* n. 53.

272 For the opinions in the controversy over the reconciling of these two canons, cf. Roberti, *De Delictis et Poenis,* nn. 49-53.

Because of the doubt whether all public sinners are also public delinquents, the strict sense will be retained in regard to the penalty of the privation of Christian burial. In other words, one is not to be considered as having incurred the penalty unless he is notoriously guilty of a delict in the strict sense of canon 2195, § 1.[273]

The difficulty is largely speculative, however, for the delicts of the Code include most of the offenses specified in the old law as punishable with the denial of Christian burial. Further, even were one not guilty of a notorious delict in the sense of canon 2195, § 1, the notoriety of his sin, presuming it were notorious, would deprive him of Christian burial because of the very probable danger of grave scandal in its concession to one so publicly unworthy. It is inconceivable that the Christian burial of one who is notoriously a public sinner would not cause grave scandal. However, when it is doubtful in view of the obscure meaning of the term "public sinner" whether one has incurred the *penalty* of privation, and scandal remains the only possible obstacle to his receiving Christian burial, there seems to be no good reason why such a one could not be granted the honors in some place where the case is entirely unknown and scandal is unlikely.

It may therefore be said that even those public sinners who in the pre-Code law were listed among that general class of persons who lived and died in sin, even if such sin were not clearly established as a delict in the present law, will incur the privation of Christian burial, if not by the notoriety of their sin, then in view of the inevitable scandal attaching to any attempt to accord it to them.

The number of delicts enumerated in the Code for the notorious perpetration of which one may incur the privation of

[273] *L'Ami du Clergé* is of the same opinion. It states that the nature of the penalty requires this; for the privation of Christian burial is so public a penalty that it should not be inflicted except for an equally public *crime;* therefore since not all those who commit notorious sins are notorious delinquents *in law,* not all are to be denied Christian burial. XL (1923), 309; XXXVIII (1921), 110.

Christian burial according to canon 1240, 1, 6, is so large that it precludes any attempt at a comprehensive enumeration or exhaustive treatment. The general principles as applied in each case will determine whether Christian burial may be granted or whether it must be denied. They will also determine whether the privation, if it be necessitated, is the result of a certainly incurred penalty for a perpetrated delict, or is due solely to the danger of unavoidable grave scandal.

The principles:

I. *In cases of perpetrated delicts.* Before an absolute denial of Christian burial is unquestionably warranted, the following conditions must obtain:

a. The deceased must have been guilty of a canonical delict.
b. The delict must be notorious, i.e.
   1. certain and indubitable,
   2. unconcealable, and
   3. inexcusable.
c. There must be wanting all evidence of any positive sign of repentance.

II. *In cases of extant or imminent scandal.* In the absence of any perpetrated delict which of itself would deprive the deceased of Christian burial, he may be granted Christian burial only on condition that all extant scandal be removed and all imminent scandal be prevented. If scandal cannot be obviated no matter what procedure is followed, then the less scandalous course of action will be the determinant factor in deciding whether Christian burial is to be granted or denied.

III. *In the cases which leave the issue doubtful.* In any case of doubt regarding the enumerated conditions, the case must be referred to the Ordinary for its ultimate solution, whenever time permits such recourse. If upon such recourse the doubt remains insoluable, the Ordinary must grant Christian burial under the proper safeguards against impending scandal. If for lack of time the Ordinary cannot be consulted, the pastor must persue the same course of action.

A few of the more common and more serious delicts for which the privation of Christian burial will be incurred according to canon 1240, § 1, 6°, under the above conditions, should be mentioned.

A. *Those Who Neglected to Make Their "Easter Duty".*

With regard to the omission in the new law of any express mention of the culpable missing of one's "Easter duty" as a delict that is punished with the privation of Christian burial, it appears that the Legislator has abolished this specific delict. The making of the "Easter duty" is commanded by canon 859 [274] but no penalty is attached to the violation of the canon, and therefore its violation does not appear to be a delict.[275]

However, the authors are agreed that while the fact of neglecting one's "Easter duty" may not of itself be a delict, it may quite possibly become the cause of the privation of Christian burial because of the scandal that it has raised in a particular case. Therefore the omission that would cover a period of years and that would appear to be the result of contempt of religion might amount to a notorious sin. In such a case it would be but an added scandal to grant Christian burial to such a person.

Furthermore, since the authors insist that contempt or hatred of religion be *notoriously* present in the omission, the failure in this duty out of simple neglect would not give rise to the penalty of privation.[276]

274 Van Hove says that it is an obligation founded on divine law. *De Legibus Ecclesiasticis*, n. 101.

275 Claeys Bouuaert-Simenon: "Hic casus enim in novo iure non iam recipitur et per se non est sufficiens ad denegandum sepulturam ecclesiasticam."—*Manuale Iuris Canonici*, n. 815; Brys: "Opinamur nudum factum non impletionis dictorum praeceptorum per aliquot annos non constituti aliquem ut peccatorem publicum et manifestum qualis a lege requiritur."—*Collationes Brugenses*, XXV (1925), 246.

276 Brys: "notorious contempt or impiety"—*Colationes Brugenses*.

B. *Gangsters*

Gangsters, in the modern sense, quite easily fit into the category of public and manifest delinquents in that their sins are usually also delicts of murder, robbery, theft, and the like. If, by chance, one or the other of them should be a notorious sinner but not a notorious delinquent in the canonical sense, the great probability of grave scandal in granting Christian burial to such would annul his possibly theoretical right to it.

Scandal may often be eliminated in these cases of notorious gangsters by the announcement of the signs of repentance and the elimination of all pomp and ceremony. The funeral could be limited to a low Mass and simple absolution, without music, organ, bells, chant. The procession itself, so often in the past a source of grave scandal in these funerals, could be restricted to the hearse and the cars containing the family and bearers. Newspaper publicity could be forbidden, especially as to the name of the church, the cemetery and the time of the ceremonies. All the above could legitimately be forbidden under penalty of total privation, for canon 1240, § 2 *orders* that scandal be obviated, although for obvious reasons it doesn't specify how that is to be done.

Few of the faithful are scandalized when even a notorious sinner is given the essentials of Christian burial, if they know that he repented. But last minute repentance does not justify, in their eyes, the granting of the same honors and suffrages

XXV (1925), 247; Cappello, *Summa*, II, n. 760; Cocchi: "ex odio religionis"—*Commentarium in Codicem*, V, n. 71; Mothon: "par haine ou mépris de la religion"—*Institutions Canoniques*, II, n. 574; Coronata: "notorious omission"—*Institutiones Iuris Canonici*, II, n. 816; Wernz-Vidal: "qui per plures annos notorie omiserunt . . ."—*Ius Canonicum*, IV, n. 586; Schaaf: ". . . therefore the mere fact that one has failed to make his Easter duty will not suffice to deny him Christian burial . . . now they (who miss their Easter duty) can and must be denied this honor only in so far as they are public and manifest sinners who depart this life without giving any sign of repentance."—*The Ecclesiastical Review*, XCV (1936), 190.

that are usually extended to those who have striven to lead a good Christian life. Untold harm has been done to religion in the past by the ostentatious Christian burial of such public sinners.

C. *Those Who Lived in Concubinage or Civil Marriage.*

Considerable difficulty may be experienced with cases that are concerned with civil marriage or concubinage. The present growth of these evils is commensurate with the decline of the respect for the sanctity of marriage. These cases are often rendered difficult by the fact that the deceased, while apparently living in sin, was faithful to Sunday Mass, charitable practices, or other commendable deeds. In such cases it should not be forgotten that there is no sign of repentance for the concubinage unless it can be directly referred to that delict. In other words, acts of piety are of little avail to nullify the notoriety of the concubinage so long as the parties persist in that state. There must be a sign that is sufficiently public to nullify the notoriety already attached to the delict. Such a sign is lacking in one who perseveres publicly in the state of illicit union, no matter how faithful he is to Mass or other religious practices. These do not touch upon the delict nor detract from its notoriety. Therefore, the general rule may be stated for these cases: If a separation was not effected or if, *in extremis*, at least the promise of a separation was not furnished, Christian burial must be denied.[277]

In the case of sudden death, however, any sign that may be interpreted as a positive indication that the deceased wished to break away from the concubinage, could be weighed to determine its value in obviating both the scandal already given, and that which might arise from the granting of Christian burial.

Once a death-bed reconciliation has been made, there is no reason why the funeral may not be had from the house where the deceased lived, even if the surviving partner in sin is to

[277] *L'Ami du Clergé*, XXXVII (1920), 615.

participate. So long as the deceased has been publicly reconciled, the right to Christian burial has been regained. To insist on the funeral's being held from another house would amount to an unjustified interdict of the place. As for the presence of the partner in sin at the obsequies, let it be remembered that even the excommunicated may attend the public services of the Church.[278]

[278] *L'Ami du Clergé*, XLII (1925), 75 ff.

D. *Divorces*

The obtaining of a divorce is not of itself a canonical delict by general law, although it may be by particular law.[279] It is, if deliberately done and willed for itself, a sin, and the sin may or may not give rise to scandal. If it were notorious, Christian burial could hardly be granted because of the unrepaired grave scandal that has been caused and that which would be caused by publicly granting ecclesiastical rites to such a person.

It must be admitted, however, that divorce no longer causes the same kind or amount of scandal which it formerly caused. Like many evils of the time, it is of a relative nature in its scandalous effects. Thus it may be gravely scandalous in one community and not in another. In most American communities, with their large number of sects and the consequent lack of religious influence on public opinion, the inevitable materialism that has tainted even Catholics has lessened the horror for this fault to the point where divorcees are no longer publicly considered as grave sinners.[280]

Moreover, to protect itself from conflict with the civil power,

[279] *L'Ami du Clergé* states that many French dioceses have legislated the sanction of excommunication and privation of Christian burial for divorcees.—XXXVIII (1921), 684; XL (1923), 309.

[280] *L'Ami du Clergé* notes that the same situation prevails in France. Although divorce remains a grave fault, there is a general growth of the opinion that tends, if not to consider it indifferently, at least to regard it with greater toleration than formerly and to consider it less worthy of grave sanctions.—XXXVIII (1921), 110.

the ecclesiastical court must at times require the presentation of a certificate of civil divorce in cases contesting the validity of a marriage. This proves that civil divorce may be of a sinless character when obtained for sufficiently worthy motives and with the right intention; that is, when it is understood as only a legal formality to which no intrinsic value is attached.

If no attempt at re-marriage follows divorce, the scandal that it may have caused will diminish with the passing of time. It may happen that, if not by public penance, at least by the public profession of religion, one may undo the scandal given. The past fault may be obliterated by years of faithful religious living. Public reception of the sacraments would undoubtedly signify a regret for the offense or scandal occasioned for the community.

Re-marriage, however, remains gravely sinful and scandalous. It is readily classified as notorious concubinage whenever the fault is known as unconcealable and inexcusable. While the scandal given by a divorce can be overcome by time and the subsequent good life of the offender, the scandal of concubinage lasts as long as the concubinage continues.

E. *Other Excluded Sinners*

Under this heading there may be mentioned those Catholics who are publicly known as enemies of the Church, Catholic officials and rulers who have notoriously betrayed the Church, or robbed her of her property or her rights, as well as those political leaders who have by their sinful lives and corrupt practices been a reproach to her. These cases may offer special difficulty. Their treatment must be determined in the individual case and it may often happen that there will be only a choice of the less scandalous course. This is particularly true in the death of such a person who is also a national figure, for then a conflict may arise between the external and official regret that the Church must express at the nation's loss and the liturgical recommendation of his soul to God in

Christian burial. In such cases the refusal of Christian burial could only too readily be publicly considered as an act of hostility to the government, particularly in those countries in which there is a strong anti-clerical element. Further, when such a national figure has been assassinated while in office, the deed may well clothe the victim in a martyr's mantle in the eyes of the people and erase the scandal caused by his faults. In such cases the harm caused by the refusal of Christian burial may quite possibly be greater than that occasioned by its concession. The ecclesiastical authorities must act according to the dictates of circumstances, and, as a last resort, choose the less scandalous course.

Included also under number 6 of canon 1240, § 1 will be those who are guilty of notorious delicts against the faith, e.g., those notoriously guilty of the crimes of heresy or schism, but who have joined no sect;[281] others included will be the notorious members of condemned societies that are not of a Masonic character,[282] or of condemned movements, such as *L'Action francaise*,[283] and those persons who are under a *latae sententiae* excommunication or interdict when the delict and the penalty are notorious.[284] Others are those who are notoriously guilty of adultery, prostitution, concubinage, whether the latter arises from civil marriage or not,[285] writers of

281 Coronata, *Institutiones Iuris Canonici*, II, n. 816; *De Locis et Temporibus Sacris*, n. 263; Wernz-Vidal, *Ius Canonicum*, IV, n. 586; Brys, *Collationes Brugenses*, XXV (1925), 243.

282 Coronata, *Institutiones Iuris Canonici*, II, n. 816; Ayrinhac, *Administrative Legislation*, n. 79; Cocchi, *Commentarium in Codicem*, V, n. 71; Brys, *Collationes Brugenses*, XXV (1925), 247.

283 The Hierarchy of the Netherlands has forbidden participation by Catholics in Liberal, Socialist, Communist and National Socialist (Nazi) movements, under pain of refusal of absolution, Extreme Unction, and Catholic burial.—N.C.W.C. News Service (Msgr. Enrico Pucci, Vatican City), 2/10/41-M.

284 Roberti, *De Delictis et Poenis*, n. 336; Blat, *Commentarium Textus*, lib. III, n. 173; Coronata, *Institutiones Iuris Canonici*, II, n. 816; *L'Ami du Clergé*, XXXVII (1920), 447.

285 Coronata, *Institutiones Iuris Canonici*, II, n. 816; *De Locis et*

obscene or impious works,[286] and those who order another's cremation.[287]

Neglect of one's religious duties and obligations will not of itself constitute one a public sinner in the canonical sense. If, however, the neglect is notorious, i.e., indubitably public and culpable, as it easily may be in a small and Catholic community, it would indirectly exclude one from Christian burial because of the probability of grave scandal to the faithful if Christian burial were granted.[288]

Ayrinhac-Lydon note that the loss of one's good name, the incurring of public contempt, or canonical infamy of fact, may imply the existence of a notorious delict from which they arise.[289] Blat also includes under canon 1240, § 1, 6°, those who are manifestly infamous in fact, such as magicians, fakers, sooth-sayers, fortune-tellers and the like.[290]

What was said of the limiting of the pomp and ceremony of the funerals of gangsters applies also to the funerals of other notorious public sinners. Their last minute reconciliation before death, after years of notorious sin, does not entitle them to the full honors of Christian burial. There may be a vast difference between Christian burial in the canonical sense, and the types of funeral ceremonies that prevail in some places, with all the added honors, decorations, customary distinctions between the various classes of funerals and the like. The essential rites are all that need be granted. Between these and the most ostentatious funeral rites there is much room for

Temporibus Sacris, n. 263; Vermeersch-Creusen, *Epitome,* II, n. 549; Ayrinhac, *Administrative Legislation*, n. 79; Buvée, *Ministère Paroissial*, n. 818; Beste, *Introductio in Codicem*, p. 605; Wernz-Vidal, IV, n. 586; Brys, *Collationes Brugenses*, XXV (1925), 246.

286 Brys, *loc. cit.*

287 Wernz-Vidal, *Ius Canonicum*, IV, n. 586; not. (43).

288 Cappello, *Summa*, II, n. 760; *Perfice Munus*, X (1935), 254; XI (1936), 397.

289 *Penal Legislation*, n. 161; Wernz-Vidal, *Ius Canonicum*, VII, n. 346.

290 *Commentarium Textus*, lib. III, n. 173.

various degrees of limitation. It must not be forgotten that even the essentials are denied by the law if scandal cannot be effectively removed or precluded. Therefore, it is well within the right of the pastor to restrict the ceremony to the essentials, commonly considered the prayers at the door of the church, a low Mass, absolution and burial in blessed ground. The funeral may also be limited to a strictly private family affair.

In this way the Church, while extending to the deceased her last blessing and recommending his soul to God, at the same time expresses her disapproval of his life and warns others not to emulate him.

CONCLUSIONS

1. Christian burial is both a right and an obligation; Catholics are not free to choose it or to refuse it, although they may decline some of the pomps and ceremonies that do not pertain to the essential rite.

2. Christian burial is defined for the first time in the Code of Canon Law.

3. The legal definition in the Code has retained the traditional concept of Christian burial as the ensemble of religious rites, prayers and suffrages, and burial in a place set aside by the ecclesiastical authority for the interment of the faithful departed.

4. The Code has transferred the emphasis from the latter element—burial in blessed ground—to the former—the liturgical rites and prayers—so that whereas formerly Christian burial signified primarily burial in blessed ground, it now connotes principally the rites and ceremonies, and only secondarily the interment. In this transfer the Church but returns to the ancient concept of Christian burial as the participation of the Church through her rites and prayers in the final honors rendered to the faithful departed.

5. The Code has removed any doubt about the nature of the privation of Christian burial. It may be incurred as a public penalty for a public delict, or it may proceed from the absence of a right on the part of the deceased to the honors of Christian burial.

6. As a *latae sententiae* penalty it will be incurred at the moment that the delict is completely constituted according to the requirements of canon 1240, § 1, regardless of whether the penalty is executed later.

7. As proceeding from the absence of a right to Christian burial, the privation may arise from the lack of baptism, from the presence of an impediment to full ecclesiastical communion with the visible Church of Christ, as in the case of those who are baptized outside the Catholic Church, or from the prior

right of the common good over that of the individual, as in those cases in which the imminent danger of grave scandal that would follow the concession of Christian burial cannot be prevented.

8. The requirement that the delicts, for the perpetration of which the penalty is incurred, be notorious will render the privation of Christian burial, as a penalty, rare.

9. In doubtful cases, or in those in which there is established any positive sign of repentance for the delict, the deceased is entitled by law to Christian burial, due precautions being taken to prevent scandal.

10. The necessity of preventing scandal, an obligation founded on divine law, will be the more frequent cause of the privation, and not infrequently of the non-privation of Christian burial.

11. The law leaves to the ecclesiastical authorities the determining of whether, and how, scandal can be prevented.

12. The privation of Christian burial is exclusively a matter of the external forum and there are no occult cases. The decision as to whether the penalty has been incurred will depend entirely upon the evidence at it appears to a judge in the external forum.

13. The privation will depend upon the notoriety of the delict, that is, on the fact that the delict is publicly known as culpable beyond any doubt.

14. The privation of Christian burial is a measure of public order to repair the damage done to the social order and to prevent others from committing similar damage.

15. It may happen, however, that the common good will be better served by the non-execution of the penalty than by its execution; in such cases the execution of the penalty should be omitted.

APPENDIX

Article 1.—May Baptized Non-Catholics Be Granted Christian Burial?

In Chapter Three, Article Four, the problem of the baptized non-Catholics was considered from the point of view of their denial of Christian burial because of their lack of a clear right to it. An entirely new light is thrown upon the problem if it is considered from another point of view: are there times when they may, because of signs of conversion, be granted it? From this point of view the problem is of immediate concern when it is a question of a non-Catholic member of a Catholic family. In our country two circumstances especially make it to be of interest: the great number of mixed marriages and the consequently unusually large number of non-Catholic spouses to be found in thoroughly Catholic families. A contributory circumstance, also, is the fact that great numbers of these non-Catholic spouses may be, as in the case of the non-Catholic father considered above, not only not Protestant in the true sense of the word, but, faithful to their prenuptial promises, sympathetic, friendly and inclined toward the Church. It may very easily happen that one or another of these may arrive at the point where he desires to set aright his relations with God, to learn what the Church demands of him, or to become, possibly at some future date, a member of his family's Church.

Manifestation of this state of mind may be established by signs that, although they may leave something to be desired, cannot but indicate the inclination of a puzzled mind toward what it only vaguely understands but toward which it is being indubitably attracted. The following may be given as frequent signs: "If ever I join any Church, it will be the Catholic;" "I intend to die in the Church;" "I am beginning to see my way but I must have time to know what I am doing, I will not join until I can be a good Catholic;" "I regret anything in my life that the Church disapproves;" "I intend to see a priest some day and find out where I belong." The number of such remarks could be multiplied, but the purpose is served with these.

Whether such remarks will amount to an implied desire for communion with the Church can only be ascertained in the individual case, after consideration of individual circumstances. Even without an expression of the sort enumerated, one's whole life could be a powerful argument in favor of a presumption that he was seeking the truth and was on his way to the Church.

On the contrary, such expressions could largely be robbed of any deep significance, if a considerable amount of time elapsed after them without any serious attempt on the part of the speaker to realize the indicated desire.[1]

In the consideration of this problem it should be recalled that much less is demanded by the Church for the granting of Christian burial than for the reception of the sacraments, apart from their conditional administration in extreme circumstances.[2] In the matter of Christian burial, as is clearly manifested in canons 1239 and 1240, the Church is most generous. In fact, she may be said to be reluctant to refuse Christian burial until it is obvious that it must be refused. If the proof of *any* sign of repentance, or if the fact that there is doubt about either the delict or the sign of repentance, is sufficient to cause the law to command that Christian burial be not denied even to notorious apostates, heretics, public sinners and even excommunicates who are *vitandi,* it may very reasonably be questioned just what is asked of by the Church of one whose right to Christian burial is only suspended by his baptism in a heretical sect; who is separated from communion with the faithful only by good faith or by ignorance; whose life is a public testimony of his good intentions. There is certainly the widest degree of dissimilarity between the two groups.

In the consideration of this matter let it be recalled that for

1 Schaaf—*The Ecclesiastical Review,* XCV (1936), 189.

2 Mahoney, "Ecclesiastical Burial" — *The Clergy Review,* XVIII (1940), 547.

the granting of Christian burial the law does not demand any specific retractation, abjuration, reparation, restitution or satisfaction, beyond what is absolutely necessary to allay scandal in the external forum; and that may usually be accomplished by the public announcement that the deceased died reconciled with the Church.

Again, it must be borne in mind that the question of granting Christian burial is one that is completely concerned with the external forum, having nothing to do with the internal. Canon 1240 demands that Christian burial be not denied to even the worst of public sinners if there is enough evidence of repentance for a judge in the external forum to decide that it is sufficient in the circumstances.[3] And even if the evidence is doubtful, the benefit of a positive doubt is in favor of the delinquent.

The common law, in canon 2314, § 2, amply provides for the bishop to absolve from all delicts of apostasy, heresy and schism, provided that the examination of them has been brought in to the external forum in any way. Since the law presumes that baptized non-Catholics are not without the taint of heresy—although proof to the contrary may readily be establish that they are but material heretics—they come under the absolving power of the local Ordinary, and even of the Vicar-General when he is properly authorized with a special mandate.[4] Although canon 2314 requires the usual abjuration

[3] *L'Ami du Clergé*, XXXVIII (1921), 684.

[4] Chelodi gives an interesting explanation of the reason why the power of the Ordinary is so broad in the external forum, when it is restricted in the internal forum by the fact that the absolution from the excommunication incurred by those guilty of these delicts is reserved in a special way to the Holy See. This power in the external forum, he states, is a survival of that power which bishops had in the days of the inquisitions, when they were the ordinary inquisitors who were empowered to absolve those heretics who appeared before them and renounced their errors. Th Council of Trent wished them to retain this power (sess. XXIV, *de ref.*, c. 6), and it has been confirmed in the most recent times by a decision of the Holy Office (16 feb. 1916—*AAS*, VIII [1916], 61).—*Ius Poenale*, n. 58.

before the absolution, in the case under discussion the evidence of abjuration would be found in the signs of repentance given some time before death.

Vermeersch-Creusen note that an absolution from the penalties incurred by heresy, apostasy or schism, when it is given after death, does not absolve from the censure, for the case has been referred to a Higher Tribunal, but it amounts to a remission of the effects of the censure, or *obex,* as the case may be, one of which is the privation of Christian burial.[5] However, this absolution after death is no longer required.[6]

The process therefore seems to be reduced to an administrative action by which the Ordinary decides that the evidence presented is, or is not, sufficient to constitute a sign of repentance, on the part of the deceased, for his heresy or his lack of communion with the Church.

In view of these considerations there seems to be no reason why the bishop could not grant Christian burial, in whole or in part, as the circumstances dictated, to a baptized non-Catholic who is publicly known, or can be publicly known by the announcement of his wish, to have desired, in so far as he was able in the circumstances, to be united to the Church of Christ. The granting of such a favor will depend very largely on circumstances, both those in the case itself and those in the diocese. As head of the diocese, it is the bishop's duty to determine what is for the good of religion in his territory.[7] Thus the favor granted in one diocese, with beneficial results

[5] "Quare censura non cessat sola delinquentis poenitentia et satisfactione, aut morte subiecti vel auctoris poenae. Qui censura innodatus mortuus fuerit, si signa poenitentiae dederit, per se post mortem absolvi potest. Neque sic Ecclesia eum qui suo iudicio eripitur proprie et directe absolvit, sed effectus consurae qui eum respiciunt et perdurant, tollit, v.g., prohibitionem sepulturae ecclesiasticae, privationem suffragiorum, etc."—*Epitome,* III, n. 447.

[6] Cf. *Rit. Rom.,* tit. III, cap. IV, n. 1; Vermeersch-Creusen: "Sed huiusmodi absolutio iam necessaria non est ut defunctus sepulturae ecclesiasticae mandetur (c. 1240)."—*loc. cit.*

[7] Cc. 329, § 1; 334, § 1; 335, § 1; *L'Ami du Clergé,* XL (1923), 309.

for religion, might not be warranted in another, for fear of the opposite effects.

Considerations motivating a granting of the benefit may possibly be found in the following reasons: to prevent a non-Catholic minister from claiming the funeral, to the scandal and sorrow of the Catholic family; to prevent an entirely irreligious funeral in a Catholic family; to avoid scandal among the faithful, who cannot understand the legal provisions by which the worst sinners may receive Christian burial by last-minute repentance, while "good men," who have been friendly to the Church and who may be said to have been on the way to conversion, are denied it because they did not find the opportunity to take the final step.

The extent to which the mercy of the Church has been accorded in the past is illustrated by a case in which a non-Catholic was granted full Christian burial because of his desire to see the priest, who however arrived only after the man's sudden death.[8]

In another instance, an unbaptized non-Catholic was granted Christian burial because of an interpretative desire for Baptism. The man's Catholic daughter had baptized her dying father while he was unconscious, after an accident, on the strength of his earlier remark: "If I ever join any Church, it will be the Catholic." The bishop ruled this an interpretative desire of Baptism.[9]

There need be no fear of violation of the cemetery, for the ordinary baptized non-Catholic is not excommunicated by personal sentence, nor is he a *vitandus;* therefore canon 1172 would not apply.[10]

8 *Theologisch-praktische Quartalschrift,* LXXXVII (1934), 797-804. For a similar decision by the Holy Office, cf. *Fontes,* n. 1200.

9 *The Ecclesiastical Review,* LIX (1918), 419.

10 "Responsa,"—*Collationes Brugenses,* XXIX (1929), 76; Coronata, *Inst. Iur. Can.,* II, n. 748.

Article II.—May Unbaptized Non-Catholics Be Buried In Catholic Cemeteries?

Obviously, in the discussion of the burial of unbaptized non-Catholics, there is no question of their being granted Christian burial in the canonical sense as it is defined in canon 1204, except under the conditions considered in the preceding article. It should be understood clearly that what is tolerated is the mere interment in blessed ground, and even that is tolerated only to avoid a greater evil. To consider that they have received Christian burial by such a concession is to fail to appreciate the meaning of the term as it is understood in the new law: that assistance which the Church renders, by her liturgy and prayers, in the obsequies of her children.[11]

With regard to the unbaptized non-Catholic, he is, of course, deprived by law of Christian burial by the very fact of his not being baptized.[12]

However, instances are not lacking of a partial relaxation of this prohibition, a relaxation that cannot be called a privilege, but merely the choosing of the lesser of two evils. There are several replies of the ecclesiastical authorities in regard to the necessity—which must be faced at times—of allowing the burial in consecrated ground of those to whom it is denied by law. It has always been insisted however, that the toleration was merely a passive one. The tenor of the replies to questions submitted to the Holy See has clearly demonstrated a consistent and unvarying attitude that may be considered to be the mind of the Church in this matter. As far back as the sixteenth and seventeenth centuries the problem was submitted to Rome, according to two decisions of the Congregation of the Council, which declare that the burial of non-Catholics in blessed ground is to be tolerated only when it cannot be avoided.[13] In 1744 Benedict XIV ordered that the burial of

[11] Cf. Chapter I, p. 120.

[12] Canon 1239, § 1.

[13] S. C. C., 24 aug. 1579; 16 iun. 1668—Pallottini, *Collectio . . . S. C. C.*, "*Sepultura*," III, nn. 42, 43.

non-Catholics in Catholic cemeteries was to be suffered only to avoid a greater evil.[14] During the same century the Holy Office granted the most passive toleration of the burial of non-Catholics under strict necessity. No consent or approval was to be given and the act was to be permitted only to prevent a greater evil.[15]

Again in 1859, in reply to a question as to whether non-Catholics and Catholics might share the same private burial place, the Holy Office replied that the decree of 1781 was to be the norm in such cases: *"Curent episcopi totis viribus ut cuncta fiant ad norman sacrorum canonum; quatenus vero absque scandalo et periculo id obtineri non possit, tolerari potest."* [16]

When some doubt arose as to whether that reply of the Holy Office, as interpreted by the II Plenary Council of Baltimore,[17] was a privilege or a toleration, the Holy Office clarified all doubt by its reply of 1888 wherein it ordered that the Baltimore decree be understood in the light of the decree of the Holy Office of 1859, and added: *"adeo ut tolerantia de qua agitur sit tolerantia mere passiva ad praecavenda maiora mala."* [18]

Donnelly has very well outlined the significance of the correction by the Holy Office:

> Consequently the exception made by the Holy Office was intended solely as passive tolerance to prevent

14 Const. *"Inter Omnigenas,"* 2 febr. 1744—*Fontes*, n. 339.

15 S. C. C. Off., instr. (*ad Ep. Scepusien.*), 16 aug. 1781—*Fontes*, 843.

16 S. C. C. Off., 30 mart. 1859—*Fontes*, n. 949. In re the use of this decree by the Provincial Council of Prague (1860) and the II Plenary Council of Baltimore (1866) with regard to family plots, cf. pp. 63-65 in the Historical Part of this work; also, Donnelly, "Certain Problems of Ecclesiastical Burial"—*The Ecclesiastical Review*, CIII (1940), 2-5.

17 "Ex mente Sedis Apostolicae toleratur, ut in sepulchris gentilitiis, quae videlicet privata et peculiaria pro Catholicis laicorum familiis aedificantur, cognatorum et affinium etiam acatholicorum corpora tumulentur." n. 389.

18 S. C. C. Off., 4 iul. 1888—*Coll. S. C. P. F.*, n. 1178.

> greater harm, a case of choosing the lesser of two evils. It was not meant to be a special *privilege,* conceding a *positive* right at variance with the common law. However it was an official interpretation of how the general law was to be applied, and for that reason, can be appealed to in the enforcement of the law of the Code . . . but the principle can be applied only in so far as the interment of the non-Catholic is necessary to prevent the evils that are feared. For that reason each case must be decided separately and on its own merits, lest the passive tolerance assume the form of a positive privilege and be extended when circumstances do not warrant it. Beste (*Introductio in Codicem,* p. 603) considers that the fear of arousing hatred toward the Church, or of alienating the people from the Church, or of causing disturbance or other serious trouble would be enough to justify tolerance of the burial of a non-Catholic in a Catholic *sepulchrum gentilitium.* In all cases, the spiritual good of the persons concerned should be the paramount consideration." [19]

Some may feel that since the II Plenary Council of Baltimore spoke only of burial in Catholic family plots, it limited the interpretation of the decree of the Holy Office to burial of non-Catholics in only such plots. But there seems to be no foundation for such a restriction, for the Baltimore decree was based upon the decree of the Council of Prague,[20] which, in turn, was but a formulation of the reply of the Holy Office of 1859. Moreover, it is evident from the terms of that reply of the Holy Office that more is implied than was asked in the original question: may non-Catholics be buried in Catholic family burial places? The Holy Office permitted that non-Catholics may be buried in blessed ground when it is necessary to avoid scandal or greater evil. For to draw a distinction between blessed plots or tombs or cemeteries is quite useless; blessed ground or blessed places are of the same character whether they be a building, ground or a stone vault. It is the blessing that matters and it is the blessing that is in question:

19 *The Ecclesiastical Review,* CIII (1940), *loc. cit.*

20 Tit. III, c. 13, n. 2—*Coll. Lac.,* V, 468.

"Evidently the extent of its [the Holy Office] *toleratio* is not dependent on the material character of the place of burial. If interment in a family vault, even outside the cemetery, can be tolerated *ad maiora mala vitanda,* why should it be forbidden in an ordinary grave? The reason why the burial of a non-Catholic in a Catholic cemetery is not allowed is *because of the sacredness of the place.* Certainly a family plot is no more sacred than a mausoleum. What is tolerated in one may for the same reason be tolerated in the other. *Ubi eadem est ratio, ibi eadem debet esse iuris dispositio.*" [21]

The reasons therefore, for such a toleration are two; to avoid scandal or greater evil.

It may seem strange that scandal can be given the faithful by the refusal of the Church to permit the burial of non-Catholics in Catholic cemeteries, and may be given to such an extent that its avoidance is a matter of major concern. That such is the case, however, is amply demonstrated by evidence that is contemporary with the legislation just considered:

"If there is danger of scandal, then the bishop is free to exercise his discretion by admitting into consecrated ground one or another of those who, though belonging to Catholic families, have, nevertheless, neglected to prove their right to rest there by embracing the Catholic faith. This is a passive toleration to avoid greater evil" . . . "If, as in the case of a mixed marriage, it happen that a non-Catholic dies in the bosom of a Catholic family, the Church, rather than see dissension and public scandal arise, would for the time yield a measure of her right and of her sacred discipline for the sake of peace and order." [22]

The Fathers of the III Plenary Council of Baltimore (1884) had to take cognizance of the possibility of this type of scandal in reference to the necessity of tolerating the burial of converts in non-Catholic cemeteries:

[21] Donnelly, *ibid.*, pp. 4-5; cf. above, pp. 64-65.

[22] *The American Ecclesiastical Review,* I (1889), 207, 208.

> "Hinc plurium acatholicorum animi ab Ecclesia alienantur, aliquando etiam fideles et conversorum consanquinei, qui inter ipsius mortis tristitias legis rigorem incusant, odia adversus Ecclesiae ministros suscipiunt et quandoque a fide omnino deficiunt." [23]

That the times have not lessened this possibility of grave harm to souls and to the Church by a too severe enforcement of the burial law is further proved by the fact that in these days Catholics are all too frequently indifferent to Catholic burial because of family or temporal ties.[24] Therefore there remain many cases in which toleration of both evils is rendered necessary to avoid a greater evil.[25] Among the greater evils may be considered the possibility of the loss of the family to the Church; or the danger of the eventual burial of the whole family in a non-Catholic cemetery if the non-Catholic has to be buried there.

This evil may be obviated if a separate part of new cemeteries be set aside, unblessed, for those who are united in mixed marriages, and the blessing of the grave of the Catholic party be deferred until the time of interment.

It cannot be made too clear that the toleration is not a concession of a privilege or of a favor; it is not to be used by any pastor without the permission of the bishop; it must be referred to the bishop for his approval in each individual case; it is not to be allowed if the evil anticipated can in any other way be avoided.

Since none of the replies of the Holy Office distinguished between the burial of baptized and unbaptized non-Catholics, it would seem that no distinction is to be made.[26]

It has already been noted in regard to the violation of the cemetery [27] that there need be no concern felt over the burial of a baptized non-Catholic in a Catholic cemetery, but it may

23 *Concilii Plenarii Baltimorensis Tertii Decreta*, n. 317.

24 Raus—*Theologisch-practische Quartalschrift*, LXXX (1927), 122.

25 *Loc. cit.*

26 Donnelly, *ibid.*, p. 3, not. 5.

27 P. 239.

now be asked if the burial of one who is not baptized will not violate the cemetery? A conflict would therefore appear to exist between the toleration granted and the law on violation.

The contradiction is only apparent, however, for even in the new law the Legislator has provided for the burial of non-Catholics of all sorts in a blessed cemetery,[28] on condition, it is true, that Catholics will constitute a major portion of those buried there, and also that there be no other way for Catholics to have burial places of their own. Despite these conditions the fact remains that there is provision made for a blessed cemetery in which there will be buried not only Catholics, but others, whether they be baptized or unbaptized. There is apparent here a derogation, at least in part, by the Legislator himself, of canon 1172, § 1, unless one were prepared to hold that the Church would allow the blessing of a cemetery which she clearly foresaw was to be frequently, even daily, violated.[29]

If the Legislator has gone so far to allow the blessing of cemeteries for the use of the faithful which he clearly forsees will be used by others, there is the greater likelihood that the legitimate toleration of the burial of an unbaptized person, to prevent a greater evil, would not violate a blessed cemetery.

The strongest evidence that such a burial would not constitute the violation is to be found in the nature of the violation

28 Canon 1206, § 2.

29 Wernz-Vidal: "Difficultas potius est circa characterem coemeterii benedicti, in quo toleratur inhumatio acatholici (c. 1206, § 2): estne locus sacer ex benedictione? Ex tenore citati canonis videtur asserendum; sed tunc videtur dicendum, ex necessitate illius tolerantiae, derogari partialiter canoni 1172, § 1, 4°, secus coemeterium et fere quotidie esset reconciliandum." *Ius Canonicum*, IV, n. 563; " . . . quod non videtur pollui ex sepultura infidelis vel acatholici, secus Ecclesia, canone 1206, § 2, permitteret coemeterii benedictionem cum praevisione certae frequentissimae pollutionis." *Op. cit.*, IV, n. 567, not. (27); Coronata: "In canone 1206, § 2, contineri videtur partialis dispensatio a c. 1172, § 1, 4°; . . . "—*Inst. Iur. Can.*, II, n. 792; "Exceptio a lege generali . . . hic tolerari videtur, enim dicitur benedicendum coemeterium, etsi supponitur corpora haereticorum aut infidelium sepelienda esse."—*De Locis et Temporibus Sacris*, n. 137.

itself. In the old law it was disputed under which circumstances the burial of an unbaptized person polluted the cemetery.[30] But in the new law a cemetery is violated only when the conditions prescribed by the law have been fulfilled. Thus the actual burial of an infidel *does not in itself constitute violation.* The act must be a *delict,* and the delict must be *notorious.*[31]

Further, the infidelity itself must be gravely culpable.[32] Therefore, if there is any doubt about the certitude of the breach of law, whether this doubt be one of law or one of fact, or if there is any doubt of the gravity of the act or of the place where it was committed there is no violation.[33]

Even if a tolerated burial were a breach of the law, and even were it a grave one, the necessity for the publicity of the grave breach of law is so great that if the act was not public there is no violation; but if the act later becomes public, violation exists only from that moment.[34]

Beyond the concession already made, there seems to be no legal reason why the Bishop could not, for reasons that to him seemed valid, permit a priest to offer a few prayers, not liturgical, and in private, over the deceased non-Catholic. The act must be dissociated in every way from the appearance of a Catholic ceremony; nor could it be allowed if there were any probability that it would be interpreted as Christian burial.

30 Coronata: "Hanc violationis ex infidelium sepultura causam, ex Decreto Gratiani excerptam, ante Codicem non omnes admittebant, quia Decretum vi obligandi carebat, et proinde ut casus violationis dubiae dubio iuris habebatur."—*De Locis et Temporibus Sacris*, n. 28.

31 Canon 2329; Coronata: "Violatio ecclesiae aut coemeterii est *delictum* ecclesiasticum."—*Inst. Iur. Can.*, II, n. 747; "Ecclesia (or cemetery, cf. canon 1207) violatur infra recensitis tantum actibus, dummodo certi sint, notorii . . . "—canon 1172, § 1.

32 Coronata, *op. cit.*, II, n. 748; Vermeersch-Creusen, *Epitome*, II, n. 478; Gasparri, *Tractatus Canonicus de SS. Eucharistia*, I, n. 253; Many, *De Locis Sacris*, n. 34.

33 Coronata, *Inst. Iur. Can.*, II, n. 748; Many, *De Locis Sacris*, 36-37; Gasparri, *De SS. Eucharistia*, I, n. 246.

34 Coronata, *loc. cit.;* Many, *loc. cit.;* Gasparri, *loc. cit.*

All due precautions would have to be taken that it would be understood as it was meant: as a mere act of charity, in no way to be considered as an official act or ceremony.

The necessity of restricting such actions, so precariously liable to be associated with contempt of the law, to only those cases wherein they are clearly justified in the eyes of the Ordinary need hardly be stressed any further.

ARTICLE III.—THE BURIAL OF CATHOLICS IN NON-CATHOLIC CEMETERIES

A matter so closely connected with the present discussion that it merits being considered at this point is that of the granting of or the refusing of Christian burial to Catholics who are to be buried in a non-Catholic cemetery when a Catholic one is available. The two questions are so intimately associated that they will be considered together, and only from the point of view of the practice in this country. The fact that European cemeteries are largely public property, set aside for the common use of all the citizens, precludes the need of any consideration of that question here.[35]

A brief review of the law of the Baltimore Councils is in order here before the law of the Code is considered. The I Plenary Council of Baltimore (1852) denied Christian burial to all who were not to be buried in Catholic cemeteries wherever these were available.[36]

The II Plenary Council (1866) mitigated the rigor of the law of the earlier Council by adding two amendments of its own, and one at the direction of the Sacred Congregation for the Propagation of the Faith. It decreed that exception may be made for converts who have non-Catholic relatives surviving them and who have a lot in a non-Catholic cemetery. They

35 Cf. Maroto—*Apollinaris,* I (1928), 278, not. (43) ; *L'Ami du Clergé,* XXXVII (1920), 192.

36 This provision of the I Plenary Council was repeated in the II Plenary Council (1866) before certain amendments were attached to it.—*Concilii Plenarii Baltimorensis II Decreta,* n. 391.

may be granted the rites of Christian burial at the house or in the church, if the pastor believes that it will be for the good of souls, or that it is necessary for any other reason. It decreed also that Catholics who had acquired a lot in a non-Catholic cemetery *sine fraude legis* or at a time prior to 1853, in which bodies already have been interred, may have the rites of Christian burial performed in the house, if the pastor either chooses to grant this or feels that in conscience he can grant it.[37] But services for the latter could not be held in the Church without the specific permission of the Ordinary.[38]

The last amendment ordered that when the Catholic must be buried in a non-Catholic cemetery, and when no Catholic portion can be obtained therein, the grave is to be blessed according to the rites prescribed by the Ritual.[39] The II Plenary Council finally urged that the common law on Christian burial be observed "as soon and as far as possible."[40] This Council, therefore wished to enforce the common law of the Church in so far as it was possible under the circumstances prevailing in our country, one of which was the large number of converts to whom some consideration had to be given for the good of the Church itself.

The III Plenary Council (1884) further mitigated the law as formulated by the two preceding councils. It noted that the great number of converts to the faith raised a special problem here; that it appeared harsh to them and to Catholics who had obtained a lot in a non-Catholic cemetery prior to 1853, or *sine fraude legis,* in which relatives were already buried, that they should have to be buried apart from their relatives and kinfolk. It therefore amended the law to permit the granting of Christian burial rites to the two classes of people above specified, *either* in the house or in the Church, *unless* the bishop

[37] " . . . pastoris arbitrio et conscientiae relinquimus . . . ,"—*Conc. Plen. Balt. II Decreta*, n. 392.

[38] *Loc. cit.*

[39] "Additum ex Instructione I, S. C. Prop. Fide, Jan. 24, 1868, Art. 17,"—*op. cit.*, n. 392, not. 2.

[40] *Op. cit.*, n. 393.

had forbidden the concession for grave reasons. It thus gave the pastor the liberty to perform the services in either place unless the bishop had prohibited it. Finally, it ordered that, with these exceptions, no Christian burial was to be granted to a Catholic who was to be buried in a non-Catholic cemetery, without the express permission of the Ordinary.[41]

It should not pass unnoticed that the mitigations of the law of the I Plenary Council, which was but the common law of the Church, were introduced by the II and III Councils only because of the force of circumstances peculiar to this country.[42]

Since the exceptions to the common law legislated by the Councils of Baltimore are particular law, this consiliar law is now abrogated [43] because of its opposition to the law of the Code.[44]

Despite this abrogation the fact remains that the conditions that called for the exceptions, and the motives that prompted the granting of the concessions made in the Baltimore Councils, remain the same today as then. Non-Catholic relatives of Catholic converts still feel that it is a harsh law that separates the convert from final rest with the other members of his family in the family lot in the non-Catholic cemetery. They

41 *Decreta Concilii Plenarii Baltimorensis Tertii*, nn. 317, 318.

42 "Cum tamen conditionem, in qua nostrates versantur, consideremus, legis huius (of the I Plenary Council) rigor mitigari aliquantulum posse videtur."—*Concilii Plenarii Baltimorensis II Decreta*, n. 392; " . . . ob conditionem in qua nostrates versantur . . . "—*Decreta Concilii Plenarii Baltimorensis Tertii*, n. 317.

43 Canon 6, 1°: Leges quaelibet sive universales, sive particulares, praescriptis huius Codicis oppositae, abrogantur, nisi de particularibus legibus aliud expresse caveatur;" Cf. Barrett, "*A Comparative Study of the Councils of Baltimore and the Code of Canon Law*, The Catholic University of America Canon Law Studies, n. 83, Washington, D. C.: The Catholic University of America, 1932.

44 Canons 1205, § 1 and 1206, §§ 2, 3, command that the faithful be buried in blessed cemeteries, unless the right of the Church to have such is impeded; in the latter event, their grave, wherever it be, is to be blessed.

feel it is an arbitrary application of a law to an exceptional case. They are often incensed by the rigor of the law, and the Church appears cruel and overbearing in their eyes. It is of no avail to assert that the law is the law; much harm is done, particularly because of the sorrow and bitterness that are added to the family at a time when trial is already pressing heavily upon them. This was the opinion of the Fathers of the III Plenary Council and it was this opinion that motivated their mitigation of the law.[45]

There are still Catholics who obtain lots in non-Catholic cemeteries through ignorance of the law. The number is fewer, no doubt, than in the days of the Baltimore Councils, but the fact remains that they should not be punished for something for which they were not fully responsible. For Catholics especially, the refusal of Christian burial is a severe penalty, and one that, from the clearest indications in the law itself, should not be inflicted unless for the most serious delicts.

It is quite clear, then, that the same conditions which caused the Fathers of the Baltimore Councils to see the necessity of a mitigation of the law *in particular instances, at the discretion of the bishop,* may be encountered today as they were then.

Although the law of the Baltimore Councils is abrogated, the practice that that law sanctioned both ante-dated its enactment and follows its abrogation. It is indisputable that the custom has been for the bishops of this country to administer this law in accordance with what, in their view, the good of religion required. That is quite as true today, wherever the necessity arises, as it ever was. Although some dioceses have forbidden Christian burial to those who are not to be buried in Catholic cemeteries, this is not the rule for the whole country. It is not difficult to understand that, where Catholic cemeteries are sufficiently provided, it is according to the spirit of the law that they be used exclusively. But where they are deficient in number, as they still may be in portions of the United States, exceptions must be made.

45 Cf. above, p. 244.

The practice that has prevailed in the United States is quite justifiable. It is legal as a custom that is immemorial, and one concerning which the bishops may feel, in certain circumstances as they may arise in this country, that it cannot prudently be discontinued.[46]

It may be objected that one hundred years have not elapsed between the I Plenary Council of Baltimore in 1852 and the coming into effect of the Code in 1918. But it is not to be ignored that the fact that the Council took action on the matter is of itself proof that the practice was then already prevalent. Nor is it hard to conceive that the further back one goes in the history of the nation, the greater must have been the necessity for the exception to the common law, because of the greater scarcity of Catholic cemeteries.

It is questionable whether the decree of the I Plenary Council broke the custom that was so soon thereafter sanctioned by the II Plenary Council, in clear and explicit terms, as a necessity that had been proved by the fact that the law of the I Council was too rigorous for the conditions of the United States. In looking back, therefore, throughout the entire span of the history of the Church in America, one notes that the one and sole attempt to enforce the common law was that made by the I Plenary Council, an attempt which fourteen years later was officially admitted as an unsuccessful one by the Fathers of the II Plenary Council.

Further, even if it be maintained that the action of the I Plenary Council broke the possibility of a hundred year precedent, it should not be overlooked that a custom may be valid before the lapse of the time required by the law, if the tacit consent to it may be deduced from conclusive facts.[47] The

[46] "Vigentes in praesens contra horum statuta consuetudines sive universales sive particulares . . . quae quidem centenariae et immemorabiles sint, tolerari poterunt, si Ordinarii pro locorum ac personarum adiunctis existiment eas prudenter submoveri non posse; . . . "—canon 5.

[47] Wernz: "Quamprimum enim de illo tacito consensu ex factis concludentibus constat, iam ante lapsum temporis ad praescriptionem legi-

tacit consent of the Holy See to the practice of the bishops of this country of making necessary exemptions from the burial law is clearly deducible. Not only is there no instance of the Holy See's objection to this practice, but there is a clear sign of at least implied consent in the addition that was made to the decrees of the II Plenary Council by the Sacred Congregation for the Propagation of the Faith, when it amended the statutes of that Council to include the blessing of the grave in such instances when Catholics were not being buried in Catholic cemeteries.[48]

This at least tacit consent has been indubitably demonstrated since the Code in the approval by the Holy See of the decree of the IV Provincial of Portland (1932), in which it was provided that all cases of the burial of a Catholic in a non-Catholic cemetery, or of a non-Catholic in a Catholic cemetery are to be referred to the Ordinary.[49] The Synods of Spokane (1939) and of Seattle (1938) have identical decrees in which it is ordered that any question of the burial of a non-Catholic member of a lot owner's family is to be decided by the Bishop.[50] The Portland Council likewise provided for the ecclesiastical rites in a non-Catholic cemetery, with the permission of the Ordinary.[51]

The recent reply of the Holy Office[52] does not militate against the assertion that the Holy See has not reproved the practice prevailing here. That decision declares that the simple desire of a converted non-Catholic to be buried with his relatives or parents is not sufficient to justify his burial in a non-Catholic cemetery. It has never been the practice here to

time requisiti validum habetur ius consuetudinarium." — *Ius Decretalium*, I, n.190.

48 Cf. above, p. 248, note 39.

49 *Acta et Decreta Provincialis Portlandensis Quarti*, Decretum n. 352.

50 *Synodus Diocesana Spokanensis Prima*, Appendix XVII, 206A; *Synodus Diocesana Seattlensis, Quinta*, Appendix III, n. 33.

51 *Op. cit., Decretum* n. 346.

52 *Periodica*, XXVI (1937), 467-468.

permit such a burial solely for such a reason. But the reason for any and all exceptions to the common law has always been: to prevent the greater evil for the Church, and religion, that would arise in an individual case from the full application of the law on Christian burial. This is a reason that the Holy See itself advanced for the necessary toleration of the burial of non-Catholics in Catholic cemeteries,[53] and the only one that prompted the exceptions made by the Fathers of the Councils of Baltimore.

The practice of American bishops in dispensing from the law on Christian burial in the individual case, whether it be to allow a non-Catholic's burial in a Catholic cemetery or a Catholic's burial in a non-Catholic cemetery may be also justified by canon 81.[54] For the three conditions required by the canon may be present in an individual case: recourse to the Holy See is out of the question in the matter of Christian burial which will brook no delay; there may be danger of grave harm in delay in deciding the case; it is a matter in which the Holy See has been accustomed to dispense, evidence of which is present in the attitude of the Holy See in approving the decrees of the Plenary Councils of Baltimore and of the Portland Council in regard to giving the bishops discretionary powers in individual cases. Evidence is also found in the at least tacit toleration of the situation that prevails in those countries in which cemeteries are the property of the state and in which these cemeteries are used for the burial both of the baptized and of the unbaptized, of Catholics, of Protestants, and of such who were of no faith. In both instances, the toleration is one that is born of necessity.

Moreover, there is the interesting opinion that the bishops

53 Cf. p. 241.

54 "A generalibus Ecclesiae legibus Ordinarii infra Romanum Pontificem dispensare nequeunt, ne in casu quidem particulari, nisi haec potestas eisdem fuerit explicite vel implicite concessa, aut nisi difficilis sit recursus ad Sanctam Sedem et simul in mora sit periculum gravis damni, et de dispensatione agatur quae a Sede Apostolica concedi solet."

of a country may, through customs, acquire the right to dispense from a universal law.[55] According to this opinion, Donnelly believes that such a custom could now be recognized as fully established in favor of the American Hierarchy, if the American Bishops have continuously been making the exceptions which were sanctioned by the III Plenary Council of Baltimore.[56]

Finally, with regard to denying Christian burial to Catholics who are to be buried in a non-Catholic cemetery, it should be recalled that the law always leaves to the bishops and judges the discretionary power to moderate penalties.[57] Furthermore, penalties are inflicted for justice's sake, but within the limits of social usefulness.[58] Therefore it may happen that at times society is helped much more by the remission than by the execution of a penalty.[59]

It may therefore be safely concluded that the granting or the refusing of Christian burial, in so far as such action would be the result of the choice of the place of burial, depends by force of circumstances in this country, wherever no diocesan statutes have regulated it, upon the discretion of the Ordinary,

55 Van Hove, *De Privilegiis—De Dispensationibus* (*Commentarium Lovaniense*, vol. I, tom. V, Mechliniae-Romae: Dessain, 1939), n. 391; Vermeersch-Creusen, *Epitome*, I, n. 191. Reilly, *The General Norms of Dispensation*, The Catholic University of America Canon Law Studies, n. 119, Washington, D. C.: The Catholic University of America, 1939, pp. 84, 85.

56 "Certain Problems of Ecclesiastical Burial,"—*The Ecclesiastical Review*, CIII (1940), 8.

57 Roberti: "Idem (ius Canonicum) semper episcopis ac iudicibus reliquit discretam potestatem moderandi poenas." — *De Delictis et Poenis*, n. 237.

58 Roberti: "Poenae dantur ex iustitia sed iuxta limites utilitatis socialis," *op. cit.*, n. 267; "Limites iustitiae humanae definiuntur necessitate societatis . . . Igitur potestas puniendi humana habet fundamentum in iustitia, limites in necessitate sociali. Quae propositio converti nequit quia utilitas non potest esse fundamentum poenae." *op. ct.*, n. 32.

59 Roberti, *op. cit.*, n. 267; Cocchi, *Commentarium in Codicem*, V, n. 71; Beste, *Introductio in Codicem*, p. 603.

who is to be governed by the exigencies of places and persons, that he may decide what will be to the best interests of souls in his diocese.[60]

[60] *L'Ami du Clergé*: "en face de la décadence regrettable des moeurs de nos temps, nous avons toujours défendu et justifié Pattitude de l'Eglise et de tous ceux qui à leur suite mettent en pratique les tolérances nécessaires *ad maiora mala vitanda*, c'est à dire, pour le plus grand bien général de la société chrétienne." XXXVIII (1921), 554.

BIBLIOGRAPHY

Sources

Acta Apostolicae Sedis, Commentarium Officiale, Romae, 1909-

Acta Sanctae Sedis, 41 vols., Romae, 1865-1908.

Bullarium Diplomatum et Privilegiorum Romanorum Pontificum Taurinensis Editio, 25 vols., Augustae Taurinorum, 1857-1872.

Codex Iuris Canonici Pii X Pontificis Maximi iussu digestus Benedicti XV Papae auctoritate promulgatus, Romae, Typis Polyglottis Vaticanis, 1917.

Codex Theodosianus, ed. P. Kreuger, Th. Mommsen, P. M. Meyer, 3 vols., Berolini, 1905.

Codex Iuris Canonici Fontes cura Emi. Petri Card. Gasparri editi, 9 vols., Romae (later Civitate Vaticana) : Typis Polyglottis Vaticanis, 1923-1939. (Vols. VII, VIII, IX ed. *cura et studio* Emi. Iustiniani Card. Serédi).

Collectanea in Usum Secretariae Sacrae Congregationis Episcoporum et Regularium, cura A. Bizzarri, secretarii, Romae, 1885.

Collectanea Sacrae Congregationis de Propaganda Fide, 2 vols., Romae, 1907.

Concilia Provincialia Baltimori, 1829-1846, Baltimore, 1847.

Concilii Plenarii Baltimorensis II Decreta. Baltimore, 1875.

Corpus Iuris Civilis (Kreuger-Mommsen-Schoell-Kroll), 5. ed., 3 vols., Berolini, 1928-1929.

Corpus Iuris Canonici, ed. Lipsiensis 2., Aemilius Ludovicus Richter-Aemilius Friedburg, ed. anastatice repetita, 2 vols., Lipsiae: Tauchnitz, 1928.

Corpus Scriptorum Ecclesiasticorum Latinorum, ed. consilio et impensis Academiae Litterarum Caesariae Vindobonensis, Vindobonae, 1865-

Decreta Concilii Plenarii Baltimorensis Tertii, Baltimore, 1886.

Decretales D. Gregorii Papae IX una cum Glossis Restitutae, Romae, 1582.

Didascalia et Constitutiones Apostolorum, ed. Funk, 2 vols., Paderbornae, 1905.

Hardouin, Jean, *Acta Conciliorum et Epistolae Decretales ac Constitutiones Summorum Pontificum,* 12 vols., Parisiis, 1715.

Liber Sextus Decretalium, una cum Clementinis et Extravagantibus Earumque Glossis Restitutis, Romae, 1582.

Jaffé, Philippus, *Regesta Pontificum Romanorum ab condita Ecclesia ad annum post Christum MCXCVIII,* 2. ed., 2 vols. in 1, Lipsiae, 1885-1888.

Mansi, Joannes, *Sacrorum Conciliorum Nova et Amplissima Collectio*, 53 vols., Parisiis, 1901-1927.

Migne, Jacques Paul, *Patrologiae Cursus Completus, Series Graeca*, 161 vols., Parisiis, 1856-1866.

————, *Patrologiae Cursus Completus, Series Latina*, 221 vols., 1844-1864.

Pallottini, Salvator, *Collectio Omnium Conclusionum et Resolutionum Quae in Causis Propositis apud S. Congr. Cardinalium S. Consilii Tridentini Interpretum prodierunt ab anno 1564 ad annum 1860*, 17 vols., Romae, 1868-1893.

Rituale Romanum iussu editum Pauli V Pontificis Maximi, Romae, 1614.

Rituale Romanum Pauli V Pontificis Maximi iussu editum, a Benedicto XIV et a Pio X castigatum et auctum, Romae, 1903.

Rituale Romanum Pauli V Pontificis Maximi iussu editum aliorumque Pontificum cura recognitum atque auctoritate Sanctissimi D. N. Pii Papae XI ad normam codicis iuris canonici accomodatum, Romae, 1935.

Reference Works

Alterius, Marius, *Disputationes de Censuris Ecclesiasticis*, 2 vols., Romae, 1616.

André, l'Abbé, *Dictionnaire de Droit Canonique*, 2 vols. in 1, Paris, 1844.

André-Condis, *Dictionnaire de Droit Canonique*, 4 vols., Paris, 1901.

Ayrinhac, H. A., *Administrative Legislation in the New Code of Canon Law*, New York, Longmans Green, 1930.

———— and Lydon, P. J., *Penal Legislation in the New Code of Canon Law*, New York, Benziger Bros., 1936.

(Bachofen), Charles Augustine, *A Commentary on the New Code of Canon Law*, 8 vols., St. Louis: Herder, 1931-1938.

Barbosa, Augustinus, *Iuris Ecclesiastici Universi Libri Tres*, Lugduni, 1660.

————, *De Officio et Potestate Parochi*, 2 vols., Lugduni, 1656.

Barrett, John D., *A Comparative Study of The Third Plenary Council of Baltimore and The Code*, The Catholic University of America Canon Law Studies, n. 83, Washington, D. C.: The Catholic University of America, 1932.

Bernard, Antoine, *La Sépulture en Droit Canonique*, Paris, Loviton, 1933.

Beste, Udalricus, *Introductio in Codicem*, Collegeville, Minn.: St. John's Abbey Press, 1938.

Blat, Albertus, *Commentarium Textus Codicis Iuris Canonici*, 5 vols. in 7, Romae: Collegio "Angelico," 1921-1938. Vol. III, partes II-VI, 2. ed., 1934; vol. V, 1. ed., 1924.

Buvée, H., *Memento Pratique du Ministère Paroissial*, Paris, Maison de la Bonne Presse, 1921.

Bingham, Joseph, *The Antiquities of The Christian Church*, 2 vols., London, 1878.

Cabrol, F. Dom, and Leclercq, H., Dom, *Dictionnaire d'Archéologie Chrétienne et de Liturgie*, 14 vols., Paris, Letouzey et Ané, 1924-

Cappello, Felix, *De Censuris iuxta Codicem Iuris Canonici*, 3. ed., Augustae Taurinorum: Marietti, 1933.

————, *Summa Iuris Canonici*, 3 vols., Romae, Universitas Gregoriana, Vol. I, 3. ed., 1938; vol. II, 3. ed., 1939; vol. III, 1. ed., 1936.

————, *Tractatus Canonico-Moralis de Sacramentis*, 3 vols. in 6, Taurini: Marietti, 1932-1939. Vol. I, 3. ed., 1938; vol. II, pars I, 3. ed., 1938; vol. II, pars II, 1. ed., 1932; vol. II, pars III, 1935; vol. III, partes I et II, 4. ed., 1939.

Catholic Encyclopedia, The, 15 vols., New York, 1907-1912.

Cavagnis, Felix, *Institutiones Iuris Publici Ecclesiastici*, Romae, 1882.

Cavigioli, Joannes, *De Censuris Latae Sententiae Quae in Codice Iuris Canonici continentur Commentarium*, Taurino: Librería Editrice Internazionale, 1918.

Cerato, Prosdocimus, *Censurae Vigentes*, 2. ed., Patavii: Typis Seminarii, 1921.

Chelodi, Joannes, *Ius Poenale et Ordo Procedendi in Iudiciis Criminalibus iuxta Codicem Iuris Canonici*, 4. ed., recognita et aucta a Vigilio Dalpiaz, Tridenti: Libr. Moderna. Edit. A. Ardesi, 1935.

Cicognani, Amleto, *Canon Law*, authorized translation by J. O'Hara and F. Brennan, Philadelphia: Dolphin Press, 1934.

Cippolini, A., *De Censuris Latae Sententiae*, Taurini, 1925.

Claeys-Bouuaert, F., et Simenon, G., *Manuale Iuris Canonici Ad Usum Seminariorum*, 2. ed., I vol., Gandae et Leodii, 1926.

Clinton, Connell, *The Paschal Precept*, The Catholic University of America, Canon Law Studies, n. 73, Washington, D. C.: The Catholic University of America, 1932.

Cocchi, Guidus, *Commentarium in Codicem Iuris Canonici*, 8 vols., Taurinorum Augustae: Marietti, 1931-1940. Vol. I, 5. ed., 1938; vol. II, 4. ed., 1937; vol. III, 5. ed., 1931, vol. IV et V, 3. ed., 1932; vol. VI, 3. ed., 1933; vol. VII, 3. ed., 1940; vol. VIII, 4. ed., 1938.

Conran, Edward, *The Interdict*, The Catholic University of America, Canon Law Studies, n. 56, Washington, D. C.: The Catholic University of America, 1930.

Coronata, Matthaeus Conte a, *Institutiones Iuris Canonici*, 5 vols.. Taurini: Marietti, 1928-1936; Vol. I, 1928; vol. II, 1933; vol. IV, 1935.

————,*De Locis et Temporibus Sacris*, Taurini, Marietti, 1922.

Crnica, A., *Modificationes in Tractatu de Censuris Iuris Canonici Introductae*, St. Mauritii Agaunensis, 1919.

D'Annibale, J., *Summula Theologiae Moralis*, 5. ed., 3 vols., Romae, 1908.

DeMeester, Alphonsus, *Juris Canonici et Juris Canonico-Civilis Compendium*, nova ed., 3 vols. in 4, Brugis, 1921-1928.

Devoti, Joannes, *Institutionum Canonicarum Libri IV*, Romae, 1830.

Ducange, Charles DeFresne, *Glossarium Mediae et Infimae Latinitatis*, 10 vols., nova editio aucta pluribus verbis aliorum scriptorum a Leopold Fauré, Librarie des Sciences et des Arts, Paris, 1937-1938.

Duchesne, Louis, *Christian Worship*, translated by M. J. McClure, 5. ed., Society for the Promotion of Christian Knowledge: London, 1931.

————, *Le Liber Pontificalis*, 2 vols., Paris, 1892.

Durandus, Gulielmus, *Speculum Iuris*, 3 vols., Venetiis, 1577.

Duranti, Joannes, *De Ritibus Ecclesiae Catholicae Libri Tres*, Romae: 1591.

Eichmann, E., *Lehrbuch des Kirchenrechts auf Grund des Codex Iuris Canonici*, 4. ed., 2 vols., Paderborn: Schöningh, 1934.

Fagnanus, Prosper, *Commentaria Super Quinque Libros Decretalium*, 4 vols., Venetiis, 1697.

Galtier, Paulus, *De Poenitentia*, Parisiis: Beauchesne, 1923.

Gasparri, Pietro, *De SS. Eucharistia*, 3. ed., 2 vols., Parisiis, 1897.

Giraldi, Ubaldus, *Expositio Iuris Pontificii iuxta Recentiorem Ecclesiae Disciplinam*, 3 vols., Romae, 1769.

————, *Animadversiones ad Augustinum Barbosa De Officio et Potestate Parochi*, Romae, 1774.

Gonzalez-Tellez, Emanuel, *Commentaria Perpetua in Singulos Textus Quinque Librorum Decretalium Gregorii IX*, 5 vol. in 4, 1673.

Guérin, Pierre, *Les Conciles Généraux et Particuliers*, 3. ed., 3 vols., Paris, 1897.

Hastings, James, *Encyclopedia of Religion and Ethics*, 10 vols., New York: Scribner's Sons, 1908-1927.

Hefele, Carolus and Leclercq, Henricus, *Histoire des Conciles*, 10 vols. in 18, Paris, 1907, 1921.

Hinschius, Paul, *Das Kirchenrecht der Katholiken und Protestanten in Deutschland*, 6 vols., Berlin, 1869-1897.

Hollweck, Joseph, *Die kirchlichen Strafgesetze*, Mainz 1899.

Hornstein, Edouard, *Les Sépultures*, Paris, 1886.

————, *La Crémation*, Paris, 1886.

Hostiensis, Cardinalis (Henricus de Segusio), *Commentaria in Quinque Libros Decretalium*, 5 vols. in 3, Venetiis, 1581.

————, *Summa Aurea*, Lugduni, 1503.

Hyland, Francis, *Excommunication, Its Nature, Historical Development, and Effects*, The Catholic University of America, Canon Law Studies, n. 49, Washington, D. C.: The Catholic University of America, 1928.

Joannes Andreae, *In Sex Decretalium Libros Novella Commentaria*, 6 vols. in 5, Venetiis, 1581.

Jordanus, Pax, *Elucubrationes Diversae*, 3 vols., Lugduni, 1729.

Lehmkuhl, A., *Theologia Moralis*, 11. ed., 2 vols., Friburgi Bresgoviae, 1910.

Lex, Peter, *Das kirchliche Begräbnisrecht, historisch-kanonistisch dargestellt*, Regensburg, 1904.

MacKenzie, Eric, *The Delict of Heresy*, The Catholic University of America, Canon Law Studies, n. 77, Washington, D. C.: The Catholic University of America, 1932.

Many, S., *De Locis Sacris*, Paris, 1904.

Martène, Dom, *De Antiquis Ritibus Ecclesiae*, 4 vols., Anvers, 1736-1738.

Martigny, l'Abbé, *Dictionnaire des Antiquitées Chrétiennes*, Paris, 1889.

Moriarty, Francis, *The Extraordinary Absolution from Censures*, The Catholic University of America, Canon Law Studies, n. 113, Washington, D. C.: The Catholic University of America, 1938.

Morinus, Joannes, *Commentarius Historicus de Disciplina in Administratione Sacramenti Poenitentiae Tredecim Primis Saeculis in Ecclesia Occidentali, et huc usque in Orientali Observata*, Parisiis, 1651.

Mothon, Joseph, *Institutions Canoniques*, 3 vols., Paris, Desclée-Brouwer et Cie., 1934.

Moulart, F. J., *De Sepultura et Coemeteriis*, Lovanii. 1862.

Murga (De), Petrus, *Disquisitiones Morales et Canonicae de Sepulturis*, 2 vols., Lugduni, 1666.

O'Reilly, John, *Ecclesiastical Sepulture in the New Code of Canon Law*, The Catholic University of America, Canon Law Studies, n. 18. Washington, D. C.: The Catholic University of America, 1923.

Panormitanus, Abbas (Nicolaus De Tudeschis), *Commentaria in Quinque Libros Decretalium*, 5 vols. in 7, Venetiis, 1588.

Petra, Vincentius, *Commentaria in Constitutiones Apostolicas*, 5 vols. in 2, Venetiis, 1729.

Piatus Montensis (Jean Joseph Loiseaux), *Commentarius in Constitutionem Apostolicae Sedis*, Parisiis, 1881.

Pirhing, Enricus, *Ius Canonicum Novo Methodo Explicatum*, 5 vols. in 4, Dilingae, 1674-1678.

Pistocchi, Mario, *I Canoni Penali del Codice Ecclesiastico*, Torino: Marietti, 1925.

Pollock and Maitland, *A History of English Law before the Time of Edward I*, 2 vols., Cambridge, 1899.

Praelectiones Iuris Canonici Habitae in Seminario Sancti Sulpitii, 6. ed., 3 vols., Parisiis, 1886.

Prümmer, Dominicus, *Manuale Iuris Canonici*, 4. et 5. eds., Friburgi Brisgoviae: Herder, 1927.

Quigley, Joseph, *Condemned Societies*, The Catholic University of America, Canon Law Studies, n. 46, Washington, D. C.: The Catholic University of America, 1927.

Raymundus de Pennafort, *Summa*, Veronae, 1744.

Reiffenstuel, Anacletus, *Ius Canonicum Universum*, 5 vols. in 7, Parisiis, 1864-1870.

Roberti, F., *De Delictis et Poenis*, 2. ed., Romae: apud Universitatem Utriusque Iuris, 1938.

Rossi, Giuseppe, *La "Sepultura" e l' "Ius Funerum" nel Diritto Canonico*, Bergamo: Arnaldi, 1920.

Salucci, R., *Il Diritto Penale secondo il Codice de Diritto Canonico*, 2 vols., Subiaco: Tipografia dei Monasteri, 1926-1930.

Santi, Franciscus, *Praelectiones Iuris Canonici*, 4. ed., 5 vols. in 3, Ratisbonae-Romae, 1904.

Schmalzgrueber, Franciscus, *Ius Ecclesiasticum Universum*, 5 vols. in 12, Romae, 1843-1845.

Schroeder, H. J., *Disciplinary Decrees of the General Councils*, St. Louis: Herder, 1937.

Sole, Iacobus, *De Delictis et Poenis-Praelectiones in Lib. V Codicis Iuris Canonici*, Romae: Pustet, 1920.

Thesaurus, Carolus, *De Poenis Ecclesiasticis Praxis Absoluta et Universalis*, nova ed., U. Giraldi, Romae, 1831.

Thomassinus, Ludovicus, *Vetus et Nova Ecclesiae Disciplina circa Beneficia et Beneficiarios*, 10 vols., Parisiis, 1786-1787.

Vacant, A., et Mangenot, E., *Dictionnaire de Théologie Catholique*, 13 vols., Paris, 1903-

Van Espen, Zegerus, *Scripta Omnia*, 4 vols., Lovanii, 1753.

Van Hove, A., *Commentarium Lovaniense in Codicem Iuris Canonici*, vol. I, tom. I, *Prolegomena*, Mechliniae: Dessain, 1928; tom. II, *De Legibus Ecclesiasticis*, Mechliniae: Dessain, 1930; tom. V, *De Privilegiis-De Dispensationibus*, Mechliniae: Dessain, 1939.

Vermeersch, A., et Creusen, J., *Epitome Iuris Canonici*, 3 vols., Vol. I, 6. ed., Vols. II-III, 5. ed., Mechliniae-Romae: Dessain, 1934-1937.

Vito, P., *Questioni Canoniche*, 4 vols. in 1, Napoli: Picone, 1926.

Watkins, Oscar, *A History of Penance*, 2 vols., London: Longmans, 1920.

Wernz, Franciscus, *Ius Decretalium*, 2. ed., 6 vols., Prati, 1906-1913.

———, et Vidal, Petrus, *Ius Canonicum ad Codicis Normam Exactum*, 7 vols. in 8, Romae: apud Universitatem Gregorianum, 1923-1938.

Periodicals

Apollinaris, Romae, 1928-

Archiv für katholisches Kirchenrecht, Innsbruck, 1857-1861; Mainz, 1862-

Collationes Brugenses, Bruges, 1895-

Diritto Ecclesiastico, Il, Romae, 1890-

Ecclesiastical Review, The (originally, *The American Ecclesiastical Review*), Philadelphia, 1889-

Homiletic and Pastoral Review, The, New York, 1900-

Ephemerides Theologicae Lovanienses, Lovanii, 1924-

Jus Pontificium, Romae, 1921-

L'Ami du Clergé, Paris, 1878-

Monitore Ecclesiastico, Il, Romae, 1876-

Nouvelle Revue Théologique, Paris, 1869-

Palestra del Clero, Rovigo, 1922-

Perfice Munus!, Torino, 1926-

Periodica de Re Canonica et Morali utili praesertim Religiosis et Missionariis, Bruges, 1905-

Sal Terrae, Santander, 1912-

Theologisch-praktische Quartalschrift, Linz, 1832-

Principal Articles

Aichner, "Das kirchliche Begräbnis,"—*Archiv für katholisches Kirchenrecht*, I (1857), 25-32, 80-93.

Bernardini, C., "Privatio Sepulturae Ecclesiasticae,"—*Il Diritto Ecclesiastico* XL (1929), 473-479.

Brys, J., "De Corporis Crematione," — *Collationes Brugenses*, XXV (1925), 41-45, 65-67.

———, "De Obligatione Ritus Sepulturae Sacrae," *Collationes Brugenses*, XXVI (1926), 319-321.

———, "De Poenis Latae Sententiae," — *Collationes Brugenses*, XXXIII (1933), 183-185.

———, "De Sepultura Ecclesiastica,"—*Collationes Brugenses*, XXV (1925), 159-163, 241-247.

Cancstri, A., "An concedenda sit sepultura ecclesiastica infantibus defunctis sine baptismo?"—*Apollinaris*, IV (1931), 128-136.

Ciprotti, P., "De Consummatione Delicti," *Apollinaris*, VIII (1935), 224-248; 377-427.

Donnelly, F., "Certain Problems of Ecclesiastical Burial,"—*The Ecclesiastical Review*, CIII (1940), 1-16.

Maroto, P., "De axiomate 'ubi tumulus ibi funus',"—*Apollinaris*, I (1928), 22-35, 125-139, 263-279.

Mostaza, M., "Denegacion de sepultura ecclesiastica," *Sal Terrae*, XIV (1930), 332-338.

Prümmer, D., "Die Feuerbestattung menschlicher Leichen vom Standpunkt der Moral betrachtet,"—*Theologisch-praktische Quartalschrift*, LXXXI (1928), 539-546.

Raus, J., "Bestattung von Katholiken auf einem akatholischen Friedhof, und von Akatholischen auf einem katholischen Gottesacker,"—*Theologisch-praktische Quartalschrift*, LXXX (1927), 122-127.

Schaaf, V., "Catholic Burial of Public Sinners,"—*The Ecclesiastical Review*, XCV (1936), 189-194.

Teodori, I., "Secta Massonica,"—*Apollinaris*, IV (1931), 579-582.

Woywod, S., "The Refusal of Christian Burial,"—*The Homiletic and Pastoral Review*, XXVI (1926), 832-838.

———, "Deniego de la Sepultura Ecclesiastica,"—*Il Monitore Ecclesiastico*, XLIX (1937), 151-158.

ABREVIATIONS

AAS — *Acta Apostolicae Sedis.*
ASS — *Acta Sanctae Sedis.*
C. — *Codex Iustinianus.*
C. Th. — *Codex Theodosianus.*
c. — canon; caput.
cc. — canones; capita.
Coll. Brug. — *Collationes Brugenses.*
Coll. S. C. P. F. — *Collectanea S. C. de Propaganda Fide.*
Coll. S. C. Ep. et Reg. — *Collectanea S. C. Episcorum et Regularium.*
CSCL — *Corpus Scriptorum Ecclesiasticorum Latinorum.*
Fontes — *Codicis Iuris Canonici Fontes cura . . . Gasparri editi.*
Harduin — *Acta Conciliorum et Epistolae Decretales ac Constitutiones Summorum Pontificum.*
MPG — Migne, *Patrologia Graeca.*
MPL — Migne, *Patrologia Latina.*
Mansi — *Sacrorum Conciliorum Nova et Amplissima Collectio.*
P. C. I. — Pontificia Commissio Interpretationis.
S. Poenit. Ap. — Sacra Poenitentia Apostolica.
S. C. C. — Sacra Congregatio Concilii.
S. S. C. Off. — Sacra Congregatio Sancti Officii.

BIOGRAPHICAL NOTE

Charles Augustine Kerin was born on August 30, 1905, at Montpelier, Vermont. Upon completing his studies at Montpelier High School he made his preparatory seminary course at St. Charles College, Catonsville, Md., and graduated in 1926. His two years' course in philosophy he made at the Séminaire de Philosophie, Montreal, 1926-1928. His first year in theology he made at the Grand Séminaire in the same city, 1928-1929. He completed his theological course at St. Mary's Seminary, Baltimore, where he received the degrees of Master of Arts, 1930, of Bachelor of Theology, 1931, and of Bachelor of Canon Law, 1932. He was ordained to the priesthood in 1932 and one year later was admitted into the Society of St. Sulpice. After teaching for five years at St. Charles College, he entered the Catholic University of America at Washington, D. C., in the fall of 1938, to follow a graduate course of studies in the School of Canon Law. He received the degree of the Licentiate in Canon Law in June, 1940.

INDEX

CANON LAW STUDIES

1. Freriks, Rev. Celestine A., C.PP.S., J.C.D., Religious Congregations in Their External Relations, 121 pp., 1916.
2. Galliher, Rev. Daniel M., O.P., J.C.D., Canonical Elections, 117 pp., 1917.
3. Borkowski, Rev. Aurelius L., O.F.M., J.C.D., De Confraternitatibus Ecclesiasticis, 136 pp., 1918.
4. Castillo, Rev. Cayo, J.C.D., Disertacion Historico-Canonica sobre la Potestad del Cabildo en Sede Vacante o Impedida del Vicario Capitular, 99 pp., 1919 (1918).
5. Kubelbeck, Rev. William J., S.T.B., J.C.D., The Sacred Pentitentiaria and Its Relations to Faculties of Ordinaries and Priests, 129 pp., 1918.
6. Petrovits, Rev. Joseph J.C., S.T.D., J.C.D., The New Church Law On Matrimony, X-461 pp., 1919.
7. Hickey, Rev. John J., S.T.B., J.C.D., Irregularities and Simple Impediments in the New Code of Canon Law, 100 pp., 120.
8. Klekotka, Rev. Peter J., S.T.B., J.C.D., Diocesan Consultors, 179 pp., 1920.
9. Wanenmacher, Rev. Francis, J.C.D., The Evidence in Ecclesiastical Procedure Affecting the Marriage Bond, 1920 (Printed 1935).
10. Golden, Rev. Henry Francis, J.C.D., Parochial Benefices in the New Code, IV-119 pp., 1921 (Printed 1925).
11. Koudelka, Rev. Charles J., J.C.D., Pastors, Their Rights and Duties According to the New Code of Canon Law, 211 pp., 1921.
12. Melo, Rev. Antonius, O.F.M., J.C.D., De Exemptione Regularium, X-188 pp., 1921.
13. Schaaf, Rev. Valentine Theodore, O.F.M., S.T.B., J.C.D., The Cloister, X-180 pp., 1921.
14. Burke, Rev. Thomas Joseph, S.T.D., J.C.D., Competence in Ecclesiastical Tribunals, IV-117 pp., 1922.
15. Leech, Rev. George Leo, J.C.D., A Comparative Study of the Constitution, "Apostolicae Sedis" and the "Codex Juris Canonici," 179 pp., 1922.
16. Motry, Rev. Hubert Louis, S.T.D., J.C.D., Diocesan Faculties According to the Code of Canon Law, II-167 pp., 1922.
17. Murphy, Rev. George Lawrence, J.C.D., Delinquencies and Penalties in the Administration and Reception of the Sacraments, IV-121 pp., 1923.
18. O'Reilly, Rev. John Anthony, S.T.B., J.C.D., Ecclesiastical Sepulture in the New Code of Canon Law, II-129 pp., 1923.

19. Michalicka, Rev. Wenceslas Cyrill, O.S.B., J.C.D., Judicial Procedure in Dismissal of Clerical Exempt Religious, 107 pp., 1923.
20. Dargin, Rev. Edward Vincent, S.T.B., J.C.D., Reserved Cases According to the Code of Canon Law, IV-103, pp., 1924.
21. Godfrey, Rev. John A., S.T.B., J.C.D., The Right of Patronage According to the Code of Canon Law, 153 pp., 1924.
22. Hagedorn, Rev. Francis Edward, J.C.D., General Legislation on Indulgences, II-154 pp., 1924.
23. King, Rev. James Ignatius, J.C.D., The Administration of the Sacraments to Dying Non-Catholics, V-141 pp., 1924.
24. Winslow, Rev. Francis Joseph, A.F.M., J.C.D., Vicars and Prefects Apostolic, IV-149 pp., 1924.
25. Correa, Rev. Jose Servelion, S.T.L., J.C.D., La Potestad Legislativa de la Iglesia Catolica, IV-127 pp., 1925.
26. Dugan, Rev. Henry Francis, A.M., J.C.D., The Judiciary Department of the Diocesan Curia, 87 pp., 1925.
27. Keller, Rev. Charles Frederick, S.T.B., J.C.D., Mass Stipends, 167 pp., 1925.
28. Paschang, Rev. John Linus, J.C.D., The Sacramentals According to the Code of Canon Law, 129 pp., 1925.
29. Pointek, Rev. Cyrillus, O.F.M., S.T.B., J.C.D., De Indulto Exclaustrationis necnon Saecularizationis, XIII-289 pp., 1925.
30. Kearney, Rev. Richard Joseph, S.T.B., J.C.D., Sponsors at Baptism According to the Code of Canon Law, IV-127 pp., 1925.
31. Bartlett, Rev. Chester Joseph, A.M., LL.B., J.C.D., The Tenure of Parochial Property in the United States of America, V-108 pp., 1926.
32. Kilker, Rev. Adrian Jerome, J.C.D., Extreme Unction, V-425 pp., 1926.
33. McCormick, Rev. Robert Emmett, J.C.D., Confessors of Religious, VIII-266 pp., 1926.
34. Miller, Rev. Newton Thomas, J.C.D., Founded Masses According to the Code of Canon Law, VII-93 pp., 1926.
35. Roelker, Rev. Edward G., S.T.D., J.C.D., Principles of Privilege According to the Code of Canon Law, XI-166 pp., 1926.
36. Bakalarczyk, Rev. Richardus, M.I.C., J.U.D., De Novitiatu, VIII-208 pp., 1927.
37. Pizzuti, Rev. Lawrence, O.F.M., J.U.L., De Parochis Religiosis, 1927. (Not printed).
38. Bliley, Rev. Nicholas Martin, O.S.B., J.C.D., Altars According to the Code of Canon Law, XIX-132 pp., 1927.
39. Brown, Mr. Brendan Francis, A.B. LL.M., J.U.D., The Canonical Juristic Personality with Special Reference to Its Status in the United States of America, V-212 pp., 1927.

40. Cavanaugh, Rev. William Thomas, C.P., J.U.D., The Reservation of the Blessed Sacrament, VIII-101 pp., 1927.
41. Doheny, Rev. William J., C.S.C., A.B., J.U.D., Church Property: Modes of Acquisition, X-118 pp., 1927.
42. Feldhaus, Rev. Aloysius H., C.PP.S., J.C.D., Oratories, IX-141 pp., 1927.
43. Kelly, Rev. James Patrick, A.B., J.C.D., The Jurisdiction of the Simple Confessor, X-208 pp., 1927.
44. Neuberger, Rev. Nicholas J., J.C.D., Canon 6 or the Relation of the Codex Juris Canonici to the Preceding Legislation, V-95 pp., 1927.
45. O'Keefe, Rev. Gerald Michael, J.C.D., Matrimonial Dispensations, Powers of Bishops, Priests and Confessors, VIII-232 pp., 1927.
46. Quigley, Rev. Joseph A.M., A.B., J.C.B., Condemned Societies, 139 pp., 1927.
47. Zaplotnik, Rev. Johannes Leo, J.C.D., De Vicariis Foraneis, X-142 pp., 1927.
48. Duskie, Rev. John Aloysius, A.B., J.C.D., The Canonical Status of the Orientals in the United States, VIII-196 pp., 1928.
49. Hyland, Rev. Francis Edward, J.C.D., Excommunication, Its Nature, Historical Development and Effects, VIII-181 pp., 1928.
50. Reinmann, Rev. Gerald Joseph, O.M.C., J.C.D., The Third Order Secular of Saint Francis, 201 pp., 1928.
51. Schenk, Rev. Francis J., J.C.D., The Matrimonial Impediments of Mixed Religion and Disparity of Cult, XVI-318 pp., 1929.
52. Coady, Rev. John Joseph, S.T.D., J.U.D., A.M., The Appointment of Pastors, VIII-150 pp., 1929.
53. Kay, Rev. Thomas Henry, J.C.D., Competence in Matrimonial Procedure, VIII-164 pp., 1929.
54. Turner, Rev. Sidney Joseph, C.P., J.U.D., The Vow of Poverty, XLIX-217 pp., 1929.
55. Kearney, Rev. Raymond, A., A.B., S.T.D., J.C.D., The Principles, of Delegation, VII-149 pp., 1929.
56. Conran, Rev. Edward James, A.B., J.C.D., The Interdict, V-163 pp., 1930.
57. O'Neil, Rev. William H., J.C.D., Papal Rescripts of Favor, VII-218 pp., 1930.
58. Bastnagel, Rev. Clement Vincent, J.U.D., The Appointment of Parochial Adjutants and Assistants, XV-257 pp., 1930.
59. Ferry, Rev. William A., A.B., J.C.D., Stole Fees, V-135 pp., 1930.
60. Costello, Rev. John Michael, A.B., J.C.D., Domicile and Quasi-domicile, VII-201 pp., 1930.
61. Kremer, Rev. Michael Nicholas, A.B., S.T.B., J.C.D., Church Support in the United States, VI-1930.

62. Angulo, Rev. Luis, C.M., J.C.D., Legislation de la Iglesia sobre la intencion en la application de la Santa Misa, VII-104 pp., 1931.
63. Frey, Rev. Wolfgang Norbert, O.S.B., A.B., J.C.D., The Act of Religious Profession, VIII-174 pp., 1931.
64. Roberts, Rev. James Brendan, A.B., J.C.D., The Banns of Marriage, XIV-140 pp., 1931.
65. Ryder, Rev. Raymond Aloysius, A.B., J.C.D., Simony, IX-151 pp., 1931.
66. Campagna, Rev. Angelo, Ph.D., J.U.D., Il Vicario Generale del Vescovo, VII-205 pp., 1931.
67. Cox, Rev. Joseph Godfrey, A.B., J.C.D., The Administration ot Seminaries, VI-124 pp., 1931.
68. Gregory, Rev. Donald J., J.U.D., The Pauline Privilege, XV-165 pp., 1931.
69. Donohue, Rev. John F., J.C.D., The Impediment of Crime, VII-110 pp., 1931.
70. Dooley, Rev. Eugene A., O.M.I., J.C.D., Church Law On Sacred Relics, IX-143 pp., 1931.
71. Orth, Rev. Raymond Clement, O.M.C., J.C.D., The Approbation of Religious Institutes, 171 pp., 1931.
72. Pernicone, Rev. Joseph M., A.B., J.C.D., The Ecclesiastical Prohibition of Books, XII-267 pp., 1932.
73. Clinton, Rev. Connell, A.B., J.C.D., The Paschal Precept, IX-108 pp., 1932.
74. Donnelly, Rev. Francis B., A.M., S.T.L., J.C.D., The Diocesan Synod, VIII-125 pp., 1932.
75. Torrente, Rev. Camilo, C.M.F., J.C.D., Las Processiones Sagradas, V-145 pp., 1932.
76. Murphy, Rev. Edwin J., C.PP.S., J.C.D., Suspension Ex Informata Conscientia, XI-122, pp., 1932.
77. Mackenzie, Rev. Eric F., A.M., S.T.L., J.C.D., The Delict of Heresy in its Commission Penalization, Absolution, VII-124 pp., 1932.
78. Lyons Rev. Avitus E., S.T.B., J.C.D., The Collegiate Tribunal of First Instance, XI-147 pp., 1932.
79. Connolly, Rev. Thomas A., J.C.D., Appeals, XI-195 pp., 1932.
80. Sangmeister, Rev. Joseph V., A.B., J.C.D., Force and Fear as Precluding Matrimonial Consent, V-211 pp., 1932.
81. Jaeger, Rev. Leo A., A.B., J.C.D., The Administration of Vacant and Quasi-vacant Episcopal Sees in the United States, IX-229 pp., 1932.
82. Rimlinger, Rev. Herbert T., J.C.D., Error Invalidating Matrimonial Consent, VII-79 pp., 1932.
83. Barrett, Rev. John D.M., S.S., J.C.D., A Comparative Study of the Third Plenary Council of Baltimore and the Code, IX-221 pp., 1932.

84. Carberry, Rev. John J., Ph.D., S.T.D., J.C.D., The Juridical Form of Marriage, X-177 pp., 1934.
85. Dolan, Rev. John L., A.B., J.C.D., The Defensor Vinculi, XII-157 pp., 1934.
86. Hannan, Rev. Jerome D., A.M., S.T.D., LL.B., J.C.D., The Canon Law of Wills, IX-517 pp., 1934.
87. Lemieux, Rev. Delisle A., A.M., J.C.D., The Sentence in Ecclesiastical Procedure, IX-131 pp., 1934.
88. O'Rourke, Rev. James J., A.B., J.C.D., Parish Registers, VII-109 pp., 1934.
89. Timlin, Rev. Bartholomew, O.F.M., A.M., J.C.D., Conditional Matrimonial Consent, X-381 pp., 1934.
90. Wahl, Rev. Francis X., A.B., J.C.D., The Matrimonial Impediments of Consanguinity and Affinity, VI-125 pp., 1934.
91. White, Rev. Robert J., A.B., LL.B., S.T.B., J.C.D., Canonical Ante-Nuptial Promises and the Civil Law, VI-152 pp., 1934.
92. Herrera, Rev. Antonio Parra, O.C.D., J.C.D., Legislation Ecclesiastica sobra el Ayuno y la Abstinencia, XI-191 pp., 1935.
93. Kennedy, Rev. Edwin J., J.C.D., The Special Matrimonial Process in Cases of Evident Nullity, X-165 pp., 1935.
94. Manning, Rev. John J., A.B., J.C.D., Presumption of Law in Matrimonial Procedure, XI-111 pp., 1935.
95. Moeder, Rev. John M., J.C.D., The Proper Bishop for Ordination and Dismissorial Letters, VII-135 pp., 1935.
96. O'Mara, Rev. William A., A.B., J.C.D., Canonical Causes For Matrimonial Dispensations, IX-155 pp., 1935.
97. Reilly, Rev. Peter, J.C.D., Residence of Pastors, IX-81 pp., 1935.
98. Smith, Rev. Mariner T., O.P., S.T.L., J.C.D., The Penal Law For Religious, VII-169 pp., 1935.
99. Whalen, Rev. Donald W., A.M., J.C.D., The Value of Testimonial Evidence in Matrimonial Procedure, XIII-297 pp., 1935.
100. Cleary, Rev. Joseph F., J.C.D., Canonical Limitations on the Alienation of Church Property, VIII-141 pp., 1936.
101. Glynn, Rev. John C., J.C.D., The Promoter of Justice, XX-337 pp., 1936.
102. Brennan, Rev. James H., S.S., A.M., S.T.B., J.C.D., The Simple Convalidation of Marriage, VI-135 pp, 1937.
103. Brunini, Rev. Joseph Bernard, J.C.D., The Clerical Obligations of Canons, 139 and 142, X-121 pp., 1937.
104. Connor, Rev. Maurice, A.B., J.C.D., The Administrative Removal of Pastors, VIII-159 pp., 1937.
105. Guilfoyle, Rev. Merlin Joseph, J.C.D., Custom, XI-144 pp., 1937.
106. Hughes, Rev. James Austin, A.B., A.M., J.C.D., Witnesses in Criminal Trials of Clerics, IX-140 pp., 1937.

107. Jansen, Rev. Raymond J., A.B., S.T.L., J.C.D., Canonical Provisions for Catechetical Instruction, VII-153 pp., 1937.
108. Kealy, Rev. John James, A.B., J.C.D,, The Introductory Libellus in Church Court Procedure, XI-121 pp., 1937.
109. McManus, Rev. James Edward, C.SS.R., J.C.D., The Administration of Temporal Goods in Religious Institutes, XVI-196 pp., 1937.
110. Moriarity, Rev. Eugene James, J.C.D., Oaths in Ecclesiastical Courts, X-115 pp., 1937.
111. Rainer, Rev. Eligius George, C.SS.R., J.C.D., Suspension of Clerics, XVII-249 pp., 1937.
112. Reilly, Rev. Thomas F., C.SS.R., J.C.D., Visitation of Religious, VI-195 pp., 1938.
113. Moriarty, Rev. Francis E., C.SS.R., J.C.D., The Extraordinary Absolution from Censures, XV-334 pp., 1938.
114. Connolly, Rev. Nicholas P., J.C.D., The Canonical Erection of Parishes, X-132 pp., 1938.
115. Donovan, Rev. James Joseph, J.C.D., The Pastor's Obligation in Prenuptial Investigation, XII-322 pp., 1938.
116. Harrigan, Rev. Robert J., M.A., S.T.B., J.C.D., The Radical Sanation of Invalid Marriages, VIII-208 pp., 1938.
117. Boffa, Rev. Conrad Humbert, J.C.D., Canonical Provisions for Catholic Schools, X-211 pp., 1939.
118. Parsons, Rev. Anscar John, O.M. Cap., J.C.D., Canonical Elections, XII-236 pp., 1939.
119. Reilly, Rev. Edward Michael, A.B., J.C.D., The General Norms of Dispensation, X-156 pp., 1939.
120. Ryan, Rev. Gerald Aloysius, A.B., J.C.D., Principles of Episcopal Jurisdiction, XII-172 pp., 1939.
121. Burton, Rev. Francis James, C.S.C., A.B., J.C.D., A Commentary on Canon 1125, X-222 pp., 1940.
122. Miaskiewicz, Rev. Francis Sigismund, J.C.D., Supplied Jurisdiction according to Canon 209, XII-340 pp., 1940.
123. Rice, Rev. Patrick William, A.B., J.C.D., Proof of Death in Prenuptial Investigation, VIII-156 pp., 1940.
124. Anglin, Rev. Thomas Francis, M.S., J.C.L., The Eucharistic Fast.
125. Coleman, Rev. John Jerome, J.C.L., The Minister of Confirmation.
126. Downs, Rev. John Emmanuel, A.B., J.C.L., The Concept of Clerical Immunity.
127. Esswein, Rev. Anthony Albert, J.C.L., Extrajudicial Penal Powers of Ecclesiastical Superiors.
128. Farrell, Rev. Benjamin Francis, M.A., S.T.L., J.C.L., The Rights and Duties of the Local Ordinary Regarding Congregations of Women Religious of Pontifical Approval.

129. Feeney, Rev. Thomas John, A.B., S.T.L., J.C.L., Restitutio in Integrum.
130. Findlay, Rev. Stephen William, O.S.B., A.B., J.C.L., Canonical Norms Governing the Deposition and Degradation of Clerics.
131. Goodwine, Rev. John, A.B., S.T.L., J.C.L., The Right of the Church to Acquire Property.
132. Heston, Rev. Edward Louis, C.S.C., Ph.D., S.T.D., J.C.L., The Alienation of Church Property in the United States .
133. Hogan, Rev. James John, S.T.L., J.C.L.,, Judicial Advocates and Procurators.
134. Kealy, Rev. Thomas M., A.B., Litt. B., J.C.L., Dowry of Women Religious.
135. Keene, Rev. Michael James, O.S.B., J.C.L., Religious Ordinaries and Canon 198.
136. Kerin, Rev. Charles A., S.S., M.A., S.T.B., J.C.L., The Privation of Christian Burial.
137. Louis, Rev. William Francis, M.A., J.C.L., Diocesan Archives.
138. McDevitt, Rev. Gilbert Joseph, A.B., J.C.L., Legitimacy and Legitimation.
139. McDonough, Rev. Thomas Joseph, A.B., J.C.L., Apostolic Administrators.
140. Meier, Rev. Carl Anthony, A.B., J.C.L., Penal Administrative Procedure Against Negligent Pastors.
141. Schmidt, Rev. John Rogg, A.B., J.C.L., The Principles of Authentic Interpretation in Canon 17 of the Code of Canon Law.
142. Slafkosky, Rev. Andrew Leonard, A.B., J.C.L., The Canonical Episcopal Visitation of the Diocese.
143. Swoboda, Rev. Innocent Robert, O.F.M., J.C.L., Ignorance in Relation to the Imputability of Delicts.
144. Dubé, Rev. Arthur Joseph, A.B., J.C.L., The General Principles for the Reckoning of Time in Canon Law.
145. McBride, Rev. James T., A.B., J.C.L., Incardination and Excardination of Seculars.

www.ingramcontent.com/pod-product-compliance
Lightning Source LLC
LaVergne TN
LVHW050255080826
844660LV00012B/643

* 9 7 8 0 8 1 3 2 2 3 2 5 4 *